Second Edition

GRIEF AND LOSS

THEORIES AND SKILLS FOR THE HELPING PROFESSIONS

Katherine Walsh
Westfield State University

D0141553

PEARSON

Boston   Columbus   Indianapolis   New York   San Francisco   Upper Saddle River
Amsterdam   Cape Town   Dubai   London   Madrid   Milan   Munich   Paris   Montreal   Toronto
Delhi   Mexico City   Sao Paulo   Sydney   Hong Kong   Seoul   Singapore   Taipei   Tokyo

Editorial Director: Craig Campanella
Editor in Chief: Dickson Musslewhite
Executive Editor: Ashley Dodge
Editorial Product Manager: Carly Czech
Director of Marketing: Brandy Dawson
Executive Marketing Manager: Jeanette Koskinas
Senior Marketing Manager: Wendy Albert
Marketing Assistant: Jessica Warren
Media Project Manager: Felicia Halpert
Production Project Manager: Debbie Ryan
Art Director: Jayne Conte
Cover Designer: Suzanne Duda
Composition: PreMediaGlobal

Library of Congress Cataloging-in-Publication Data

Walsh-Burke, Katherine.
 Grief and loss : theories and skills for the helping professions / Katherine Walsh. — 2nd ed.
     p. cm.
 Includes bibliographical references and index.
 ISBN-13: 978-0-205-82709-1 (alk. paper)
 ISBN-10: 0-205-82709-8 (alk. paper)
 1. Loss (Psychology)   2. Grief.   3. Counseling.   I. Title.
 BF724.3.L66W35 2012
 155.9'37—dc23

                                                              2011018684

14 2019

ISBN-10: 0-205-82709-8
ISBN-13: 978-0-205-82709-1

CONTENTS

PREFACE

It is another snowy morning in January, the beginning of a new year and 5 years have passed since the first edition of this text was published. In 2006, I had been blessed with the gift of Julie and Mickey's house in Vermont to complete the book. In that edition's prologue I wrote, "The falling snow makes everything appear peaceful. I begin my retreat by opening the door and embracing the view—I look out to a vast field, circled by gently sloping hills. Smoke curls from the chimney of a house in the distance. I breathe in the cold, refreshing air and as I do I call to mind the recent letters and phone calls I have received. One is from the mother of a teenager who died 20 years ago of leukemia, following a hard-fought battle. She has written every Christmas since I met her while a social worker at the Dana Farber Cancer Institute. This year she writes, "...I still can't believe that David has been gone from us for so long. I think of him everyday. His little nephews have heard all about him and know that his spirit is with us all. Dear Kathy, you were such a lifeline to us during our darkest hours. We love you and thank you still." I recall also a phone message, left out of the blue from Dotti. I met her family when her 43-year-old husband was treated for cancer—more than 20 years ago. Although we kept in touch for the first year after his death, I have not had contact with her since I moved from Boston to Western Mass 18 years ago. "I am moving and was going through my address book," she says on the machine. " I don't know if you remember me but you helped me in ways I will never forget and I just wanted to call and tell you that and wish you and your family well." My daughters smile at the tears that inevitably spring up when I receive these words from families who have endured the most painful of losses with a mixture of bemusement and concern as they put their arms around me and reassure each other and me with the words, "Its ok, mom. It means you helped.' "

Since that time I have accumulated significant personal losses in my own life and as they have occurred, it has not been lost on me that so much of what was included in the text about loss and grief has been applicable. In these 5 years the world has changed dramatically in many ways that have influenced the content of this second edition. Tsunamis, hurricanes, and earthquakes have added to our understanding of the impact of trauma and grief. A new edition of the *Diagnostic and Statistical Manual* is being produced, which finally addresses complicated grieving, the role of advanced directives and grief in palliative and end-of-life care has grown, and the Internet has profoundly changed the ways in which people connect and communicate with one another, as evidenced by a Facebook message I received this year from a former client, a bone marrow transplant recipient I had worked with in 1983. She wrote asking me if I was the same Kathy Walsh who was her social worker at the Dana Farber Cancer Institute when she was 24 and treated for acute leukemia. If I was, she wanted to let me know she remembered my attending her wedding following her transplant and that she was still happily married, with two college-age children and very grateful for her life. I was, and it was of course a great joy to hear from her again. When one of my very best friends, Pauline, was dying in 2007, our friend Magui and I maintained her Caring Bridge Web page while she was hospitalized and maintained it following her death so the wide community of friends she had accumulated could post memorial messages. I have also accumulated 5 more years of inspiring examples from my students and colleagues of how we as professionals can help our clients who are experiencing loss, as well as attend to our own grief. All of these new experiences have helped inform this second edition.

And so, once again, this book is dedicated to my family—especially Lauren and Jessy—and to all the families, students, friends, and colleagues who have helped me to live and learn. I hope, once again, that the content of this book will help others to risk and reap the rewards of helping with grief and loss as well.

CHAPTER 1

Introduction to Grief and Loss

CHAPTER OUTLINE

A journey of a thousand miles begins with the first step.

Chinese Proverb

BASIC FACTS ABOUT LOSS

Did you know that every year 2 million people die in America? And if each of those deaths affects just five other people, at least 10 million people are affected by loss each year.

This is just one of the reasons that the study of grief is so important for helping professionals. Others that you may not have been aware of include:

- Chronic illnesses, such as cancer, heart disease, and diabetes, account for two of every three deaths. These illnesses create many losses before death is anticipated.
- Accidents are the leading cause of death for children under age 18. They are also the cause of many disabling injuries, creating loss of mobility, fine motor skills, and cognitive functions.
- In 2008 (the most recent year for which statistics have been published by the U.S. Department of Health and Human Services), 463,000 children were living

in foster care. These children, their biological and foster families, their siblings, teachers, and social workers are all affected by loss and grief.

- According to predictions based on the U.S. Census, approximately 43% of marriages in the United States will end in divorce.
- Some parents and children who experience divorce consider adjusting to the losses associated with it to be as challenging as the losses associated with death.
- Each year, there are approximately 33,000–34,000 suicides in the United States, leaving over 180,000 suicide survivors. Suicide impacts families, communities, and society as a whole.
- The tragic events of September 11, 2001, immediately affected people all over the world, and particularly in the United States. The traumatic losses associated with these terrorist attacks, along with natural disasters such as Hurricane Katrina, earthquakes, and tsunamis, have an impact on individuals and communities far beyond what can be currently understood.

How many times have you heard the phrase, "Loss is a part of life"? Yet, have you thought about how loss will impact the work you have chosen to do and how you will respond when someone you are working with is grieving? If you are reading this text, you are most likely a student in training or already working with people in the fields of education, law, health care, mental health, or social services. If so, you will be better prepared than many professionals to help those who are grieving.

Many professionals report a lack of training in grief and loss. In 1997, the Institute of Medicine released a report (*Approaching Death: Improving Care at the End of Life*) that identified multiple causes for the deficiencies in professional preparation including legal, organizational, and economic barriers; a public uncomfortable with discussions about death; and education and training programs for health care professionals that do not teach knowledge, skills, and attitudes needed to care for dying people (Field & Cassel, 1997).

WHY STUDY GRIEF AND LOSS?

If you have chosen a profession in which you will be helping people through teaching, human service administration, human resource management, coaching, rehabilitation therapy, medicine, social work, or even through law or corrections, it is inevitable that you will encounter loss and the grief reactions that loss engenders.

This book is written for a broad professional audience because loss is encountered everywhere. Loss through death is encountered in hospitals, hospices and skilled nursing facilities, schools, businesses, community clinics, prisons, and every possible setting in which you will find yourself working as a professional. You may find yourself coaching a child whose parent or grandparent has died, teaching in a school where a teacher or student has died, serving as a probation officer to an adolescent whose best friend has been killed, providing legal counsel to a family that has sustained a death through natural causes or domestic violence, or coordinating home care services in a senior center for an elderly woman whose husband has died and whose children have concerns about her ability to live independently in her home of 50 years.

Mildred, a substance abuse counselor, wrote the following description of her encounter with a grieving client for an assignment in our grief and loss class.

CASE EXAMPLE: DEBBIE

Debbie, a thirteen-year-old, really impacted me, not only as a professional case worker, but also as a mother of two who at an early age lost her mother in a tragic accident.

Debbie was attending middle school and was an A student. She lived with her parents and two siblings. Both were younger than her. Her mother was an active participant in the Relapse Prevention Program where I was working. Debbie, like many adolescents, gets involved and participates in different activities while they wait for their parents. Even though she was aware of her mother's past substance abuse, she felt highly about her mother. She was very attached to her father and maintains a good relationship with her siblings. There was never a complaint about Debbie. It was not until one day Debbie's mother dropped her off at the mall. Debbie didn't know that would be the last time she would see her mother. While her mother drove away from the parking lot, she waved goodbye and smiled at her. That day, fifteen minutes after, her mother's car was impacted by another car that left the scene where the accident occurred. Later that day, Debbie arrived at the Medical Center with her maternal aunt and other relatives. She was told that her mother was in surgery and doctors were doing all they could. Debbie felt everything was ok. She has seen accidents happen every day. Two hours later doctors called the family to a private room and notified them they did everything possible to save her, but they couldn't. Debbie thought it was a nightmare and she was going to wake up any moment. She couldn't understand why that was happening to her. This was the third death in Debbie's life. When she was three, she lost her maternal grandmother. At age seven, her paternal grandfather died. None of them impacted her as hard as the death of her mother.

(Mildred Arroyo, 2009)

These types of losses represent only a very few of the many losses due to death that helping professionals encounter. They are actually quite typical of the kinds of deaths that occur every day in our communities. If you are wondering about what you might gain from this textbook, you might ask yourself the following questions:

- How comfortable and confident am I in my own ability to deal with grief and loss?
- How well do I understand the impact of death on people of different ages, genders, cultures, and spiritual orientations?
- How familiar am I with other life events and losses that cause grief reactions?
- Am I confident that I can identify when an individual or family is expressing normal grief or when their grief may be complicated?
- How prepared am I to respond effectively to those who are grieving around me?
- What types of grief reactions might trigger my own grief reactions and how will I handle them?
- Do I know how to directly acknowledge grief and make a referral to an appropriate resource when necessary?

As we will discuss in Chapter 3, self-awareness regarding our own grief reactions is essential to working with others who are experiencing a loss. These losses may result from a variety of causes, just as our clients' losses do.

In addition to preparing you to address the grief in reaction to death that you will inevitably encounter in your practice, this text is intended to prepare you to identify and assist individuals and families who may be coping with grief that is due to causes other than death. Loss and grief are experienced in reaction to divorce, foster care placement, job loss, changes in health care status, substance dependence, domestic violence, the diagnosis of a child with a serious disability, children leaving home for independent living, and older adults leaving their lifelong homes for nursing homes or alternative care. These types of losses are termed *symbolic losses* and often trigger grief reactions that are similar to those that occur in reaction to death. These will be discussed in Chapter 2 and it is important to be aware of all of the losses that may cause grief reactions in order to respond effectively to those who may need your help.

LOSS EXPERIENCES THAT GENERATE GRIEF REACTIONS
Grief in every practice setting

After many years of teaching social work and providing consultation about grief to a wide variety of programs and agencies, I have come to appreciate how much loss impacts work in every practice setting where professionals are helping others. As a hospital social worker and hospice program director, I frequently collaborated with other disciplines, so I knew that nurses, physicians, employee assistance program managers, pastoral counselors, and funeral directors are almost always closely involved in helping people who grieve when someone dies. But as I began teaching classes on loss to personnel in schools, child welfare agencies, and correctional programs, I realized how important it is for professionals in every discipline to be well prepared to deal with loss and grief—our own as well as others'.

Rachael Kessler, a teacher who created an institute and a Web site to support *teachers* in their professional development, identified several reasons *teachers* should learn about grief. She noted that most students experience unexpressed grief stemming from traumatic losses, family deaths, divorce, geographic relocation, and dislocation. She also discussed the losses that students experience through abuse and pregnancy as well as those routinely experienced through growing up, such as saying goodbye at the end of the school year or leaving for college (Kessler, 2004).

Brandon Hunt (2007) has written about the need for *rehabilitation counselors* to learn about grief due to the multiple losses they encounter in their clients. He identifies loss of employment, loss of independence, and death of loved ones as just a few of the experiences that generate grief reactions to which rehabilitation specialists must be prepared to respond.

LIMITED TRAINING IN GRIEF   Like teachers and counselors, nurses and physicians, rehabilitation therapists, child life specialists, and legal professionals encounter loss and grief every day. When my own daughter became a children's rights lawyer and began working with young victims of human trafficking, our conversations about her work inevitably involved grief reactions to traumatic losses—her clients' as well as her own in reaction to their experiences. Unfortunately, most professional training programs do not adequately address issues of grief and loss in their programs, even though so many will be faced with grieving clients. Without the opportunity to learn how to assess and address grief, many professionals may lack confidence in acknowledging loss and providing support. This lack of confidence and understanding can make professionals uncomfortable discussing death and loss. Avoidance or reluctance can adversely affect clients who look to professionals for "truth, knowledge and support" (Naierman, 1997).

Even in training programs whose focus includes the populations most vulnerable to loss and grief, class discussion is usually limited to grief related to death or relegated to a "death and dying" elective that few students have the opportunity or room in their schedules to register for.

Professional organizations as well as researchers have become increasingly aware that grief and bereavement have a significant impact on the clients we work with. The National Center for the Advancement of Health published a Report on Grief and Bereavement that recognizes that there is a need for health care professionals to be prepared to respond to grief. The report notes that there are relatively few studies that address the education and training of health care professionals in this area and that those that do address it are focused primarily on physicians. The studies that have been conducted, according to the report, indicate that training is inadequate, but health care providers who do receive training are more comfortable with death (National Center for Advancement of Health, 2003).

These findings are supported by a recent study by genetics professionals (Rushton et al., 2010). Genetic counselors work closely with families who have members with birth defects, genetic disorders, and a variety of life-threatening inherited conditions such as *BRCA* gene–related breast cancer and Huntington's disease. The study was undertaken because the majority of *genetic counselors* have clinical interactions with patients and families who are seeking genetic counseling while experiencing grief, loss, and/or death. Almost 20% of the study participants reported discomfort with grief and loss and 29% reported that their training in grief had not been adequate. However, when study participants reported their training in grief and loss was adequate, they also reported higher levels of comfort with grief.

This has been my experience in teaching this content to a variety of helping professionals who express relief at finally feeling equipped to address the distress they so frequently encounter in their work with grieving clients. A seasoned crisis counselor pointed out how grief training had helped her become better prepared for her role:

> I believe that I have a good idea of my limitations. ... I know that even with my absolute best efforts, I cannot "cure" someone of his or her grief or the emotional pain. What I can do, however, is offer my help, guidance, advocacy, and care during an incredibly difficult time and help them begin to find their own way out of the pain. If I can make the journey a bit easier, though, that would be success. Three most difficult

aspects: First, letting go of (and allowing myself to grieve for) people who have come to be a part of my life. Second, dealing with a certain amount of helplessness. Third, keeping myself in the land of the living when I'm not working-avoiding the tendency to dwell on death. How will I cope? I couldn't possibly do it alone. I will definitely use any support that is available to me-from coworkers or employers, friends, family, etc. I'll have to acknowledge and accept my frustration and stress and grief when they arise. And I'll have to give myself permission to do things I enjoy even when I'm in the midst of death or others' pain. (Townsend, 2002)

BENEFITS OF TRAINING IN GRIEF   Without sensitization to, and training in, grief and loss, even seasoned mental health professionals may have difficulty identifying and responding effectively to grief-related problems that clients present. Clients may have sealed over their grief from previous losses, sometimes masking it with alcohol or drugs. Children and teens may develop other maladaptive behaviors such as aggression to cope with anger due to a significant unresolved loss. Grief and loss issues can be obscured or neglected in the treatment of clients who present other primary problems when seeking treatment. Professionals who are not attuned to grief may miss the opportunity to identify and assist with loss and grief associated with these problems. When they are attuned, it is not uncommon to identify loss as well as unresolved grief embedded in the problems that clients struggle with in many settings. Haven and Pearlman (2003), trauma therapists, write about a 37-year-old professional woman who had experienced sexual abuse and a forced abortion of a pregnancy resulting from incest. In therapy she mourned this pregnancy and dealt with the painful feelings of loss that came from the experience of sexual abuse. In describing her mourning, the client stated "my heart hurts," indicating the depth of pain that accompanied the grieving process. This type of grief is not always acknowledged, even in the therapy of sexual abuse survivors and yet, as in this case, addressing unresolved loss can bring relief and restoration.

While research on the outcomes of grief training programs for professionals is sparse, I have found over the past ten years of teaching courses on grief and loss, that the responses of students and seasoned professionals regarding inclusion of this content in their training have been universally positive.

They identify many areas of increased competence including:

- The ability to ask questions that lead to identification of loss experiences
- The ability to identify what types of grief reactions clients are experiencing
- Recognition of symbolic losses in addition to losses through death
- Increased comfort in listening to clients speak about their losses
- Increased understanding and utilization of theories related to grief
- Improved skill in working with families in crisis whose symbolic and actual losses impact their current coping

While this text addresses the literature and research on grieving in reaction to death, some of the losses our clients experience are symbolic. Symbolic losses, which will be discussed in Chapter 2, are losses that do not result from death and not all clients will experience these losses. Loss due to death, however, is inevitable in each of our clients' lives. These losses vary and include sudden, unanticipated, anticipated, accidental, and illness-related deaths as well as deaths of infants, parents, children, and older adults. Even if we have not been directly exposed to these types of deaths in our personal or professional roles, we, and our clients, are exposed daily to media announcements of military deaths, deaths due to natural disasters, and deaths due to crimes. Even when these deaths are remote—like the deaths in Haiti following a massive earthquake in 2010—they have an impact on our communities and often on our clients. With some deaths—those that are anticipated or publicly acknowledged—there may be a good deal of support offered to the grieving family and friends, even to us as professional members of a caring community. But there are many deaths that are not anticipated or publicly acknowledged and there may be little or no support for the grief experienced by significant others. Stillbirth, death from HIV, and suicide are examples of deaths that are often accompanied by stigma, which can result in "disenfranchised" grief. These and other complicated grief reactions are addressed in depth in Chapter 7.

The grief that families and workers experience when death results from violence is also important to recognize and is another type of grief situation that may be accompanied by stigma and not publicly acknowledged. Dr. Michael Durfee (1997) has written one of the few articles about this type of experience in a Web-based publication for the International Child Abuse Network. He recognizes that there is often too little recognition of the grief reactions of survivors of fatal child abuse and neglect. These survivors include the siblings and grandparents who need acknowledgment and understanding of their losses and who may need counseling, particularly in the critical first year following the death. Families who have experienced death due to intimate partner violence, which results in approximately 1,500 deaths per year in the United States, may also be deprived of support due to social stigma.

Through many years of training child protective workers I have also learned that the grief-related needs of this population of professionals are too often unacknowledged or unaddressed.

Although some organizations do recognize the impact that dealing with trauma and grief have on their frontline staff, too often staff do not receive support for the trauma they witness or their own grief reactions. When support is offered, there may be barriers, such as stigma, that impede worker access (Bernier, 1998).

This is not dissimilar from the experiences reported by health care practitioners who also come in close contact with loss through caring for dying patients. The National Center for the Advancement of Health Report (2003), cited earlier, reviewed several studies that indicate that while health care workers experience emotional reactions to the deaths of patients and the "emotional intensity" of their work, support to health care providers in the workplace is lacking. The report also underscores that professionals will be better able to work effectively with individuals and families in need with knowledge of grief and how to assist someone in the process.

While other texts are written for those who are training for a specialized career in bereavement counseling or grief therapy, this text is designed for those students and professionals who find themselves in the position of working in proximity to loss, trauma, and grief in a variety of capacities—educator, advocate, case manager, or counselor. You will need the basic knowledge and skills addressed here to respond effectively to those you encounter in the course of your daily work. I am confident that when you complete this text, you will feel better equipped to understand and assist your clients with their grief and to deal with your own inevitable losses as well.

SUMMARY

Professionals in every service setting will inevitably encounter clients who are experiencing grief in reaction to losses. These losses will include deaths of significant others such as parents, children, grandparents, partners, classmates, coworkers, and friends as well as losses that do not result from death but are considered symbolic losses. Despite the fact that we will all encounter loss and grief in our work, relatively few helping professionals report feeling adequately prepared in their training to effectively address the complex needs of grieving clients. Without training in grief and loss, even seasoned mental health professionals may have difficulty identifying and responding effectively to grief-related problems that clients present. This text and the accompanying exercises and resources are available in MySocialWorkLab for Advancing Core Competencies under Resources in the "Grief and Loss" section will help to prepare you to identify and address grief-related needs from a variety of perspectives, in a wide array of service settings.

Symbolic Loss

CHAPTER OUTLINE

> *Be kind-for everyone you meet is fighting a hard battle.*
>
> Anonymous

SYMBOLIC LOSS

> The three most difficult situations that I have had to deal with in my life are divorce, selling my home, and losing my dog. My reaction to my divorce was a terrible feeling of loss. I lost my husband, my role as a wife, my identity, and my last name! I felt like it was a death more than a divorce. It was the worst pain that I have ever encountered in my life! I had to grieve for all of the dreams that will never be met. I had numerous symptoms as a result. I experienced weight loss, disturbance in sleep, crying, lack of strength, physical exhaustion, feelings of emptiness and heaviness, indications of anxiety, and lastly, lack of energy. (Kroeber, 2004).

As we discussed in Chapter 1, there are many different losses in life that engender grief reactions. While many helping professionals report they do not feel adequately prepared to deal with grief reactions, when they are prepared it has often been through course content on death and dying. For many years content on grief in textbooks and elective courses has focused on **bereavement**, which is defined as *the state of having experienced the death of a significant person.* Much of the research that has informed our understanding of grief reactions has been conducted with bereaved individuals who are grieving a death. This research and the theories about grief that have been formulated from the research findings have been most important in guiding professionals in assisting grieving individuals and families who are grieving a death.

In addition to loss related to death, there are many types of significant losses that are not due to death, but rather represent the loss of relationships, intact systems, and even dreams for the future. These types of losses are considered symbolic losses. Dr. Therese Rando was one of the first grief experts to identify grief in reaction to symbolic losses in her seminal text *Grief, Dying and Death: Clinical Interventions for Caregivers* (1984). Although the text was written primarily about grief due to death, Rando acknowledged that grief is experienced in reaction to symbolic losses as well. She gave examples of divorce and losing status because of a job demotion and identified the lack of acknowledgment that often accompanies a symbolic, or psychological, loss. According to Rando, symbolic loss is not always identified as a loss per se, so those who experience a symbolic loss may not realize they need to take time to grieve and deal with the feelings that are engendered by it.

While there has not been nearly as much research to inform our understanding of reactions to symbolic loss as research on reactions to death, grief reactions to symbolic loss are more frequently being identified in the literature for professional caregivers and in publications of organizations that assist grieving individuals and families. The Veterans' Administration Web site, for example, includes information about the symbolic losses experienced by veterans injured during the war in Iraq. Examples that are highlighted are injuries that result in amputations and blindness, which cause loss of bodily functions and bodily integrity. Since these losses have a major impact on the lives of those who sustain them, as well as their family members, it is not difficult to see how they would engender grief reactions. The same feelings of anger, sadness, and guilt that are experienced in reaction to loss through death are experienced in reaction to these symbolic losses (Wain et al., 2011).

SIMILARITIES AND DIFFERENCES IN SYMBOLIC AND ACTUAL LOSSES

Death is acknowledged; symbolic loss often is not

While anger, sadness, guilt, and yearning are common grief reactions to both a death and a symbolic loss, there is a major difference between loss due to death and symbolic losses. Because symbolic losses so often go unacknowledged by others, the grieving individual does not receive the same kind or amount of support that those grieving a death may receive. Children placed in foster care, biological and foster parents from whose homes children are removed, families experiencing a divorce, parents whose children have been diagnosed with a disabling medical or mental condition, or even adults whose children are leaving home or whose parents must be moved from the family home to a nursing home can be expected to express a variety of grief reactions.

They, as well as many others who experience symbolic loss, will need your understanding and will benefit from your ability to listen and provide assistance.

Whether we are in a professional role in which we are responsible for providing psychosocial or mental health services to clients affected by loss, or we are in a position to refer clients to, or work collaboratively with, a grief counselor, it is essential for all of us who work with people to be aware of the types of losses that generate grief reactions, as well as the range of responses of individuals, families, and communities who are grieving so that we are prepared to work with them effectively as well as refer them, when needed, for additional help. As noted in Chapter 1, it is not uncommon for teachers, nurses and other medical personnel, and individuals working in law enforcement, correctional settings, child welfare, and senior service settings to encounter individuals who have experienced symbolic losses but have not had an opportunity to grieve them, for a variety of reasons. Often, after a period of heightened distress, these clients are referred to or seek services for other reasons and in the course of assessment we learn that they are still experiencing grief reactions, both "normal" and "complicated" because their grief has not been acknowledged or processed.

This is especially true for symbolic losses such as the loss of identity that comes with retirement or emigration, the loss of a relationship outside the formal legal or family system, and the loss of anticipated relationships or accomplishments that come with stillbirth or disability. There is, however, increasing recognition on the part of grief professionals that these losses are important and therefore the chances are greater now that individuals grieving symbolic losses will receive intervention if the losses are identified. An example of how organizations serving populations at risk are attending to symbolic loss can be seen in a Web-based education program for Marine officers entitled "The Marine Leaders Guide" (United States Marine Corps, 2011) that defines a symbolic, or psychosocial, loss as the loss of something intangible. Divorce, the end of a unit relationship, and separation or retirement from the Marine Corps are identified as symbolic losses that might be experienced by Marines in addition to injuries and illness. Even the loss of innocence following combat or the loss of a dream for the future is viewed as causes of grief. The guide points out that the loss may not be recognized by others around the marine, but notes that the readiness of the marine or even the entire unit can be impacted by the feelings, thoughts, physical, social, and behavioral reactions to the loss.

Loss due to life transitions

In addition to veterans of war who experience both tangible and symbolic losses, whole populations of people who have fled their countries of origin following war or economic hardship are increasingly being recognized by nongovernmental advocacy and service organizations as populations experiencing grief, as the following example illustrates.

> With my volunteer work at IRIS, (Integrated Immigrant and Refugee Services) every time I have a new client I encounter physical losses as well as symbolic losses, especially with refugees. These losses are usually very profound, sometimes involving violent death of family members,

friends, neighbors. Beside deaths, other losses involve loss of friendships, losses of support systems they have back home, losses of cultural identities (especially for young children), losses of status, losses of things they own, financial changes. After working with these families for years, we become very close and once they (some of them) decide to move to another state, we (my clients and I) always feel sad. In my heart I always know that they are moving away looking for a better future, but again I always feel the loss. (Chantal Ndikunkiko, 2010)

A student working with families who had fled rural and arid Somalia and were resettled in an urban center in New England spoke of the parents she was meeting who were grieving the loss of their homeland, their extended families, and their whole way of life, including a family structure, partly influenced by Muslim beliefs, in which men had primary authority in decision-making as well as responsibility for income earning.

Many authors who have written about vulnerable populations with refugee status have described the difficulties adults from other cultures may have in adapting to American culture. A major challenge for many is the different roles that women play in American culture where women frequently participate equally in earning income and decision-making for the family, which is not the case in many other cultures. The differences often require that families give up the role expectations they brought with them. This kind of change, as well as other changes in family functioning and structure, does represent a loss. Adults may also grieve the loss of their cultural norms when their children and adolescents adopt the mores of urban American youth (Drachman & Ryan, 2001). Yet, these losses and the grief related to them are not often given expression or acknowledged by families or the professionals who interact with them, sometimes because language is a barrier, or because the professionals are unaware of the norms and expectations of the country of origin.

Another type of symbolic loss is experienced by both adolescents and their parents during the launching phase of the family life cycle. According to Kennedy (2004), the transition to college or independent living can be seen as a significant loss and source of deep grief for parents. Kennedy notes that letting children go after 18 or so years of giving birth to, nurturing, and protecting them is a source of grief for parents that they often are not prepared for. Adolescents and young adults in the launching phase of life are not lost in the way they would be if a death had occurred, but the relationship as it was is permanently changed. Acknowledgment of this loss and tending to the grief reactions can help parents establish a new relationship with the child.

Health-related symbolic loss

My students and colleagues in allied health, human services, education, law, and social work programs have provided countless examples of the types of losses that are encountered in a diverse array of agency settings in which they carry out their work. My family members have provided many examples. My father is a retired firefighter who witnessed and provided emergency care to people coping with so many losses over his long career; families who lost their homes and possessions; business owners who lost their means of support; and in the most tragic cases, firefighters and other families who lost loved ones to fire. One of my sisters is a pediatric physical therapist and we have talked about the many children she has helped to gain mobility after the loss of a limb or the disabling effects of a condition such as cerebral palsy. They and their parents have dealt with many losses,symbolic and actual. Gitterman (2001) reviews the literature regarding the grief reactions of parents with children diagnosed with disabilities. This literature describes both the grief of parents whose children are born with a visible disability and the mourning that occurs in parents when a child has a disability that is less observable, but nevertheless is experienced as the loss of an intact child. Grief reactions may be staggered as the implications of the disability become more evident. She notes that the mourning process when a disability is gradually revealed through a child's early years or diagnosed in the school-age years is different from that experienced when a child has a readily identifiable physical difference or disability at birth. She recommends that professionals assess a parent's reactions over time and gear their interventions accordingly.

Individuals of all ages who present to us with chronic illnesses or disabling medical conditions may also manifest feelings of grief. While in some professional roles, such as physical, occupational, speech, or respiratory therapist, the focus of our work is primarily to enhance the physical abilities of the individual with a disabling condition. Recognizing anger or sadness as part of the grief reaction enables one to be a skilled listener and provider of emotional support, often essential aspects of providing rehabilitation services.

My youngest sister, Shirley, is a registered dietician who works in a dialysis center. She deals with grief on a daily basis. When clients are referred for dialysis, they are coping with the loss or impairment of their kidney functioning. Often they express the same range of feelings and reactions-including denial, anger, sadness, and fear-to this, and the accompanying losses, that people coping with imminent death express. In addition to the loss of independence that dialysis imposes, many of the people she works with face the loss of their jobs and income because the time and travel required for treatment make many jobs impossible, the loss of their bodily integrity or sense of well-being, and in many instances, the loss of cherished leisure or recreational activities and social relationships. She recently talked about the grief of a 44-year-old man, with whom she has been working for several months. Each month she reviews his lab results and counsels him on how he can best manage his diabetes and lab outcomes. He had been employed as a salesman for a manufacturing firm that required regular travel but was unable to continue in his job when dialysis began, as the treatments require 3–4 hours of travel and dialysis every other day. Initially his kidneys were partially functioning and he was coping with the loss of his job and the need to manage his diet and insulin very carefully. However, as the months have passed, his kidneys have ceased to function and he has become increasingly despondent. As is often the case in dialysis, it has become more problematic for him to manage his insulin and his lab results have become more problematic. The more stressed and despondent he has become, the less well he is able to control his eating. Although he is receiving counseling and antidepressant medication, Shirley, the clinic dietician, is the primary bearer of news about his lab results and it is inevitable that his feelings of frustration, anger, and sadness come up in their discussions. "He is grieving so many losses," she says. "It's a challenge for me to figure out how to help him focus on achieving good lab results when he's lost his job, his freedom and his faith. I really understand that he is angry and he needs to express it" (Suter, 2004).

Another professional arena where loss and grief are commonly encountered is the human resource management field. Employees generally call their human resources department with practical questions related to benefits, but may express feelings related to grief when seeking information.

CASE EXAMPLE: MS. O'CONNOR

Ms. O'Connor could be seeking help from the human resources staff of any organization. She is a 57-year-old single woman who has been the caregiver for many years for her 82-year-old father who has Alzheimer's disease. She has been employed for 25 years by a large insurance agency and has contacted the human resources office there to enquire about her employee benefits, since she is now faced with planning for her father's care during the end stage of his illness. Diagnosed 5 years before, her father was able to attend a day treatment program while she worked, but in the past 6 months his symptoms have rapidly accelerated and he now requires full-time care. Ms. O'Connor has come into the human resources office with many questions, including what her options are for family medical leave. As she begins to discuss her father's difficulties and why she needs time away from work to care for him, she becomes visibly upset, tearfully stating she is not sure how much longer this can go on. Ms. O'Connor, like most employees who are faced with this kind of family crisis, is primarily seeking practical help and information from the human resources office. Yet clearly loss and grief are manifested during her conversation with the human resource staff. It is highly likely that months later she will express as much appreciation for the understanding and supportive responses of the staff as for the information she received.

Insurance case managers, legal aid providers, and many other professionals encounter similar situations in their work. Individuals with disabling illnesses or injuries or substance dependence often experience multiple symbolic losses, including the loss of identity as a healthy person, loss of self-efficacy, loss of income and social status. Many of my students have written about their encounters with clients experiencing grief in reaction to injuries; traumatic brain injury is one that is accompanied by multiple other symbolic losses. A head injury can result in both long- and short-term memory loss, loss of mobility, stability or overall functioning of arms and legs, loss of a driver's license, and loss of employment. The consequences of these losses, such as divorce, loss of custody of one's children, and loss of self-efficacy as well as one's identity as a spouse, parent, and employee, can further compound the grief reactions that result from the injury itself.

Another common experience that can be viewed as a symbolic loss is giving up the use of alcohol or drugs on which one has become dependent. This is a loss that is accompanied by multiple other losses and often goes unacknowledged. In fact, individuals have often developed a pattern of dependence on substances to avoid or numb the painful feelings that have accompanied death, divorce, or other significant losses in their lives. When the individual then strives for sobriety and is no longer using these numbing substances, he or she can be flooded with the grief reactions that were avoided in the past with addiction. The following entry from a student journal illustrates this.

"An example from my own life was the symbolic loss that I suffered as a result of stopping using alcohol and other drugs. I was 24 years old at the time, and when I stopped using them, I definitely felt myself going through the grieving process in regards to stopping using. I read an article that describes this grieving process using Elizabeth Kubler-Ross' cycle of grief in loss in the context of addiction recovery. (Fabry, 2010)

It states that in many substance abuse recovery programs, this is known as the Forgiveness Cycle. I could see myself in my early recovery going through the stages of denial. This would have occurred prior to my stopping using drugs, not believing that I had a problem with drugs. Drugs would also help me to cover up any other feelings of loss or grief that I was experiencing, and kept those feelings buried. I also went through the stage of bargaining, where I would attempt to "just drink," or attempt to cut down my use. When I went to treatment, I really felt angry because in some ways, I felt forced to go into treatment, and I was also angry at myself for letting my addiction get this far out of hand. I also experienced serious depression when I first stopped using drugs and alcohol. Around 2 years into my recovery, I finally got to the stage of acceptance, and felt that I was free of the compulsion to use alcohol and other drugs. Now, approaching 4 years of recovery, I feel that I have moved through this cycle with my addiction, but have been re-experiencing the cycle with other losses in my life." (Anonymous, 2010)

Symbolic loss in different life stages

Understanding the meaning of these types of symbolic losses and providing effective responses to individuals who are grieving them is a skill set that every professional needs.

In many settings, such as skilled nursing facilities, child care centers, and after-school programs, children, adolescents, and adults often express grief in reaction to symbolic losses. An intern in a skilled nursing facility wrote about one type of loss family members of those afflicted with Alzheimer's experience:

I observe the child visitor huddling behind the parent, grabbing onto a sleeve, poking their fingers in their mouth, as they peer at the patients with fear. The child brightens as he spies his grandfather and darts out to him. The startled grandfather grabs at the child's arm and pushes him away. The child begins to cry. … The child is now visiting their grandparent in a "hospital." Grandpa may or may not recognize the child who has a sense of attachment to the familiar family figure who no longer interacts in the same way. I consider the reactions of children unprepared for the reality of Alzheimer's disease to be strongly equated to the mourning process associated with death. In an attempt to avoid such scenarios, I attempt to discuss the possible reaction of children with the parent before they arrive at the facility. I do not discourage the presence of children on the unit. I do encourage preparation. I want the family to be safe and secure and to benefit from meaningful interaction with their loved one. I also want the child to have an understanding of the person that Grandpa is now. (Laudette, 2003)

Symbolic loss and foster care

A worker in a residential foster care facility discussed a client whose story is similar to that of many children whom foster care workers, teachers, probation officers, and other human service workers encounter. The 14-year-old girl had been placed in a therapeutic group home for adolescents. Her mother died in a car accident when she was a toddler. Her father was incarcerated at the time. With no parents to care for her, she and her sister were moved from family member to family member as well as to foster homes where she was sexually and physically abused. Her frequent expression of anger and acting out resulted in residential placement outside of the city in which she had spent her childhood and separate from her sister. In a secure environment, and with the support of staff at the group home, she was gradually beginning to talk about the many issues of loss she had been struggling with for 12 years. She had not received grief counseling prior to the residential placement, even though she had suffered the death of her mother and many other subsequent losses including the symbolic loss of her biological family, the loss of her "childhood," and the loss of the many "potential" parents and families she experienced through impermanent and destructive foster care placements.

Unfortunately, many children in foster care are not provided with therapeutic grief interventions and secure attachment opportunities during or after placement, and instead often develop complicated grief reactions and are frequently labeled with a mental disorder such as reactive attachment disorder, depression, or oppositional defiant disorder. It is especially important for those of us who work with children in foster care to ensure that their losses are recognized and their grief is addressed appropriately. Enabling them to express their understandable feelings of anger, sadness, and anxiety related to loss and providing them with outlets for grief and stress relief can provide them with a crucial sense of being understood and cared for, and can contribute to healthy future relationships, motivation, and positive self perceptions.

A child protective worker, after participating in a course in loss and bereavement, wrote:

In the work that I do every day it is often difficult to engage a child and get them invested in their treatment because they are, understandably, so angry that they have been taken away from their parents and of course, the child believes that it is the caseworker's fault that they have been removed. Stabilization into a foster home is probably the most difficult part of the child's treatment and must precede working on disruptive behaviors and other clinical issues. This can be a lengthy process because, in a way, the child first needs to do the grief work around the transition out of their home and the separation between them and their "family." It appears to me to be very similar to having to deal with a deceased's loved one, only that these important people still exist and there is always hope in the child's mind that reunification will occur if treatment goals are reached. Part of treatment for them is like any grief work and involves acknowledging and supporting them in processing the feelings of disbelief, anger, sadness etc. that they are experiencing. (Hildreth, 2002)

This example addresses the grief from the symbolic loss that foster care placement engenders for children and the witnessing of this grief by child protective workers who are charged with assisting them. The following example illustrates how these losses can be acknowledged.

I have been working as a Treatment Social Worker for the Department of Children and Families (DCF) for the past six years. During my career with DCF, I have worked with children who have experienced losses through both short and long-term foster care placements. Sometimes, I try to prepare the children ahead of time when I know that the permanency plan is Termination of Parental Rights/Adoption, but still they are never fully prepared to deal with the loss when it occurs. When working to help children cope with losses through termination of parental rights, actively listening can be an important therapeutic intervention because it illustrates to the child that you are listening and that you are interested in what he or she has to say. Children can be very difficult to talk to, which also makes it difficult at times to get them to share their feelings. I often use active listening even in cases where the child is expressing feelings of anger, frustration and mistrust towards me because they feel that I am partly responsible for the disruption in their lives. Empathy is another therapeutic intervention that I use to help children cope with losses because it shows that as the professional working with them, I understand their losses and their struggles trying to cope with these losses. I try to avoid using phrases such as "I understand where you are coming from" or "soon you will get over it." When a child is dealing with the loss of a biological parent, he or she may not want to hear the Social Worker telling them that they will get over it soon. I find it helpful to listen and empathize with the child who is experiencing the loss rather than offering solutions to try to make them feel better.

(Georges, 2009)

The National Resource Center for Respite and Crisis Care Services is funded by the U.S. Department of Health and Human Services, Administration for Children and Families, and other organizations. In its fact sheet on grief, several different types of symbolic losses are addressed. "The family of a child considered medically fragile who is in need of respite care may experience a sense of loss over not having a 'healthy' or 'perfect' child. The spouse of a family member with Alzheimer's may grieve the loss of the life they have planned together" (Braza, 2002).

This publication emphasizes that all losses, those from death as well as symbolic losses, need to be grieved. It also underscores that professionals will be better able to work effectively with individuals and families in need with knowledge of grief and how to assist someone in the process. Subsequent chapters in this text are designed to provide you with this set of knowledge and skills.

SUMMARY

Many different losses in life engender grief reactions. Loss that is not tangible, through a death, is referred to as *symbolic loss*. Examples of symbolic loss are divorce, placement in foster care, retirement or losing a job, and diagnosis of a serious disability or chronic illness. Individuals and families at all stages of life are vulnerable to symbolic losses. A major difference between loss due to death and a symbolic loss is the lack of acknowledgment of symbolic losses. Those grieving a symbolic loss may not receive the same kind of support as those grieving a death since the loss may not be identified by the griever or others. While the majority of research on grief has focused on reaction to death, we can apply some of what we know about grief in reaction to death to help inform our understanding of grief related to symbolic losses. Sharing this understanding with clients who have experienced a symbolic loss, but not acknowledged it, may be of great help to a client who is confused by his or her own grief reactions.

CHAPTER 3

Self-Preparation and Self-Care for Professionals Encountering Loss and Grief

Everything that happens to you is your teacher. The secret is to sit at the feet of your own life and be taught by it.

Polly B. Berends

REVIEWING OUR OWN EXPERIENCES AND ATTITUDES RELATED TO GRIEF

Can you remember the very first death of someone close to you or significant in your own life? Some people, when asked this question, can retrieve this memory quite quickly. Some may recall the death of a grandparent or even a pet. Many people who were children when President John F. Kennedy was assassinated or when the space shuttle *Challenger* exploded can recall vividly these deaths as well as the reactions of those around them. More recently, almost everyone in the United States can recall their reactions to the deaths of the almost 3,000 victims of the World Trade Tower terrorist attack and the victims of Hurricane Katrina. Death, in our contemporary, media con-scious culture, is unavoidable. Yet, it is only recently that we have begun to attend to the emotional impact that loss and grief have on us as professionals and on our work.

It is important to review our own experiences, not only in order to understand and respond effectively to the grief of others, but also to ensure that we are adequately aware of, and attending to, our own grief. Almost every textbook or course in grief begins with an exploration of one's own losses. As an instructor, I assign this exer-cise to my students (similar exercises are located in MySocialWorkLab for *Advancing Core Competencies* under Resources in the "Grief and Loss" section).

EXERCISE

Instructions:

1. Take a few moments now to think about the following questions. You may want to write down your responses and reflect on them as you progress through the rest of this text or use them as the beginning of a journal that you continue to keep.

   - What was your earliest experience with death or loss? How old were you when it occurred? Where were you when you learned of the loss? Who did it involve? Describe what happened.
   - How did the people around you respond to the loss? How did they respond to your reactions?
   - How did your cultural and/or spiritual background influence your responses?
   - What about loss makes you feel vulnerable now?
   - Based on what you have learned since, what do you think can help make it easier to cope with death or loss now or in the future?

2. If there are unresolved feelings about previous experiences with death that you have not worked through, it is important to find a way to ad-dress them so they do not negatively influence your work with others. Journaling, participating in a loss specific support group, counseling, even courses like this one, on. Grief can be helpful.

3. There are many forums, chat rooms, and support groups available on the Internet that can be accessed through the Web links provided for this text. Choose the method that works best for you, but take the time you need to deal with your own losses. It will inevitably result in your providing better care for others who are coping with loss.

While students find this assignment very challenging, they also universally report that it is useful in helping to prepare them to help others. As Hooeyman and Kramer (2006) point out, "Disciplined self-awareness is necessary to ensure that we respond to the needs of our clients and not our own" (p. 355).

As discussed in Chapters 1 and 2, grief is a reaction to many different types of losses, not only loss through death. Even if you have not yet sustained the death of a significant other in your life, you have most likely experienced the loss of a relationship or other symbolic losses that will impact your reactions to others' losses. Not surprisingly, older and younger students alike report that through self-exploration, they identify issues related to loss in their own personal and professional lives that have had a major impact. The exercise has helped many to complete their own grieving process and better equip them to cope with grief and loss in their families and their workplaces. One student offered her thoughts about this process in a class discussion.

She said she had been to only two funerals in her life. Holding a wake and then a funeral was the way that her ethnic group practiced a funeral ritual. During the class, she realized she had always been afraid of death, so she avoided funerals as much as she could. What she had observed in her two experiences attending them, however, was that viewing the body and accepting the condolences of others seemed to be helpful to the mourners. She said that taking the class had helped her sort out a lot of unresolved and unanswered issues in her life about death and loss. She stated her intention to continue to deal with and sort out her own feelings, believing that it would better prepare her to help others in the internship she'd signed up for in a hospital. Many students subsequently have expressed similar feelings and fears about studying grief and loss, but they have realized the personal and professional benefits of tackling this difficult subject, just as I have.

Gerry, Gail, David, Lorenzo, Helen, Bill, and Jonathan: These are only a handful of the hundreds of people who have touched my life through my work as an oncology social worker. Theirs are the faces that I see as clearly today as I did 5 or 10 or 20 years ago when I first met each of them. Lorenzo was a young college student who came to the large Boston cancer center where I had recently begun to work at the age of 24 and was the first person to look me in the eye and tell me he was afraid to die. He was 22 years old and had just learned that the acute lymphocytic leukemia that had initially struck him during his freshman year in college had reoccurred. I wasn't much older than he was at the time and still remember how acutely inadequate I felt in trying to respond to his fear.

Forty-year-old Bill, his wife, and five children shared with me their hopes for one more Christmas together in one of our many family meetings. Bill had melanoma that had traveled to his brain and he was committed to preparing his wife and children for the possibility of his death. His 10-year-old daughter Chrissy said to me, "I want my father to be alive for Christmas and also for my birthday." Bill lived for both but died shortly after, leaving his wife Yvonne, Chrissy, and her four brothers and sisters without a husband and father. While our interdisciplinary team couldn't help Bill live longer, we did succeed in helping to make the time he spent together with his family very meaningful.

Gerry was a high school guidance counselor. Helen was a mother of eight. Gail, who I first met in the 20th year of my oncology career, was a mother just my age with two daughters my two daughters' ages when she died after a hard fought battle with breast cancer. I had the privilege of meeting each of them at a time when impending loss made time and relationships seem more precious.

The close contact with loss has affected both my work and my personal life in different ways at different times. At a St. Patrick's day parade, crouched on a curb with my two young daughters waving our flags and shamrocks at the passing dignitaries and laughing at the Melha Shriners in their tiny cars skittering wildly across the road, the combined reminders of hospitals and limousines would take my mind back to the funeral I attended for Gerry, an exceptionally popular high school guidance counselor. It seemed like hundreds of us were lined up in the procession behind a long line of limousines carrying dozens of grief stricken family members to the funeral. At the church, which couldn't hold all of the mourners, many of us stood on the steps outside, straining to hear his students speaking in his honor about the unfairness of losing their mentor. Then, my young daughter, tugging on my arm, would bring me consciously back to the parade from far away.

In a social group of young mothers, each of us pushing our toddlers on swings and sharing views on local pediatricians, the image of a stoic 17-year-old boy uprooted by leukemia from timber country in rural Maine and transplanted in Boston would suddenly be with me. I would remember him valiantly plodding the hallways of the transplant center pushing his IV pole on wheels in his hospital gown, his once muscular legs moving like shortened stilts-slowly and laboriously, his mother by his side. I would flash back to the look of bewilderment on his face when the oncology fellow who'd aggressively and optimistically offered one potential solution after another that we all clung to, finally admitted, "we can try to keep you comfortable…." In my memory I could almost feel my hand supporting his mother as her legs folded under her at the news and then I would refocus and be back with the group in my backyard, pushing my own baby in her swing.

Inevitably, certain losses would remind me of deaths in my own family. Our 10-month-old niece's death from Sudden Infant Death Syndrome (SIDS) and my sister-in-law's wrenching grief could be activated by any mother's reaction to her child's death and every elderly man could conjure up the hollow feeling of emptiness I felt at the death of my grandfather who had been such a mentor to me.

At times, over the years, when the impact of these losses has felt overwhelming, I have asked myself whether I could continue to become so close to people-a family-facing death. How many more painful memories could I accumulate? At times I have cried in my car all the way home from the hospital or a client's home, tears triggered by a song on the radio or a simple public service announcement. When this happened, I would think about changing jobs-giving up the intense emotional challenges of witnessing death, and weathering grief. At times I, like many professionals in the field, would give less than all of myself out of fear that I wouldn't be able to bear any more anguish. I read articles on "burnout" and "compassion fatigue" and questioned the wisdom of continuing, thinking maybe its time for a break or maybe I've helped as many people as I can help. Fortunately, I have had the benefit of excellent consultation from my supervisors and colleagues, attended many professional development programs, and participated in peer-support sessions where I could talk about these feelings and thoughts. I have also derived a great deal of inspiration from the grieving people I have come to know in my work.

One example of such inspiration came from a breast cancer survivor who invited me to a reading of her poetry. She is gifted with words and had written her way through multiple surgeries and chemotherapy treatments, the loss of her hair, and all of the indignities and terrors one must endure when cancer wreaks its havoc. As a celebration for 5 years of survival, she arranged a beautiful ceremony, inviting family, old friends, and new acquaintances made during her treatment. She treated us all to delicious food and then read the following poem aloud from her book, *Feeling Light in the Dark* (Walker, 1997).

"Post-op surgery six"

I raise my arm above my head,
Pulling from the heart which has been
Above it all.
Now it stops, as final as death.

There is no chance, or thought
To be Superwoman
No temptation to push a little harder,
Or defy the odds.

I have never known
The fragility of my own cells.
The starkness of reality, without denial,
Is terrifying.

(Walker, 1997)

It was encouraging to be at this celebration of life with this woman, and others, who had endured so much. As we gathered in a circle following her reading, she invited everyone to think of an affirmation in response to whatever emotions the reading and the celebration had elicited in us. We held hands and as I looked around the circle at all of the people who felt connected to this woman, many, including myself, through cancer, I was reminded of a quote I heard at a grief training. It sustained me then and has continued to sustain me in the past 8 years since this ceremony.

"Nobody has ever measured, even poets, how much a heart can hold"
Zelda Fitzgerald

It is a simple affirmation but I repeat it whenever I need inspiration to get through the difficult times. Jackie, the poet, used her experience to cofound an organization in our community, Cancer Connection, which provides support to other survivors. I experienced a tremendous sense of loss when she died in 2008 but she left a legacy and gift to our entire community and I have the privilege of honoring her every week when facilitating the breast cancer group for this organization. Finding ways to make meaning from our losses through helping others is a way that many of us cope with continuous loss. I have come to think of the human heart not as a container for emotions, with limits and boundaries and a defined area that can be overfilled. Instead, I think of our hearts as the part of each of us that connects us to others, giving and receiving the life force that sustains us in human relationships. I believe that in order to work effectively with others who are sustaining, or have sustained, losses, we must do what Marion Stonberg (1980), a leader in the field of oncology social work, advises us to do: listen *to* our hearts and listen *with* our hearts.

Our own losses can revisit us, triggered by a familiar smell, expression, or experience. We need to acknowledge the feelings related to these losses and yet allow ourselves to be free enough to feel new feelings for new people and relationships. If we can learn to do this, we can do the important work of helping others do the same.

ASSESSING AND ENHANCING OUR READINESS TO ADDRESS GRIEF IN OUR WORK

What is of greatest importance in a person's life is not just the nature and extent of his or her experiences but what has been learned from them.

Norman Cousins

How do we know if we are ready to help others with their grief? Our own thoughts, feelings, and beliefs inevitably impact the way we approach those who are experiencing grief. That is why self-assessment and self-awareness are so important for every professional who interacts with others experiencing loss. This includes physical, speech, respiratory, and occupational therapists working with those who have experienced the loss of bodily integrity that comes from stroke, auto accidents, or war injury. It also includes teachers, probation officers, and residential group home workers who encounter children who have sustained the loss of family through death, foster care placement, divorce, or even the fleeing of one's country of origin to escape political oppression. What memories or experiences in our own lives are likely to be activated when we hear of these losses? What physical and emotional reactions in our bodies, our minds, or our hearts give us clues that we are reacting to our own losses as well as theirs?

The more aware we are, the more able we will be to identify when a client's situation is making us feel uncomfortable and what to do about it. On the positive side, self-awareness can also increase our capacity to understand and empathize with the unique responses of others to loss. Bill Moyers helped many of us in America to think about issues of dying and loss in his PBS series *On Our Own Terms*. The Web site for the program offers a wealth of information and resources to both professionals and the public. You may wish to use the link to this site provided in the Internet Resources of this text to complete an interactive self-assessment.

BRINGING UP PERSONAL EMOTIONS AND MEMORIES FOR EVERY PROFESSIONAL

Those of us who choose to work with others have chosen our work because we genuinely like and want to help others. Many of us establish strong connections with the people we work with and we, too, need to grieve when facing the loss of these relationships. This can be difficult because many patients and families facing slowly progressive or chronic diseases, or those with injuries that are not immediately life threatening, are not able to directly acknowledge their reactions to loss. They may react initially with denial or anger, common reactions which will be discussed more fully in the next several chapters. This can make our work with them more challenging. Understanding their reactions, as well as our own, makes it possible for us to reach out and help, despite the challenges. One seasoned substance abuse counselor discusses how grief and loss enter into his work and professional practice.

> Reading about grief has forced me to reflect on the deaths of clients that I have built therapeutic relationships with during the course of my work as a substance abuse counselor. Although I maintain a professional therapeutic

relationship with clients, it is still a relationship, nonetheless. The reason that these relationships become so intense is because I have been working for the same company for 10+ years, and have worked in all of our available modalities of treatment. Out-pt 2-yrs, long-term tx. 1-yr, halfway house manager/counselor 3-yrs, and detox/evaluation 4-yrs. During this time period I have had a lot of clients. But, most of the clients are repeaters, coming through detox or treatment, in most cases, multiple times. Therefore, there are many clients that I have known for my entire 10-yr experience. The reason this is so pertinent to this discussion is that sometimes they die. At one point over the years, the death of clients was so regular that our long-term facility ceased taking clients who were high risk.... One client walked, fell, or was pushed in front of a train. The circumstances of his demise are still unknown or being withheld. In our detox facility, clients are in and out multiple times, until one day, they just don't come back. Eventually, someone will recognize the name in the paper or hear about the death at an AA meeting. A lot of times, the fatality is passed on to us by a returning client. Worden states that a counselor can avoid burnout by practicing "active grieving." I practice active grieving often. The death of a client affects me in multiple ways; first, I wonder if there is more I could have done that would have made a difference, second, I become angry, thinking how senseless the death was, and it could have been avoided if the client would have gone to treatment on their previous detox, third, I go through what Worden describes as "existential anxiety" or awareness of my own mortality. Fortunately, I have found ways to process my thoughts and emotions related to the loss. (Ward, 2003)

Limited preparation and support for grief in organizations

Unfortunately, despite the frequency and intensity of loss that professional helpers sustain in their work, many of the institutions and organizations that provide services to individuals and families who are grieving fail to provide training and ongoing support to their own staff for processing grief. Paul Brenner (1999) attributes this to the medical model that is practiced within many organizations, in which death is viewed as the enemy and therefore the needs of grieving staff are acknowledged only through a very brief bereavement leave with little or no formal support for processing grief. He suggests that institutions and agencies must create a new culture that trains and supports their staff in grief and grief care.

Therese Rando (1984) points to the organizational constraints that make it difficult for professional helpers who work with those who are dying to grieve themselves, noting the lack of understanding of mourning in caregivers that occurs when patients die. While progress has been made in the more than two decades since Rando published *Grief, Dying and Death*, evidence-based models for professional preparation and staff support are not practiced in every setting, particularly outside hospice and palliative care programs (Rezenbrink, 2004). Even in the literature on staff support and coping, emphasis is placed on the professional's own self-preparation and self-care (Hooyman, & Kramer, 2006, Worden, 2009) and *individual* resilience (Finck-Samnick, 2010) rather than on building resilient workplaces that are structured and function in ways that promote staff resilience (van Breda, 2011).

INCREASED RECOGNITION OF THE IMPACT OF GRIEF ON PROFESSIONALS

Since the first edition of this textbook was published in 2006, there has been new interest in the impact of loss and grief on professional caretakers and increased recognition of the need for professionals to be prepared to cope with loss. During the conflicts in the Middle East in the first decade of the 21st century, both civilian and military medical personnel have been involved in caretaking severely injured and dying military personnel as well as their grieving family members. While this is no different than in past wars, the intensity of caring for physically injured combat personnel, and the grief that results from working so closely with loss and death, has been recognized by the U.S. military in the Afghanistan and Iraq wars. Administrative personnel are now encouraged to be vigilant in addressing therapeutic needs related to the emotional reactions, including grief (Wain et al., 2011).

Similar to the military, we would expect that in hospitals, nursing homes, and other medical settings where caregivers experience close and frequent proximity to loss, staff grief reactions would be recognized. The findings of a study of grief related symptoms and the need for bereavement support among long-term care staff show that too often bereavement support is not provided. This study report entitled "How Well Are We Caring for the Caregivers?" indicates that 72% of the 236 staff surveyed across six programs experienced at least one grief-related symptom in the month prior to the survey and the symptoms varied. The longer the staff worked in the organization and cared for patients, the more symptoms they reported. While staff in the study identified several informal sources of bereavement support, 96% said they would use additional support services if they were offered (Rickerson et al., 2005).

Support may be even less available in organizations in which death or loss is not as frequent an occurrence. Child protective workers are expected to support children who are experiencing the loss of a biological parent, sometimes through death and sometimes through foster care placement due to abuse or neglect. Yet these workers are rarely provided training or adequate time to assist children or families with grief reactions. Often those who receive the least support for their grief are helping professionals themselves, whose employers, or even coworkers, do not acknowledge the grief of helping professionals. Guidelines and methods for assessing and assisting with grief reactions are included in subsequent chapters. These are applicable both to ourselves as helping professionals and to our clients. Increasing awareness and acknowledgment of our feelings related to grief is the first step to providing care to others. The next step is equipping ourselves with the knowledge and skills that will make our work with others who are grieving more effective. Reading this book, and this chapter in particular, is an important part of the process of self-preparation. After reading this chapter and Chapter 13 on professional resilience, you will have been challenged to identify and process your own grief experiences as well as developing an ongoing plan for professional sustainment both for yourself and all those in your employment or practice setting.

Sources of education and support

Considerable investment has been made in the past two decades in studying and promoting professional development in the arena of end-of-life care and grief (Csikai, & Walsh-Burke, 2005).

Supportive Care of the Dying is an advocacy organization involved in a national initiative to improve care and services to those who are dealing with dying and death in America. This organization, along with others, has begun to establish standards and competencies for end-of-life care for professionals and organizations. Grief care is included in the concept of end-of-life care, since those who are anticipating the end of life as well as those who have experienced a death experience grief.

Tools for Change is a set of assessment tools that are available on the organization's Web site. (This link is found in Pearson's MySocialWorkLab for Advancing Core Competencies under Resources in the "Grief and Loss" section). Competencies have been established for people dealing with the end of life in the physical, spiritual, emotional, relationship, and communication realms of care. These competencies can serve as an important self-check to determine readiness to help in the arena of grief.

For example, competence in the emotional aspects of care includes the ability to:

- Support clients in their expression of emotional needs,
- Actively listen,
- Refer to support groups, peer-support programs, and professional experts,
- Ask open-ended questions such as "how are you doing?" (Supportive Care of the Dying, 2004)

Many professional organizations have also established standards or competencies for those who practice specific disciplines such as nursing, physical therapy, education, and social work. While many of the allied health professions have established competencies in the arena of end-of-life care, those outside the health field may not yet specifically address grief and loss. It is useful to contact the professional organization in your discipline to see what has been established as well as what training resources it offers. The intervention chapters in this text provide you with some basic skills and strategies that you can use as well.

SUPERVISION, CONSULTATION, AND COLLABORATION WITH OTHER HELPING PROFESSIONALS

Supervision, consultation, and collaboration are important in all helping professionals' work. However, they can be especially important when we are working with clients who have experienced trauma or loss. Supervision provides an opportunity to assess, in an ongoing way, both the effectiveness of our work and the effect of our work on us. Most of us, in training internships, have the benefit of supervision and consultation with experienced staff in our own disciplines who can answer our questions, provide information and expertise, and address concerns about our work. In the teaching profession, many systems include "Master Teachers," seasoned classroom instructors who provide modeling and consultation to those newer to the profession in addition to the modeling and consultation that occur during teacher training experiences.

In education and other professions, supervision and consultation can be used to examine the feelings and thoughts that we experience as we interact with others in distress. It is especially important to seek the help of a supervisor when our exposure to the distress of others is prolonged, frequent, or intense. Staff in long-term care and emergency room settings, inner-city schools, and child protective and residential treatment settings are among those who work with students and clients who are repeatedly exposed to trauma and loss, and thus may experience *vicarious trauma* or *secondary trauma* with repeated or intense exposure to loss.

Secondary trauma

Vicarious trauma or "secondary trauma" is now recognized as a common reaction in professionals who work closely with individuals or groups who have directly experienced trauma. While the mental health professions have identified stress and trauma associated with working closely with distressed clients for some time, other professions have only recently begun to identify these phenomena in their training programs. Even the legal profession has begun to recognize that lawyers, judges, court staff, and interpreters can be affected (Gelvick, 2011).

In a study of vicarious trauma in attorneys, mental health workers, and social service workers, Levin and Greisberg (2003) found that attorneys had higher levels of secondary trauma than the other professionals and attributed this in part to the lack of training that attorneys receive in working with traumatized clients. Child protective workers who hear graphic details of child abuse, teachers who read what their students have written about traumatic events, health care workers who witness the traumatic physical and emotional effects of illness and injury are all likely to experience some degree of secondary trauma, and experience grief reactions as a result. Supervisors, peers, and consultants can help us to recognize when our own reactions may be distressed. This is important because we may not ourselves always recognize when our avoidance, anger, or tearfulness is a reaction to the distress we have witnessed in our clients or students. Supervision and consultation can also help us to identify strategies to make the best use of our knowledge, skill, and natural helping instincts and to manage our own stress as well as the stress of those we are helping.

One student's internship at a women's prison brought her into close contact with inmates whose lives had been filled with losses—loss due to deaths of family and friends, loss of their children to protective service placements, loss of their freedom and sense of personal self-efficacy, and even losses of the close relationships some formed in prison. She found that these losses activated strong feelings in her—feelings related to her own life as well as the losses these women had sustained. In her loss and bereavement journal she wrote that she had learned about loss quickly at the jail. It was such a drastic change from anything else she had ever experienced that she said she would have been lost without the help of her supervisor and fellow workers because she was just beginning to learn about her emotional limitations and the importance of recognizing the need for a break or time out.

In addition to the consultation and support that is provided in supervision, in most settings, professionals work alongside professionals from other disciplines. Many times this occurs in the context of a multi-disciplinary or interdisciplinary team. The term *interdisciplinary team* is often used now to describe a team of professionals from different disciplines who have a formal structure for communication and collaboration in developing a comprehensive plan and carrying it out. The term *multidisciplinary team* is generally used in settings in which there is not a formally established structure, such as a team meeting, to facilitate communication and collaboration among team members. In both interdisciplinary and multidisciplinary team settings, there is acknowledgment that professionals and paraprofessionals from a variety of disciplines may be working to help a single child, client, or student to achieve goals. In a multidisciplinary setting, however, the emphasis is on the *multiple* disciplines in the system rather than on *inter*disciplinary communication. This is an important distinction because it may be more difficult for the professionals in a multidisciplinary setting to have direct communication with one another.

In the absence of a team meeting or other formal structure for collaboration that is often present in an interdisciplinary team setting, individual team members may have to take more initiative to communicate and collaborate with other specialties. There also may be less opportunity for providing each other with support or information in relation to a client's grief reactions. For example, in a school setting the team may include teachers, guidance personnel, special education staff, and even rehabilitation specialists such as physical therapists, occupational, and speech and language therapists. These team members may formally meet if a child has an individual education plan (IEP), when team meetings are mandated. Without a formal IEP that mandates meetings, however, professionals in multidisciplinary settings may not have an opportunity to formally meet to discuss a student's challenges and contribute their ideas.

It is therefore most important that helping professionals identify their own grief-related needs as part of their professional development and find ways to address them as they arise in the work.

In medical settings the team often includes a physician, nurse, social worker, pharmacist, chaplain, and other allied health professionals. In corrections and child welfare settings, the team may not be as formally structured, but lawyers, parole or probation officers, child welfare workers, and psychologists or addictions specialists may all be involved in working with a client, and therefore must communicate or collaborate with one another. All may be affected by the client's losses and grief reactions but may not have an opportunity to process their own feelings.

The benefit of an interdisciplinary team model is that each member of the team contributes expertise to the treatment (or education) plan. Not all members of the team are expected to work directly to address emotional concerns. Yet, each must be prepared to understand and respond effectively to the various types of distress expressed by those the team is trying to help. This is particularly true when a death or significant loss is causing distress, because each of us plays an important role in the overall treatment and every person on the team is likely to encounter emotional reactions in carrying out our roles and functions. For example, occupational and physical therapists, like teachers, need to be prepared to listen supportively and help problem solve when emotional distress is evident, and in particular, when it negatively impacts their patients' or students' ability to carry out important tasks.

Similarly, professionals in the legal arena may find that unresolved grief may be making it impossible for their client to move toward necessary change. An elderly client, for example, who is facing multiple losses and experiencing complicated grief, may appear to have memory or other deficits that bring competency into question. Adolescents experiencing traumatic losses may act out aggressively and be unable to effectively adapt until their grief issues are addressed. Chapter 4 will review grief reactions that are considered by grief experts to be normal and complicated responses for individuals of various cultures and stages of the life span; this information will enable you to more effectively respond to those who have sustained losses. It is important to remember, however, that there are many sources of help for you, your students/clients, and organizations.

Often, when case histories are shared in an interdisciplinary team context, social workers or other mental health professionals can help to identify when grief reactions are in evidence and can recommend specific interventions to address them. Every professional, however, who is attuned to the various manifestations of grief, can make an effective intervention through acknowledging loss and the distress he or she observes in reaction to it. Often this goes a long way toward establishing an effective working relationship in which you are viewed as someone who understands. In addition, being attuned to and acknowledging grief can enable you to help a client or student get expert help when needed. Sharing important information with other disciplines and making referrals when necessary is an important kind of interdisciplinary collaboration that can be carried out in any setting, even in the absence of a formal team.

More information about specific interventions for grief and the roles of various disciplines is included in Chapters 11, 12, and 13.

SUMMARY

As professional helpers, it is important to review our own experiences with loss and grief, not only to understand and respond effectively to the grief of others, but also to ensure that we are adequately aware of, and attending to, our own grief. It is also essential to be aware of the feelings that are stimulated in us when we work closely with clients who have experienced trauma and loss. Our own thoughts, feelings, and beliefs inevitably impact the way we approach those who are experiencing grief. Unfortunately, despite the frequency and intensity of loss that professional helpers in every discipline sustain in their work, many professional training programs and organizations that employ these professionals fail to provide training and ongoing support to their own staff for processing grief. Professional organizations and even organizations devoted to grief and loss, however, do offer training and support in this area. Supervision as well as collaboration with other committed professionals can ameliorate the stress and secondary trauma that can result from the intensity of the work.

CHAPTER **4**

Loss and Grief Across the Life Span: Childhood and Adolescence

CHAPTER OUTLINE

My story is about my mom. She had a disease. It was called leukemia. She had to go in the hospital for a long time. Then she came home. That was the best day. The worst day was when she had to go back in the hospital. I was crying when my dad told me. Then a month later, my dad said my mom was dying. I was crying and my dad was too.

A child, age 8, speaking in a children's bereavement group

LOSS IN THE FORMATIVE YEARS

As discussed in the preceding chapters, grief is experienced in reaction to many kinds of losses people experience over a lifetime. Young children may accumulate multiple losses, both symbolic and actual, depending on their family situation, community, and events taking place in the world during their formative years.

31

While grief experts acknowledge that grief is a reaction to many different kinds of losses, symbolic as well as physical, research does not yet adequately tell us how reactions to symbolic losses differ from reactions to death. Most of the empirical studies that inform our understanding of grief in children and teens have examined reactions to deaths of significant others (Christ, 2000; Christ, 2006; Worden, 1996). These studies are helpful because they can guide us in understanding the grief reactions of children of different ages, cultural backgrounds, and genders to loss. If we understand, for example, how 7-year-old children typically react to loss due to a parent's or grandparent's death, we can be better prepared to support and assist them through their mourning process. We can also extrapolate from these studies to construct research to better inform our understanding of the similarities and differences between grief in reaction to death and grief in reaction to symbolic loss such as the loss of intact family through divorce or foster care placement. With 43% of marriages ending in divorce and almost half a million children in foster care, we can see that these life events affect a significant number of children and adolescents.

The focus of this chapter is on the early years of the lifespan and how grief, as a reaction to death, is generally experienced and expressed by children and adolescents. This information is based on empirical studies and theoretical frameworks addressing "normal grief." Specific grief theories and information about *complicated* grief is included in Chapter 7. In this chapter common losses are reviewed, as well as external and developmental factors that influence grief reactions in these life stages. Also included are suggestions for those of us who are in a position to help children, adolescents, and families to cope with loss and grief. Specific evidence-based intervention models are identified along with sources of additional information that can be useful to both the professional helper and children and parents themselves. It is hoped that learning how to identify normal grief reactions and facilitate coping with grief resulting from loss through death can also help you to be attuned and responsive to the grief-related emotions and behaviors that are expressed in reaction to other types of losses.

EXTERNAL FACTORS INFLUENCING GRIEF REACTIONS IN CHILDREN AND ADOLESCENTS

Growing up in a virtual world of multiple telecommunications is most certainly an influential factor in the development of children and adolescents as well as their grief reactions. Most current adults were children when President John F. Kennedy died and they were directly exposed to their own families' and communities' reactions as well as the reactions of millions of people documented through radio and television, and print media. For some, the president's death was an actual loss, for others it constituted a symbolic loss of a safe and secure nation. The federal government, the national media, and the president's family each played an instrumental role in influencing the responses and grief reactions of children as well as adults to this loss. On a national day of "mourning," all government offices and schools were closed, allowing the people affected by his death to attend his funeral mass or view it on television, which helped many to grasp the reality of the president's death and express their grief. Everyone in the nation, along with Kennedy's family, were considered to be "bereaved," having experienced the loss of their president.

The terrorist attacks of September 11, 2001, represented a similar combination of symbolic and actual losses for those who were children and adolescents in a later generation who have been growing up with the addition of more extensive media exposure through the Internet. The intense exposure to multiple information outlets, including Facebook, blogs, and millions of Web sites, means that few, even the youngest, in our culture can avoid exposure to loss and grief particularly related to deaths of celebrities, and traumatic national and international events. In a single day in 2010, children may see dying animals coated with oil on television, watch reactions to a celebrity death on an Internet home page pop-up, hear descriptions of bombing mortalities in Afghanistan on the car radio, see pictures of a teenager who committed suicide due to bullying on a national magazine cover, and read a local newspaper headline decrying a local murder, which they might also be receiving through a news alert on their cell phones.

Although the impact of the media on grief reactions is still underresearched, emerging data suggests that it does impact children and adolescents in both positive and negative ways (Hall & Reid, 2009; Williams & Merten, 2009). This influence, in addition to gender, culture, developmental stage, and social supports, must be considered in work with children in every setting. One of the contributions that helping professionals can make is to attune children and parents to the helpful as well as harmful influences children may be exposed to through telecommunications.

Family systems also have a significant influence on children's and teens' reactions. Social learning theory stresses the importance of modeling on the way that children learn all kinds of behaviors, including those related to grief and loss. In the exercise (available online) for Chapter 3 you were encouraged to look back at your own early loss experiences. Inevitably when I assign this exercise in class, a substantial number of students report they have felt uncomfortable with death and expressing feelings related to loss because death was not talked about openly and feelings were not expressed directly in their families of origin when they were children. A family's cultural background and spiritual orientation are important influences in the way that they respond to loss and communicate about it. These influences will be discussed in more depth in Chapter 8.

The relationship between children and the person who dies, or in the case of divorce or foster care placement, the people they are separated from, also influences the grief reaction. Children and adolescents are more dependent on family members for their safety, shelter, and love than individuals at other stages of the life cycle, and therefore loss at an earlier, more dependent stage of development affects multiple aspects of their life and for a greater portion of their life to come. In the case of a parent's death due to illness, factors such as longer duration of illness and intensity of symptoms have been shown to have a greater impact on children. However, in my grief therapy practice I see many adults who still experience conflict about trust in relationships many years after a parent died suddenly in their early childhood. Much of this depends on the emotional availability and support for grieving provided by the surviving parent and other significant adults.

THE INFLUENCE OF DEVELOPMENT ON GRIEF REACTIONS

Responses to death are influenced by age and developmental stage in addition to gender, cultural, and spiritual background and an individual's relationship to the person who died. The more dependent a person is on the person who has died, for example, the more he or she will be affected by changes in roles and functioning that the loss imposes.

The quote at the beginning of this chapter by an 8-year-old whose mother died is an example of a primary attachment, the loss of which has a profound impact. If the relationship between two individuals was conflicted before the loss occurred, perhaps due to alcohol abuse or domestic violence, the grieving child may experience a complicated grief reaction. More information about the factors that influence complicated grief reactions will be discussed in Chapter 7, but it is important to keep in mind that there is no single factor such as age that is important. All of these influences are important to keep in mind when working with children and teens at different ages and developmental stages.

Some of the factors that influence a child's cognitive, emotional, and behavioral reactions to death, in addition to his or her chronological age, include earlier experiences with death, the reactions of adults and the other children around them, and the child's own unique personality and coping style. The National Cancer Institute provides an excellent overview of grief reactions in children on its Web site. The opportunity a child has to share his or her feelings and memories during the illness and following the death of his or her parent, the surviving parent's ability to cope with stress and his or her own reactions, and consistent positive relationships with other adults are identified as factors that influence grief (National Cancer Institute, 2010).

Many adults misinterpret children's behavior following a loss, thinking that if a child does not directly express sadness, he or she is not grieving. While children do experience grief reactions, they may not show their feelings, or articulate them, as openly as adults. Young children, even those grieving the loss of a very significant person such as a parent, may not outwardly evidence their grief. They may throw themselves into activities unrelated to those the rest of the family is undertaking, for example, engaging in play activities at the funeral home while other members of the family are crying. Adults in the family may interpret this to mean that the child doesn't really understand, or is not emotionally affected by the death. This behavior does not necessarily indicate that the child is not experiencing grief, however. Often, young children are less able to put their feelings into words, the way that older children and adults can. Young children are also highly distractible and they transition easily from one topic of thought, or one feeling, to another. Sometimes this protects them from painful feelings or thoughts that are too overwhelming.

Because young children may not have the same acquisition of language as older children or adults, feelings or fears may be expressed through behaviors rather than words. School-age children, who may have more language but who also may be sensitive to others' reactions, may not verbalize directly, but may express their feelings and thoughts through artwork, play, or somatic (physical) complaints. Understanding common reactions of children at different stages of development, and being attuned to expressions of these as one observes and interacts with them, can prepare family members, teachers, and other helping professionals to assist them.

GRIEF REACTIONS AT DIFFERENT DEVELOPMENTAL STAGES

Children at different stages of development understand death and express their grief differently. Common reactions, based on empirical and clinical literature, are described for each of these stages, although it is important to keep in mind that every individual is unique and therefore may react somewhat differently, based on a complex mix of influential factors.

Infants

Key developmental issues for infants and toddlers are dependency and attachment. At this earliest stage of development, very young children need to feel secure in the care of adults. They must develop trust that nurturing adults will provide consistent shelter, protection, and love in order to develop healthy attachment in future relationships. While very young children do not yet have the capacity to recognize death, they will react to the loss of a consistent caregiver. There are some developmental tasks they have not yet achieved that make it more difficult for them to understand and cope with loss.

DEVELOPMENTAL FACTORS

- Dependence on caregivers for all basic needs
- Limited "object constancy" (the understanding that a person/object exists, even if not physically present)
- Limited ability to verbalize
- Few coping strategies to regulate tension

UNDERSTANDING OF DEATH   Infants do not recognize death, but they do experience feelings of loss in reaction to separation that are part of developing an awareness of death.

REACTIONS TO LOSS   Infants who have been separated from their mothers or primary caregivers may be sluggish, quiet, and unresponsive to a smile or a coo. They may undergo physical changes (i.e., weight loss), be less active, and sleep less. They may also cry and appear inconsolable.

STRATEGIES TO ASSIST INFANTS

- Maintaining normal routines of care giving and familiar surroundings
- Providing a consistent caregiver who can give frequent and lengthy periods of love and attention, including holding and hugging
- Providing consistent, gentle physical and verbal reassurance and comfort
- Expressing confidence in the child and the world

Age 2–3 years (toddlers)

Like infants, toddlers also are almost completely dependent on caregivers to provide for their basic needs, although they are making attempts at mastery and independence. They show great variation in their cognitive and emotional development. While toddlers have begun to acquire language, their ability to comprehend and express ideas and feelings verbally is still quite limited. Children at this age often confuse death with sleep and may experience anxiety related to this as early as age 3. They may express distress through regression, often giving up previously acquired skills such as speaking clearly, toileting, and self-soothing at bedtime.

DEVELOPMENTAL FACTORS

- Ambivalence about independence
- Increasing comprehension and articulation of language
- Beginning mastery of motor and fine motor skills
- Learning by mimicking and following example of others

UNDERSTANDING OF DEATH   Children under age 3 cannot cognitively understand death. They cannot differentiate a parent's absence for a short time from a long time. They can sense loss or change in something but they often cannot verbally explain or discuss it.

REACTIONS TO LOSS   Children under age 3 often express discomfort or insecurity through frequent crying or protest. They express distress or sadness through withdrawal, loss of interest in usual activities, and changes in eating and sleeping patterns. They may show regression through clinging or screaming when a caregiver tries to leave, evidencing increased dependence in activities of daily living.

STRATEGIES TO ASSIST VERY YOUNG CHILDREN

- Maintaining normal routines and familiar surroundings
- Providing consistent caregivers who can give frequent and lengthy periods of love and attention including holding and hugging
- Providing consistent, gentle physical and verbal reassurance and comfort
- Providing simple, understandable verbal explanations for changes
- Naming feelings expressed by the child and those he or she observes being expressed by others, such as "daddy feels sad, that is why he is crying"

Age 3–6 years

Children at this stage of development are still thinking concretely and may perceive death as a kind of sleep; the person is alive, but only in a limited way or in a distant place. Children cannot fully separate death from life. Their concerns may be focused on how the death directly affects them. The child's concept of death may also involve magical thinking. For example, the child may think that his or her thoughts can cause another person to become sick or die. Grieving children under age 5 may have trouble eating, sleeping, and controlling bladder and bowel functions.

DEVELOPMENTAL FACTORS

- Developing a fuller mastery of language
- Learning to read
- Continuing to master fine motor and physical skills
- Expressing feelings through art and play
- Acquiring social skills through interactions with, and observation of, others

UNDERSTANDING OF DEATH   Because they cannot quite comprehend the difference between life and death, children at this age may view the deceased person as continuing to live in a limited way. They may ask questions about the deceased (e.g., how does the deceased eat, breathe, or play?). While young children may know that death occurs physically, they usually think it is temporary or reversible, and not final.

REACTIONS TO LOSS   Since children depend on parents and other adults to take care of them, a grieving child may wonder who will care for him or her or meet his or her needs after the death of an important person. They may be very anxious that something bad like death could happen to them or someone else upon whom they are dependent, such as a surviving parent. They may exhibit searching behaviors, viewing videotapes or photographs of the deceased loved one repeatedly or asking when and how the loved one might return.

STRATEGIES TO ASSIST PRESCHOOL-AGED CHILDREN (IN ADDITION TO THE STRATEGIES SUGGESTED FOR YOUNGER CHILDREN)

- Explaining death in simple and direct terms, including only as much detail as the child is able to understand
- Answering a child's questions honestly and directly, making sure that the child understands the explanations provided
- Reassuring children about their own security and explain that they will continue to be loved and cared for (they often worry that their surviving parent or caregiver will go away)
- Encouraging mastery of age-appropriate skills while allowing for regression
- Expressing confidence in the child and the world

Age 6–9 years

Children at this age range are commonly very curious about death and may ask questions about what happens to one's body when a person dies. These children are striving for mastery and are commonly very curious about death. In their attempt to make sense of events, children may attribute responsibility for death to themselves or others. They may even believe they have magical powers, thinking they have actually caused or contributed to a death if they had thought bad things or misbehaved and may view death as a punishment. Because they are striving for mastery and want to be involved in family decisions, children this age and older often benefit from being invited to contribute to memorial ceremonies or activities. If the child wants to attend the funeral, wake, or memorial service, he or she should be given, in advance, a full explanation of what to expect.

DEVELOPMENTAL FACTORS

- Relationships with peers and adults are important
- Striving for mastery of information and tasks
- Superego and a sense of responsibility are developing
- Cognitively, they are still thinking concretely

UNDERSTANDING OF DEATH   Children's questions often indicate their efforts to fully understand death. For example, a child may ask, "I know uncle Bob died, but can he still see us up in heaven?" This may be a way of testing reality and also reflects the struggle to comprehend more abstract concepts.

REACTIONS TO LOSS   Grieving children can become afraid of school or have difficulty concentrating, may behave aggressively, become overly concerned about their own health, or withdraw from others. With information and support most children are able to carry on activities of daily living with confidence and competence; however, children at this age may regress emotionally and demonstrate separation anxiety or clinging. Boys sometimes become more aggressive (i.e., acting out in school), instead of directly expressing their sadness. Girls may become withdrawn or inattentive. Children may feel abandoned by both their deceased parent and their surviving parent if the surviving parent is grieving and is unable to emotionally support the child. The presence of a caring supportive adult, a positive relationship with at least one loving caregiver, opportunities for educational achievement, and availability of strong supports in school and in the community are the most important environmental protective factors for children experiencing a significant death (Gitterman, 2001, p. 212).

The following case example, provided by a student in my grief and loss class, is illustrative of this.

> I worked with an eight-year-old girl named "Katie" this past year at my placement. She was referred to me, as the school adjustment counselor, because of her intense anxiety issues when being away from her mother, following her parents' divorce. She would leave the classroom to use the restroom to cry. It got to a point where she was leaving the classroom too frequently and her teacher asked me to come on board. I was happy to take on "Katie" as a case. She was very sweet and kind, and loved our time together. She would always ask me if it was our time when I would see her in the halls or out on the playground. I was, however, concerned for her levels of nervousness and anxiety. Our meetings would always start off the same. I would have Katie pick an activity she would like and we would go through the activity with me peppering the conversation with questions about home. She would clam up and not really want to talk about home. She usually talked about her mother and how she was never home and doing a lot of sleepovers in a nearby community (not the hometown of the family). Once I started asking Katie to draw her family, it was clear her attachment to her mother was strong. She rarely mentioned her father or little brother. She mostly spoke of her mother or her pets. I think at the time making a "feelings" journal for Katie seemed like a good idea. Instead of leaving the class to go cry, she would get out her journal and write or color her feelings. This proved successful, but when I encouraged her to take it home, she wouldn't. Katie and I also made an "anxiety thermometer" that she could point to tell herself or someone else her level of anxiety. While I think that those were good tools to use at the time, I think I would go about things a little bit differently now. After taking the

course and reading all of the information about the effects of divorce on children in school, I see more clearly the signs that children put out. The withdrawal, lack of enthusiasm in peers and activities, feelings of abandonment, intense feelings of connection to one parent are all behaviors that Katie portrayed for time that I knew her. I think she would have benefitted from more direct conversation with me about family, and I could have been in stronger contact with her mother. Learning about the stages of grieving that children go through when they lose a parent to divorce or death and how they respond to loss by using pictures and drawings was very useful.

The same principles could be used for divorce as well as death. (Sharac, 2010)

STRATEGIES TO ASSIST SCHOOLAGE CHILDREN (IN ADDITION TO STRATEGIES SUGGESTED FOR YOUNGER CHILDREN)

- Having discussions of death that include the proper words, such as *died*, and *death*. (Words or phrases, for example, *passed away, he is sleeping*, or *we lost him* can confuse children and lead to misunderstanding.)
- Providing opportunities for children to ask questions freely and to express their feelings directly or through creative activities
- Providing reassurance that the child's thoughts, feelings, and behavior did not cause death
- Reading aloud stories or books that deal with death and allowing the child to share his or her reactions or questions
- Inviting children to share memories and participate in ceremonies or remembrance activities

Age 9–12 years

This is a stage of intense exploration and mastery in physical, cognitive, social, emotional, and spiritual development. The child is developing an increasing grasp of abstract concepts and is learning about living systems in school. By the time a child is 12 years old, death is seen as final and something that happens to everyone. Cultural and spiritual beliefs of the family and community are influential. In American society, for example, many adults avoid discussion of death or feelings of grief. Those who are grieving may withdraw rather than talk to others. Children, however, often talk to the people around them (even strangers) to see the reactions of others and to get clues for their own responses.

DEVELOPMENTAL FACTORS

- Interest in and capacity to understand biological processes
- Heightened sensitivity to others' emotions (guilt, anger, shame)
- Increased awareness of vulnerability
- Regressive and impulsive behaviors indicate stress
- Prepubertal changes

UNDERSTANDING OF DEATH   By the time a child is 9 years old, death is usually known to be unavoidable and is not seen as a punishment. Children may see death as final and frightening but also may see it as something that happens mostly to old people (and not to themselves or someone younger).

REACTIONS TO LOSS   Reactions often reflect what has been learned from parents and other adults around them. The family's spiritual beliefs are often evident in the child's statements about death and coping. Although most bereaved children do not show serious emotional/behavioral disturbances, children who lose a loved one are at a greater risk for symptoms of depression, withdrawal, anxiety, conduct problems, a change in school performance, and lower self-esteem. They are also capable of empathy and expressing caring to others who are grieving or who share similar experiences.

STRATEGIES TO ASSIST PREADOLESCENTS (IN ADDITION TO THOSE USEFUL FOR YOUNGER CHILDREN)

- Talking about the loss can help children learn effective ways to cope with loss
- Providing an opportunity to explore and discuss spiritual and cultural beliefs related to loss
- Providing physical outlets for strong emotions
- Encouraging expression of feelings through different media including art, music, dance, and writing
- Letting children know they are not alone and that others experience loss and the feelings related to it
- Modeling direct and constructive expression of feelings naturally associated with loss such as anger and sadness

Schools and other child-serving systems are increasingly recognizing that children who manifest behavioral problems often can be helped by asking whether they have lost someone they love and then by responding constructively when a child appears to be grieving. Addressing the grief can influence whether the behavioral problems intensify because the problem is not accurately assessed and addressed (Viboch, 2005).

The following case example is from a school adjustment counselor and illustrates how these strategies can be applied to assist children coping with symbolic loss as well as children coping with death.

CASE EXAMPLE: ANTONY

My client is an 11-year-old boy, Antony, whose mother died suddenly from an asthma attack when he was 9 years old. He had left for school as usual and when he returned home he learned that she had died. After his mother's death, his father, who had been separated from Antony's mother, moved away from the area and did not maintain contact with him. Antony's paternal grandmother assumed custody of him. When a child's parents disappear, without saying goodbye, it can make it hard for the child to adapt. "Because the young child invests all of his feelings in his parents (in comparison with adults who distribute their love among several meaningful relationships), the impact of a parent's death in childhood is all the more devastating. Only in childhood can death deprive an individual of so much opportunity to love and be loved and faced him with such a difficult task of adaptation" (Gitterman, 2001, p. 486). Antony did not directly express his grief because in the community he was raised in, when a man or a young boy cries they are considered weak. He did, however, demonstrate anger through aggression at school. When I began working with Antony, I let him know that feelings of anger and sadness are normal grief reactions. We began to work on expressing his feeling without being so aggressive (the anger is normal and needs to be expressed in constructive ways and anger). After several of our counseling sessions, Antony cried and for the first time he was able to express the way he felt about his mother's death and his broken relationship with his father.

(Nelia Erold, 2008)

Adolescence

Adolescence is generally thought of as a time of intense change, in biological, psychological, and social development. Most adolescents want to fit in with their peers and may view a death in the family as making them appear different from their peers, or placing greater demands on them when they want, and need to be, focused on their own developmental tasks, such as career planning, exploring intimate relationships with partners, and achieving personal goals in school, athletics, or other activities. They may also be acutely aware of the discomfort others evidence in talking about death, and they modulate their reactions accordingly or feel alienated or isolated from those who don't seem to understand. The following example is illustrative of this.

> The case that I have identified is a case from my current job. My client is a 14-year-old female whose parents both struggle with alcoholism. Both she and her 13-year-old sister reside with their father, and their mother resides in another town. The symbolic loss for both my client and her sister is that of parents/an intact family. These two young ladies are missing out on the role modeling of their mother (woman) and the childhood protection by their father. One of them stated that they wondered what it would be like to be a daddy's girl. My client, especially, is grieving the symbolic loss of her parents. In the therapy sessions that I conduct with her I utilize www.teensadvisor.com/drugs-alcohol/alcoholic-parents.html. This particular website addresses adolescent issues such as having parents that are alcoholic. The website discusses the symptoms of grief such as frustration, anger, denial, embarrassment, and guilt that teens tend to display when dealing with alcoholic parents. It recognizes that some teens may be in such denial that they make excuses for their parents and some become parentified children. It also describes other areas of teens' lives that are affected, including school, with declining grades and a lack of interest due to the ongoing grief, and social lives, as teens are often embarrassed and begin to isolate (which then leads to other issues such as depression).

My client has ongoing anger at her parents for their alcoholism and her reactions have included complete disrespect toward both of her parents, declining grades in school, and emotional instability. This website has been great with helping her to understand what is going on in her life and how to deal with her grief reactions.

(Shyanna Hicks, 2010)

As this example illustrates, the Internet provides a new vehicle for connecting with others who are experiencing similar life circumstances. The newly coined term *Internet natives* conveys the centrality of the Internet in the lives of many children and most teens. The National Hospice Foundation (NHF) provides an overview of the importance of the Internet in the lives of grieving teens and encourages counselors, clergy, social workers, child life specialists, educators, guidance counselors, funeral directors, and parents to become acquainted with the advantages and disadvantages of utilizing the Internet in grief on its Web site; NHF includes strategies for opening a dialog with children and adolescents about the ways they use the Internet as they mourn (http://www.hospicefoundation.org/pages/page. asp?page_id=96019).

DEVELOPMENTAL FACTORS

- Searching for identity
- Exploring sex and intimacy
- Peer relationships are very important
- Exposure to maladaptive responses to stress
- Abstract thinking

UNDERSTANDING OF DEATH   Adolescents comprehend that death is permanent, irreversible, and affects everyone. While they cognitively understand that death is final and inevitable, their behavior may indicate denial.

REACTIONS TO LOSS   Adolescents are capable of mature and thoughtful reflections on the meaning of life and death and may struggle with existential questions. Grieving adolescents are at risk for exposure to maladaptive coping strategies such as substance use, risk taking, and sexual experimentation. They may also be at risk for "parentification" or taking on adult roles and tasks before they are developmentally ready.

STRATEGIES TO ASSIST ADOLESCENTS

- Talking openly about death, indicating that the subject is not off limits
- Verbal or written explanations that tears, sadness, anger, guilt, and confusion are all part of normal grief
- Providing opportunities for adolescents to hear from and talk with peers who have also experienced loss (bereavement groups and retreats can be very effective)

- Inviting adolescents to help plan or participate in memorial or remembrance activities in the way that feels most comfortable to them
- Connecting adolescents to peers who have similar experiences to reduce isolation
- Encouraging journaling or other methods of expression of thoughts and feelings
- Constructing memorials, memory books (including virtual, Internet-based memorials), boxes, or quilts or providing other tangible ways to memorialize significant relationships

The following is a case example of how multiple strategies may be needed.

CASE EXAMPLE: "B"

B is a 15-year-old who joined our teen grief group about 14 months after her mother died. Throughout most of B's life, her mother suffered from untreated bipolar disorder and B had had a difficult relationship with her mom for as long as she could remember up until her mother's death. B's mom ended her own life by committing suicide. From the first moment she joined the group, B displayed clear symptoms of a fairly severe depression and she had extreme difficulty connecting with the other teens in the group (even though two of the other teens had also lost a parent to suicide). B showed signs of exaggerated grief and delayed grief; possibly because she was not supported by her family and friends after the death due to this being a disenfranchised loss (suicide) with a high level of stigma.

Following the death, B's family refused to discuss her mother or the circumstances of her death and B was expected to do the same and to get on with her life. She had cut off communication with her close friends, and as a result, B had a serious lack of social support. Although the teen group was a step in the right direction, her family took the step only when B's depression had grown so severe as to prompt a referral to our support group from the school psychologist. It quickly became clear that B needed more support than the teen group could offer her.

I asked B for a meeting after group and she shared that she had been feeling really depressed lately. I was able to draw on the resources of my program director to find an appropriate local referral, and because B was only 15, we came up with a plan to meet with her family and discuss the therapy referral. The meeting went well and B has been seeing the therapist individually. In B's case, family grief therapy was also a **very** good option since the family dynamics were such a large part of her difficulty.

(Amy Grossman, 2010)

SUMMARY

Factors in addition to age and developmental stage are important influences in the reactions of children and teens to loss. While most of the research on grief reactions in childhood and adolescence has focused on grief in reaction to death, information about internal and external influences can be extrapolated from this research and applied to children experiencing symbolic losses such as divorce and foster care placement. Modeling of grief management by families, cultural and spiritual influences, and the increasing influence of the Internet and telecommunications in the lives of children and teens are important to consider when working with grieving children and adolescents. Common reactions to loss at different stages of development as well as strategies to assist with grief reactions have been outlined. While witnessing loss and grief in children and adolescents can be extremely painful, there are tremendous rewards in providing information and support to them while facilitating their coping, as indicated in our case examples. With the knowledge and skills you are gaining while utilizing this textbook, I hope that you will experience these rewards in the future, if not already.

CHAPTER 5

Grief and Loss Across the Life Span: Young and Middle Adulthood

CHAPTER OUTLINE

Of all the challenges you face in working through grief, none is more demanding than the endurance it requires. It begins with 365 days of "the first time without," but it doesn't end there.

Bob Dietz

Stage of life and the developmental tasks and responsibilities that are associated with them have a significant influence on the kinds of losses an individual will experience as well as his or her reactions to them. With changes in family structure as well as increasing life expectancy in the United States, the length of time that individuals are living and functioning in adult relationships and roles has changed from those of previous generations for many groups of individuals. Erik Erikson, a leading developmental theorist of the 20th century, proposed a model for understanding the stages of life for individuals that is still taught and considered applicable by contemporary educators and practitioners.

According to Erikson's model (1950), a young adult is generally defined as a person between the ages of 20 and 40, and an individual between the ages of 40 and

65 is considered to be in middle adulthood. The age at which an individual completes the developmental tasks identified with these life stages may differ in contemporary society from these earlier norms. Adulthood, and the responsibilities and privileges associated with it, is defined differently for different purposes, even by law. Individuals in the United States can vote in local, state, and federal elections at age 18; join the military; and are considered independent of the foster care system. Yet while considered capable of these responsibilities, they cannot purchase alcohol legally until age 21, when the law presumes responsible adult behavior. Adding to the lack of clarity about the age at which individuals are considered independent adults in the United States today is the 2010 health reform legislation, which acknowledges that children up to age 26 may not be independently self-supporting and may be dependent on their parents' health insurance.

Individual and global life events will also impact both the kinds of losses that adults experience and their reactions to these. Subscribers to the life course theory of human development (Bronfenbrenner, 1996) would also point out that contemporary events, such as economic recessions or natural disasters, such as Hurricane Katrina, influence individual development as they influence both the life tasks and the opportunities or challenges that impact individuals at every life stage. As professionals assisting them in coping with and adapting to these losses, it can be helpful to think about events that have influenced adults born between 1945, (at the end of World War II) and 1990, the cohort who are currently in early and middle adulthood.

This chapter will examine losses that are more commonly experienced at the different stages of young and middle adulthood, and the influence of gender, culture, and history on their reactions and therapeutic needs.

Many different kinds of tangible and symbolic losses occur prior to adulthood, as discussed in Chapter 4. Yet, while most children and adolescents have experienced some kind of loss-for example, the death of a grandparent or pet, or a divorce; the death of someone close or significant is not always a common occurrence in childhood. It is extremely rare, however, in young and middle adulthood not to experience the death of a close family member or friend. We can, therefore, assume that almost every young adult and certainly every middle-aged adult will have experienced, or will be experiencing, at least one significant death in addition to many symbolic losses. The deaths that are experienced in this stage of the lifespan also are experienced in relationships that are different from those in childhood and adolescence. These include the death of a spouse or partner, the death of a child (including stillbirth or miscarriage), death of a coworker, and possibly the death of a significant other by suicide (although adolescents also may experience this kind of death in their school or community). Symbolic losses are also very common in adulthood. With the high rate of divorce in contemporary families, young adults often experience the divorce of their parents and many middle adults experience the dissolution of their own marriages, and not always by mutual agreement. The symbolic loss of divorce, like the actual loss of a parent or spouse through death, is often accompanied by other symbolic losses such as the loss of income, home, and identity as well as losses of individual social supports or social networks.

CASE EXAMPLE: ERIN

When I was 20 years old, I experienced my parents going through a divorce. I turned 21 about 2 months before their divorce was finalized. While I could technically be classified as a late-stage adolescent or adult when experiencing this loss, I do recall experiencing all of the Kubler-Ross Stage Model: denial, bargaining, anger, depression, and finally, acceptance. Looking back, I didn't even think of what my parents may have been going through.

I won't go into all the details because that could take forever, but I will highlight thoughts that I remember vividly having when my parents announced their divorce and the subsequent events that happened:

Denial: "They're not getting divorced. They're so dramatic. Why don't they just go get help?"

Bargaining: "If they stay together, I'll get a 4.0 GPA and work so many hours at work that they won't even notice I'm around. They won't have to take care of me, so then they won't fight."

Anger: "Fine. If they want to get divorced, I don't care. Serves them right. They can't even work their problems out like adults."

Sadness/Depression: "I hate seeing Dad so upset. I need my mom to help me with this 'girl problem.' Why did she leave? I just want to cry."

Acceptance: "My parents have new, loving relationships, and they're much happier now. I'm happy for them. They've taught me about what is important in a relationship."

(Erin Hungerford, 2010)

Other symbolic losses such as loss of employment affect individuals in the adult stage of life more than in other life stages. This can be a particularly challenging loss when an older adult retires from a job after many years or for a middle-aged adult whose family depends on the income or social network connected with employment. As noted in Chapter 2 on symbolic loss, the loss of employment, similar to symbolic losses such as divorce, often represents the loss of an identity an individual has formed through these relationships, and thus requires significant adjustment or adaptation. As Hooeyman and Kramer (2006) note, many symbolic losses such as infertility, job loss, sexual assault, and divorce involve the loss of dreams, and that part of the grieving process involves letting go of the dream in addition to the investments that have been made in them.

FACTORS IN ADDITION TO AGE AND DEVELOPMENTAL STAGE THAT INFLUENCE GRIEF REACTIONS

Other factors from an individual's or a family's past experiences with death and loss can also be influential and complicate the grief reaction (Gitterman, 2001, p. 485). The multiple roles and responsibilities of adulthood can also mean that one's physical and emotional resources are taxed when loss or a series of losses is experienced. A spouse caring for young children or teens, with the family responsibilities of providing food, shelter, and emotional support in addition to work responsibilities, may become overwhelmed by the demands of single parenting, after the death of his or her partner or a divorce. If an adult has adopted a primary identity of spouse, that identity may change to that of "widow(er)," "divorcee," or "single parent." Sometimes one's public persona or perceived obligations to others, such as young children or employers, influence the way an individual responds to the loss (as in the case of Jackie Kennedy, following JFK's assassination). This includes deciding whether to disclose the loss to others. The challenges associated with adult responsibilities and roles can be especially inhibiting when the loss is perceived as stigmatizing.

The numbers of adults diagnosed with breast, colon, and lung cancer along with diabetes, hypertension, and other chronic illnesses increase with increasing age. These illnesses are often associated with multiple symbolic losses including the loss of bodily integrity, sometimes loss of employment, loss of physical independence or cognitive capacities, even if temporary, and loss of financial security. Many adults fear the possibility of discrimination that can occur when an individual develops a chronic or life-limiting illness, or they simply do not want to deal with the emotional reactions in others that a diagnosis can elicit. With clients who do not disclose the diagnosis or treatment effects to others, professional caregivers may be the primary source of support in dealing with these losses.

Professional caregivers may also play a crucial role in supporting clients through other types of losses that are not publicly acknowledged. The symbolic loss of a lesbian, gay, bisexual, or transgendered (LGBT) partner through separation or death may not be disclosed or feelings related to this loss may not be shared in certain environments in the open way they might be in a heterosexual relationship, due to homophobia or the dominance of heterosexism. Other individuals may have been intimately partnered with more than one individual, sometimes in relationships that have been in place, but not publicly disclosed, for years, as the following case example illustrates.

> Gina contacted a local bereavement counselor about participating in a support group after the unanticipated death of her partner following a car accident. In the screening interview on the telephone, she disclosed that she had been intimately partnered with him for eight years, despite the fact that he was married to, and had children with, another woman. She lived in a distant community and they had experienced a particularly insular relationship, due to his concerns about his family learning about this extramarital relationship. While he was her primary support and his death represented just as significant a loss to her as if they had been married, she did not have the same opportunity for participation in the mourning rituals that were carried out by his family, nor the support for grieving that are generally available to grieving partners.

Again, in instances like these, professional care providers may play a crucial role in dealing with loss. These kinds of loss and grief reactions related to them are different from the publicly acknowledged loss that occurs when a young child or an adolescent experiences the death of someone significant. Professional helpers need to be aware of the potential losses that their clients may have experienced but not disclosed to others, since accurate assessment and effective treatment involve identifying these experiences. These types of losses, identified as "disenfranchised" (Doka, 2002), can result in complicated grief reactions, which will be discussed further in Chapter 7. In working with individuals and families experiencing this type of loss, we also need to be aware of our own values, attitudes, and beliefs that can influence our sensitivity to, and engagement with, clients whose backgrounds and relationships may be different from our own. If we are truly to be of help to those grieving, we must acknowledge and empathize with each of our clients, recognizing that with every significant attachment there is significant loss that brings with it both unique and universal reactions.

Although adulthood brings with it losses that are unique to this life stage, similar to other stages of development, the nature and quality of the relationship between the survivor and the deceased influences grief reactions to the loss. If the relationship between two individuals was conflicted before the loss occurred, perhaps due to alcohol abuse or domestic violence, the grieving survivor may experience a complicated grief reaction. In conflicted relationships there may not be a process of ending or saying goodbye that facilitates the completion of the tasks of grieving, even if the death is anticipated. Although the survivor may experience relief that the conflict or the problems experienced in the relationship are no longer a burden in his or her life, the unresolved anger, shame, and guilt associated with conflicted relationships can complicate the grieving process.

CASE EXAMPLE: NANCY

Nancy, a 34-year-old widow, sought grief therapy approximately a year after her husband's death. He had a long history of drug addiction and depression that had progressed during their marriage, resulting in repeated conflicts between them and two admissions to substance treatment programs after overdoses. The couple had three young children and between his job and his addiction, he had only been episodically present as a parent to the children, although when he was present, "it was great!" according to Nancy. These periods of recovery and positive involvement, along with a strong emotional connection, had kept Nancy in the marriage, despite the conflicts and challenges. Shortly after his second discharge from a substance dependence treatment program, Nancy returned from visiting a friend with the children, "had a very strange feeling about the quiet in the house" and found that her husband had overdosed and died. Since he left no note, it was unclear whether he intended to end his own life or the death was accidental. She had been traumatized by the whole experience and left their home with the children shortly after his memorial service to travel across the country visiting relatives, "to escape." Returning home, she found herself experiencing guilt and anger that did not diminish after several months, which is why she sought grief therapy for both herself and her children. Along with individual therapy, she attended several meetings of a local support group for survivors, although she was disappointed that there were no other young spouses close to her age and from her spiritual background. She found more support from others who shared these characteristics from an Internet site for survivors that offered a professionally facilitated online group.

Nancy's case, while illustrating the complications of a conflicted relationship, also illustrates the changes in coping with grief that have occurred with contemporary media approaches and the freedom of expression and sharing of information that the Internet has produced. Individuals or families who may have felt isolated in earlier eras now have access, even anonymous if they choose, to a multitude of resources that were previously unavailable on a local community level. Online support groups, discussion boards, or blogs provide an outlet for expression of diverse grief reactions, and bereaved individuals can often benefit from the shared expression of anger, sadness, and hope that take place in these forums. Professionals often play a key role in helping to assess the suitability or credibility of these sources of information and support, since entries in some Web sites may include inaccurate information or traumatizing details that can hinder rather than help grieving individuals. Directing or guiding clients to Web sites that are a good match for their needs is increasingly part of professional roles and functions.

In adulthood it is also common to experience the death of one's parents. The quality of the relationship, both prior to and during a parent's life-limiting illness or death, impacts the adult child's grieving process. If there was a cutoff or a conflicted relationship that is not resolved prior to the parent's death, the surviving adult child will sometimes have a complicated grief reaction. If there was a close loving relationship, there may be an intense sense of yearning for a relationship that cannot be replaced.

Dionne is a 50-year-old nurse who sought counseling for "depression" half way through her chemotherapy treatment for breast cancer. Dionne had received the diagnosis on the first day of Kwanza, a holiday her family traditionally celebrated together. The year she received her diagnosis, however, she, her adult children, two sisters and brother were already stressed by the hospitalization of her mother with a stroke she'd suffered just before Thanksgiving. Dionne described the breast cancer diagnosis as "overwhelming" and she experienced it as even more so because her mother was in a rehabilitation facility, unable to provide her customary emotional support and her siblings were pre-occupied with her mother's needs for care and support. Dionne had been taking antidepressant medication for several years, prescribed by a psychiatrist after her father's death, and had managed to continue in her job and care for her teenage sons as a single parent. She described her relationship with both her parents as having been "very close, they saved me during my divorce," and she and her mother had grown even closer after her father's death, speaking by telephone or visiting every day. The relationship with her mother had served an unusually important function for Dionne, as an adult, in coping with her many life stressors. Dionne's grief was profound when her mother died unexpectedly, sending her into a major depressive episode. Grief therapy served several purposes: It helped her to (a) connect with alternate internal and external sources of support through the counselor and a support group, (b) monitor and modify her antidepressant medication as needed, (c) continue deriving the benefit of the close relationship with her mother through writing letters to, and conversing in her mind with, her deceased mother.

Cultural and spiritual values, beliefs, and practices all significantly influence an adult's reactions to loss as well as the reactions of his or her social support networks. These will be discussed in more depth in the chapter devoted to these topics, but professional caregivers must be sensitive to, and knowledgeable about, these influences in order to best understand and connect with grieving adults, just as in the case of individuals and families at other stages of development.

DEVELOPMENTAL AND EXTERNAL FACTORS INFLUENCING GRIEF REACTIONS

Young adulthood

Young adulthood is one of the most exciting and challenging periods in a person's life. Major decisions about job and career choices, choosing a partner, and bearing and raising children are being made and this may be the first time in one's life that they are truly responsible to, and for, others. Moral decisions also come into play in this developmental phase. Many young adults facing loss-their own as well as others'-may struggle with a sense of obligation to self and others. A major strength is that they have had exposure to a wide variety of coping strategies and are often open to learning new ones. While fully capable of understanding death and its impact, the multiple demands of life may distract from one's devotion of time and energy to grief. This can easily be observed in grieving soldiers who must either carry on in the battlefield immediately after experiencing the death of fellow servicemen and women or carry out multiple roles of spouse, parent, and employee when they return from tours of duty in which they often experience multiple losses from death as well as multiple symbolic losses due to separation from their country of origin, their families, and support networks. Traumatic loss, such as loss of comrades in combat, will be discussed in Chapter 12 in more detail, but it is one of the unique types of loss affecting young adults that is distinct from the losses incurred in earlier and later stages of development and is one that, as a unique life event, can significantly influence an individual's life course and the way that he or she copes with, or defends against, all subsequent losses. There is growing attention in the military and in veterans' services of the impact of grief from combat-related losses, as evidenced by the content on grief included in the VA's PTSD Web site. On this Web site, clinicians are encouraged to attend to the many reactions such as shock, emptiness, preoccupation, as well as anger and guilt that veterans may exhibit and to recognize that these are often symptoms following the loss of comrades.[1]

---

[1]Retrieved from http://www.ptsd.va.gov/professional/pages/tgs-treatment-iraq-war.asp

DEVELOPMENTAL FACTORS

- Expected to be self-sufficient (economically if not emotionally)
- Developing career/life plans
- Establishing partnerships or a family of one's own
- Expanding range of roles and coping strategies

UNDERSTANDING OF DEATH   When young people reach adult status, they fully comprehend the impact of death-both the immediate and final impact for the deceased as well as long-term impact for survivors. They are also capable of comprehending the complex range of responses of different people to different types of losses.

REACTIONS TO LOSS   Young adults may struggle with their feelings of responsibility for other family members after a loss and may be ambivalent about meeting their own needs and/or the needs of others. They may perceive tears and sadness as indicating "weakness" or evidence guilt about their own actions or inactions related to the death. Young adults are also vulnerable to the emergence of anxiety, depression, and other disorders that stress related to loss can exacerbate.

STRATEGIES TO ASSIST YOUNG ADULTS

- Acknowledging loss and grief reactions
- Encouraging individuals to take time to attend to their own feelings as well as those of others
- Acknowledging or providing opportunities for expression and/or discussion of conflicting feelings
- Promoting social connections through peer-support and group activities

Middle adulthood

Sometimes referred to as the *sandwich* generation, middle-aged adults are meeting multiple obligations in work, family, and community. They may be involved in raising and launching children, and the role of parent brings with it many responsibilities as well as complex feelings related to losses and gains. At the same time, they may be called upon to assist their own parents or older family members whose frailty can raise existential questions as well as serve as a reminder of vulnerability. Relationships are complex, and those that are conflicted may result in complicated grief reactions when they end. Seeking meaning and satisfaction, many are leaders or major contributors in their families, work settings, or community organizations. Biological changes are occurring in both men and women that influence mood and physical capacities.

DEVELOPMENTAL FACTORS

Re-examination, renewal, and/or reintegration of identity
Multiple roles and responsibilities
Long-established patterns may be difficult to change (e.g., substance dependence)
Increased vulnerability to physical disorders (cancer, heart disease, etc.) as age increases

REACTIONS TO LOSS   Middle adults may experience a "pile-up" of losses, related to deaths as well as other life-changing events. Maladaptive patterns such as use of substances and work to avoid dealing with painful feelings or intimacy may make the process of grieving complicated. Fully aware of the impact of death and the existential questions it raises, survivors may also experience increased sensitivity and openness to others and alternative ways of coping. This generative stage of development often means that satisfaction is derived from helping others. Religious or spiritual practices are often comforting. Grieving the loss of a child or a long-term marriage can be particularly painful and protracted.

STRATEGIES TO ASSIST MIDDLE ADULTS (IN ADDITION TO THOSE LISTED FOR YOUNGER INDIVIDUALS)

- Empathic listening and support
- Release time from work or school to meet family obligations and process grief
- Bereavement support groups
- Tangible expressions of support or caring such as preparing meals and assisting with care of children or elder family members
- Pastoral care or connection with a religious or spiritual community
- Identification of risk factors and offering intervention for complicated grief
- Opportunities for respite and renewal
- Opportunities to assist others, when interest in this is expressed

It is clear that multiple roles and responsibilities in the young and middle adult years can limit or deplete an adult's internal and external resources, potentially limiting the time and energy adults can allocate to grieving. On the other hand, the multiple relationships experienced in this stage of the lifespan may mean that adults have a good deal of support after a significant loss such as death of a spouse or divorce. Peers may have experienced the same kind of loss and therefore may be more sensitive and able to offer assistance or support. Part of a helping professional's assessment of an adult's grief involves identifying the support systems one already has in place and which supporting systems, such as a widow to widow group, might be available if needed. An eco map is an excellent tool for identifying both existing and potential supports for clients of all ages, including adults. A PowerPoint presentation explaining the construction and use of an eco map is included in the Web resources for this text.

SUMMARY

With changes in family structure as well as increasing life expectancy in the United States, the length of time that individuals are living and functioning in adult relationships and roles has changed from those of previous generations. Although the beginning of adulthood is not clearly defined, the length of this stage of development means that many types of significant losses, both symbolic and actual are likely to be sustained in adulthood. Some of these, such as death of a child or death of a partner, are quite different from losses sustained in earlier life stages. It is important to remember that while loss "pile up" can be an additional stressor for adults, an advantage of age and experience at this stage of development is that adults can also draw on their previous experiences to identify coping strategies and resources that have been helpful or unhelpful in the past. With this experience and awareness, clients can then either utilize or abandon strategies or influences that have not been helpful and put effective strategies and supports into practice to cope with subsequent losses. Because peers may have experienced the same kinds of losses, assistance or support may be available for the grieving adult, including in the form of support groups or programs.

CHAPTER 6

Loss and Grief Across the Life Span: Older Adults

Death ends a life, not a relationship.

Morrie Schwartz

LOSS AND GRIEF LATER IN LIFE

When an adult reaches age 65 in American Society, he or she is considered an older adult, although it must be noted that many adults this age do not consider themselves "old," and may consider this label to be stigmatizing. With advances in health care in the United States, the number of adults living beyond age 65 to advanced age is steadily increasing as longevity in the general population increases. In the mid-20th century, the life expectancy for Caucasian men in the United States was 65 years and for women it was 71. In 2010 the average life expectancy in the United States is estimated to be 75 years for men and 81 years for women. The health care disparities that, unfortunately, still exist in the United States contribute to the different life expectancy for African Americans. According to the National Vital Statistics Reports (Vol. 47, No. 28), African American life expectancy is 70.2 years, compared to an average of 76.5 years for all population groups. The difference in life expectancy is even more striking among African American men, who have a life expectancy of only 66.1 years (CDC, 2006). However, the number of persons with diverse racial and cultural backgrounds in the general population is increasing. With the increased diversity among older adults, these life expectancies are increasing and can be expected to increase further in the future. According to a recent California study, Hispanic men live an average of 2 years longer than Caucasian men and Hispanic women an average of 5 years longer than Caucasian women. Asian Americans in California live an average of 5 years longer than Caucasians.

As life expectancy increases, it can be anticipated that the numbers of individuals in the age groups of 70–79 (septuagenarians), 80–89 (octogenarians), and 90–99 (nonagenarians) from all racial and cultural backgrounds will continue to grow over the next several decades. These increasing numbers require that providers of health, mental health, and other services be equipped to understand, plan, and implement services for a larger, more diverse population of older adults with more diverse grief-related needs.

THE INFLUENCE OF ADVANCED AGE AND LONGER LIFE EXPECTANCY

The longer one lives, the more likely one is to experience the death of a spouse, an adult child, coworkers, and friends. Like their younger counterparts, older adults who experience the death of a child may experience intense grief, since most people do not expect to outlive their children. With advanced age, this is more likely to happen than in younger adulthood; thus many older adults with whom we work may be experiencing this as well as other significant deaths. Along with cumulative actual losses through the deaths of significant others, older adults are likely to experience multiple symbolic losses. Longer life expectancy means that the time in which individuals are carrying out roles such as spouse, employee, parent, and grandparent (even great grandparent) is extended. Thus, the numbers and types of symbolic losses associated with these roles will have a significant impact on grief-related needs.

In addition to living longer, many individuals are continuing or resuming paid employment longer. According to the Social Security Administration, the age of retirement is slowly increasing from 65 to 67 in the United States and many of these individuals may work multiple jobs over a lifetime, accumulating more relationships and roles that contribute to a sense of identity. More people are living past retirement, and therefore are adjusting to employment-related losses that include loss of professional identity, potential loss of income, and social status. With increasing age come more long-term and chronic illness–related losses such as loss of independence and loss of mobility. In addition, as individuals age, the likelihood of losing relationships with in-laws and grandchildren through the divorce of adult children increases. As in earlier stages of development, the cumulative experience of symbolic losses that occur as one ages increases the likelihood of "loss pileup" and complicated grief.

Cultural connections and the influence of technology

Helping professionals will increasingly encounter older adults who have experienced one or many of these losses in every health, social service, and educational setting. As diversity increases within the older population, cultural awareness and sensitivity is very important in assessment. Understanding the influence of culture on the grief reactions of older individuals who may have maintained close connections with their country of origin and adhere to culturally dictated norms for bereavement rituals and expression of grief is essential. These connections are likely to be even more common than in the past as global communication technology becomes more accessible to everyone.

Along with changes in life expectancy, another important demographic change influencing loss and grief reactions is the number of older adults utilizing the Internet and social networking sites. According to the Neilson polls, the numbers of active Internet users older than 65 are still less than 10% of all active users, but their numbers are on the rise. In the past 5 years, the number of seniors actively using the Internet has increased by more than 55%, from 11.3 million active users in November 2004 to 17.5 million in November 2009.[1] Communication portals and cell phones, Web cams, language translation programs, online support groups, blogs, and other electronic communication vehicles are becoming a more routine part of daily communication, not only for younger cohorts but for older adults as well. This has implications not only for the type and amount of information and support older adults receive when they experience loss, but also means they may experience more or more intense losses as social networking brings them in closer contact with friends and family with whom they may not have been as connected without the Internet. For example, consider Irene.

CASE EXAMPLE: IRENE

Irene is an older adult who volunteered in the gift shop of her community hospital after her retirement from her nursing career. Her husband had died just after her retirement and shortly after she reconnected online with a high school classmate who had moved across the country four decades earlier. This classmate had also lost her spouse around the same time as Irene and they formed a bond around this experience. The relationship became more important as they experienced the deaths of other classmates and family members and they shared their memories of these important people and supported each other through their grief. Irene expressed a great sense of loss when that classmate died, noting that they had e-mailed each other at least twice a week for 5 years once they had reconnected through the Internet. "I thought of her every day, every time I went on the computer, not just the three or four days a week when we exchanged e-mails," she said to the hospital chaplain. This virtual relationship represented a part of her daily life and left a more significant void than if they did not have this routine communication.

Not only does the Internet provide a vehicle to stay in close touch with friends and family with whom one already has a relationship, it also provides opportunities

[1]Retrieved from http://blog.nielsen.com/nielsenwire/online_mobile/six-million-more-seniors-using-the-web-than-five-years-ago

for establishing new and important supportive relationships (e.g., through special interests or hobbies) in older adulthood. While this represents a gain in social support, it also represents loss when these relationships end.

One client reported a sense of loss when a member of an online group for quilters became ill and eventually died. Even though they had never met in person, they had nevertheless experienced significant emotional connection through their routine exchanges of quilt patterns, anecdotes about their quilts and informal sharing of information about their work and families, creating a grief reaction in all of the surviving members of the group.

As mobility and independence outside one's home decrease with advanced age, the importance of relationships maintained through social networks and communication technology may gain more importance for many older adults who have more time to spend in virtual communication than do younger adults who are engaged in employment, raising children, and other social commitments. It is, therefore, important in assessing loss pileup or bereavement reactions to include distant relationships that may represent significant losses. It is also important to include existing or potential virtual relationships in an assessment because they can represent an important source of social support, a known mediator of stress in reaction to loss. Online and telephone bereavement support groups, chat rooms, and other telecommunication vehicles may serve as an important, if not essential, source of strength and resilience in the face of both symbolic and actual losses for every age group, for the foreseeable future.

SYMBOLIC AND ACTUAL LOSS FOR OLDER ADULTS

While older adults experience grief in reaction to loss, just as members of every other age group do, the circumstances of loss and the presentation of normal and complicated grief reactions may appear different than in younger developmental stages. Curtiss (2007) identifies key points related to loss and grief in older persons:

- Older adults often have many major losses within a short period of time. For example, older adults who lose their spouses may suffer many losses, including financial security, their best friend, and their social contacts.
- The natural aging process brings many losses, such as loss of "beauty" and physical strength.
- Older adults may seem to overreact to a minor loss. But what is considered a minor loss may bring memories and feelings about a previous greater loss.

Another aspect of loss that makes it distinctive in older adulthood is anticipation. Loss, particularly from death, is *expected* in older adulthood as individuals age and may even become a routine part of life, whereas it is often unexpected and exceptional in earlier stages of development. Older adults begin to anticipate their own or their partner's deaths, loss of employment, the gradual loss of health and mobility, hearing, sight, and social networks as the biological and social impact of aging are manifested in oneself and significant others in this stage of life.

Both actual and symbolic losses in this life stage are cumulative, and rather than adjusting to one central, less predictable, loss that can precipitate other losses (e.g., a parent's death in childhood can precipitate symbolic losses such as the loss of one's intact family or home), older adults are often reacting to a predictable sequence of actual and symbolic losses that may be anticipated during or after retirement, the diagnosis of one or more chronic illnesses, and the physiological effects of aging (Zoeller, 2006). Case managers in senior services centers as well as personnel who work in assisted living and long-term care facilities often write poignantly about the multiple losses their clients experience. When actually asked to identify losses, many older adults recount so many it is difficult to determine which are the most challenging or significant, but the impact of each, as well as the accumulated set, can all be significant.

In addition to experiencing multiple deaths of people, for example, adult children, even grandchildren, siblings, friends, and partners, older adults are often significantly impacted by the death of a pet. Pets serve a therapeutic need for most owners but for older adults, particularly those living alone, they may represent companionship as well as love when close contact with others becomes diminished by distance, disability, or a shrinking support network. Symbolic losses such as the loss of memory, sensation, and sense of identity and purpose can make the relationships one has with both people and pets extremely important. As one case manager noted, some older adults have experienced so many losses it is impossible to identify and acknowledge them all. It is key, however, to recognize the influence that losses have on the physical, emotional, and spiritual well-being of older adults and to address these losses when there is evidence that they are negatively impacting mood and quality of life.

DEVELOPMENTAL AND EXTERNAL FACTORS INFLUENCING GRIEF REACTIONS

Developmental factors

An older person's adjustment to loss may be influenced by internal factors that are unique to individuals of advanced age. The following is a list of some of these influences.

- Ill health or disabling medical conditions that often increase as biological aging progresses
- Serenity and/or wisdom may be sought
- Changes in identity occur that are related to retirement and changes in family roles
- Adaptation to changes in information processing and memory is required to maintain maximum functioning
- Ego-integrity is enhanced if life review results in a sense of having led a successful/meaningful life
- Individuals of advanced age generally begin to anticipate their own death and contemplate the end of life
- Acceptance of death may be more prevalent than anger

According to theorist Erik Erikson (1950), the developmental task for older adults is to establish ego-integrity versus experiencing despair. This is accomplished, in part, through reflection on one's life-accomplishments and relationships and experiencing a sense that these have had meaning. In his many days spent with his former professor Morrie Schwartz, Mitch Albom (1997) documented the process through which his mentor and role model accomplished this task through his visits and visits with other friends and family members prior to Morrie's death at age 78. In his book, *Tuesdays With Morrie*, Albom describes conversations with Morrie that illustrate this process. In these conversations, Morrie reflected on how many people he knew seemed to be living a life without meaning because they were "chasing" the wrong things. He explained that he found great meaning in both his work and his relationships and recommended that everyone devote his or her life to loving others, helping the community around him or her and creating something that provides a sense of purpose and meaning. He also noted that contemporary American culture, with its greater emphasis on financial success than on loving relationships, may cause an individual to devalue the meaning of his or her own accomplishments.

This reflection on life is one illustration of the perspective that older adults may have gained through many relationships and life experiences and can perhaps be interpreted as a manifestation of ego-integrity. Anger and sadness, if not despair, along with the other normal reactions to loss that are experienced in other stages of the lifespan are also experienced by older adults, particularly in the face of the death of a life partner or multiple losses that can be accumulated, often in proximity. Author Joan Didion poignantly describes her own reactions following the death of her husband of nearly 40 years, John Gregory Dunne. The couple had shared careers as writers as well as many years of accumulated routines, life events, shared passions, and relationships. John Dunne died suddenly and unexpectedly of a heart attack while the couple was eating dinner together one evening after visiting their gravely ill daughter in the hospital. The entire experience is detailed in Didion's book *A Year of Magical Thinking* (2007), and is instructive for anyone working with grieving spouses of any age. Didion noted that even though we may know that someone close to us could die, it is difficult to look beyond the death to the months and years that follow. After her husband's death, she expected to be in shock but didn't expect the shock to be "obliterative." She anticipated, when she imagined his death prior to its happening, that she would be inconsolable with loss but says she didn't expect to feel "literally crazy," thinking things like her husband would be returning and need his shoes.

Older adult clients in my own practice have described similar feelings and have wondered aloud if this might mean they are "losing" their minds. They often feel reassured to hear that many people who have been married to a person, and viewed themselves as a partnership, for all of their adult life have difficulty integrating the experience of loss when it impacts so many aspects of their lives, including their identity.

External factors affecting older adults

External factors such as culture, multiple losses in rapid succession, age discrimination, socioeconomic status, particularly in older single women who are more likely to live in poverty, and geographic distance from children or close relatives can affect the grieving process. Deaths of significant others later in life may have a serious impact on social support, particularly if one's social support network has diminished or if one's independence or activities of daily living were closely tied to the now-deceased spouse, adult child, or friend.

Multiple losses require continuing adaptation. If significant family members or friends die, the individual must adjust to the new environment in which those persons are not present. If retirement or changes in roles and responsibilities due to illness or aging are unwanted or forced, grief reactions may be intense and maladaptive. Isolation and limited social support may contribute to problems in adjustment and changes in economic status, particularly for widowed women if their income is highly dependent on their partner's, and can contribute to increased stress. It may be difficult to differentiate between grief and depression, particularly when multiple biological, psychological, and social changes are occurring in the face of multiple losses.

WORKING WITH GRIEVING OLDER ADULTS

Despite the common presence of these factors in the lives of older adults, and the increase in longevity in the United States, the literature that specifically addresses grief, and loss in septuagenarians, octogenarians, and nonagenarians is sparse. There is little existing research or clinical literature to inform the planning and delivery of grief-related services to the population of older adults. Kramer et al. (2003), in a review of social work textbooks for content on end-of-life issues, found that relatively few pages in social work texts are devoted to these topics. This is also true for the topic of grief in many contemporary texts on practice with older adults and gerontology. Other than recommending increasing connections with social support systems, participating in bereavement counseling, or general bereavement support groups, few models specifically addressing the cumulative and symbolic losses older adults experience have been developed. McInnis-Dittrich (2009) notes that skills training groups are another beneficial type of group for grieving older adults. These groups can teach homemaking skills, for example, to widowers who have relied on their spouses to take care of cooking or chores, or teach financial skills to a widowed spouse who has never handled finances. It is important to be aware that gender-assigned roles may be more prevalent in older generations or in older adults in certain cultural groups than in younger adults who have practiced a model of shared work and home responsibilities.

This dearth is significant, not only because there is less information to guide those of us who are lending assistance to older clients than there is available to those assisting younger persons, but also because there is less to guide professional caregivers who are grieving the cumulative losses that accrue when working with an older population. As noted in Chapter 3, another population with grief-related needs that directly results from the increase in the older population in the United States is the population of professional and paraprofessional caregivers of older persons who are employed in hospice and home care, medical and rehabilitation settings, mental health, and senior service agencies. It can be most challenging to work with dying older adults and their families (McInnis-Dittrich, 2009). It may be particularly challenging for you if you are a novice to this work, since health and social service professionals report that they have not been adequately trained in end-of-life issues

(Walsh-Burke & Cskai, 2005). Support for staff's own grief may not be available in every setting where workers are experiencing multiple losses, which also makes managing grief more challenging. Research conducted with staff providing care in Programs of All-inclusive Care for the Elderly (PACE), indicates that this population of caregivers do have work-related bereavement needs. Participants in the study, who represented community-based long-term care staff, reported that they experience a variety of symptoms attributable to the deaths of their patients, and would welcome additional sources of bereavement support (Rickerson et al., 2005).

Recognizing the cumulative effects of grief on staff, some hospices, senior service agencies and other agencies caring for older people do offer memorial services remembrances in weekly interdisciplinary team meetings and bereavement groups to or remembrances support their staff. One model for this is a monthly meeting held specifically to support staff in their grief needs. The meeting is facilitated by an external grief therapist so that all members of the hospice team, including the home health aides, chaplain or spiritual coordinator, social worker, medical director, and nurses can all participate and without feeling responsible for taking care of other staff. These meetings are sometimes the only forum for staff to formally share their grief reactions, since many of them work autonomously in patients' homes and may not address their own bereavement needs during their precious nonwork time with family and friends. These staff support meetings are often richer for the diverse cultures, spirituality, age, and roles of the team members and provide a forum for staff to identify relationships with patients and families that reactivate their own personal loss experiences. Reminiscence is a common activity and often brings a positive sense of closure and fulfillment to grieving caregivers as well as to their clients who are adults of advanced age.

Strategies to help older adults

- Acknowledging symbolic losses as well as losses through death
- Maintaining or augmenting social supports (including through tele-communications)
- Providing income supports or economic assistance, when needed
- Conducting informal as well as formal life review, with emphasis on strengths and contributions
- Identifying and participating in new activities, roles, and relationships to augment or replace those that have been lost, including skills training in self-care or household management
- Reminiscing through sharing of memories, with individuals and groups
- Providing concrete supports to allow expenditure of time and energy on satisfying activities and relationships (helping with household maintenance or bill paying)
- Acknowledging losses as well as identifying and reinforcing strengths and coping capacities
- Encouraging completion of advance directives (living wills, durable powers of attorney, and health care proxy directions)
- Providing opportunities and encouragement to openly discuss ideas, values, feelings, and fears related to dying and death

Rewards of grief work with older adults

It is not uncommon for professionals to avoid either work with older adults or their grief. Some workers fear that proximity to the multiple losses of older adults-of physical capacities, homes, overall health, and even life-will result in loss for the worker that is overwhelming. However, the vast number of professional and paraprofessional caregivers to older adults report that they derive great satisfaction and inspiration from work with this population and that their personal as well as work lives are enriched by the reminders that life is precious and the models for living that older adults, like Morrie Schwartz, provide.

SUMMARY

A key difference between adults of advanced age and those at earlier stages of development is the expectation of loss, including one's own death. As one 81-year-old client put it, "I never expected to live this long or to be able to enjoy my retirement as long as I have. It makes me appreciate my golf game even more than before because every day is a gift." While not all adults of advanced age have this perspective, the anticipation of death, even multiple deaths of friends and acquaintances, does afford some preparation, both psychological and pragmatic. Reminiscence as well as a focus on activities and relationships that help the older adult to make meaning of his or her life is an essential intervention by professional helpers that can assist in completing the developmental task of establishing ego integrity. As age increases, social support networks often diminish as friends and acquaintances die and physical or cognitive impairments necessitate transition from one's established home to assisted living or skilled nursing facilities. It thus becomes important not only to help older adults maintain connection with relationships and activities that provide a sense of fulfillment, but to establish new social supports, including through the use of the Internet and relationships with professional or paid caregivers. Just as schools provide a vehicle for children and adolescents to gain support and utilize strategies for coping with loss, so do senior service centers, nursing service organizations, and hospice and palliative care programs. The cumulative losses experienced by caregivers of older adults engender their own grief reactions and self-care for those of us who work in close connection with this population, including participation in memorial services and bereavement groups, may help prevent adverse effects of loss pileup for helping professionals as well.

Normal and Complicated Grief Reactions

And can it be that in a world so full and busy the loss of one creature makes a void in any heart so wide and deep that nothing but the width and depth of eternity can fill it up!

Charles Dickens

One of the most common questions grieving people ask is, "is this reaction normal?" This same question is also asked by many professionals who are attempting to determine when, and if, an individual might need specialized help in order to cope with a loss.

CASE EXAMPLE: MIKE AND MARY

Mike M. and his sister, Mary, both work in a large corporation in the community where they were raised. Mary has called the human resources department asking for a referral to the Employee Assistance Program (EAP) because of her concern about Mike. She thinks Mike may need help because he is still showing signs of depression since his wife died 2½ years ago. Prior to his wife's death, he socialized a great deal. He has since isolated himself and abandoned activities that used to interest him such as golf, gardening, and going out after work with his buddies or his siblings once or twice a week. Since the death of his wife, he has not made any changes to anything that belonged to her, including their bedroom where her clothing still hangs in the closet. Mike did hire a neighborhood boy to take over cutting the lawn and make minor repairs on the house; activities that he used to enjoy, but the inside of the house has become uncharacteristically untidy. His sister, who works at the same place of employment, has visited repeatedly and offered to help clean up but Mike has resisted her help and given her instructions not to eliminate anything that reminds him of his wife, including giving away or storing her knick-knacks, aprons, or clothes. He also visits the cemetery every Sunday rather than participating in routine family gatherings or even special events. Mary is concerned that her brother is depressed. She says that he had a strong reaction when their father died while he was in college, but had met his wife shortly before that and had married her relatively soon after. She is seeking advice about whether he might need to see a counselor and how she can best help him.

THEORIES THAT INFORM OUR UNDERSTANDING OF GRIEF

Our understanding of "normal" or expectable grief reactions comes from many sources. Over the past half-century, many theories have been constructed to explain human attachment and the grief reactions that result from loss. Some of these theories have been constructed by researchers studying large groups of grieving people. Other theories have been constructed by psychiatrists, psychologists, and other mental health professionals providing treatment to grieving individuals. All of these theories have the potential for cultural bias, as they have been constructed by individuals who have lived and studied in a particular location at a particular time in history. Because of this, it is important to be sensitive to diverse cultures and aware that there are limitations to the applicability of every theory.

Many reactions that are considered a natural part of a culturally prescribed grief reaction in one cultural group may seem highly unusual, even distressing, to members of another cultural group. Culture is a very significant influence in the ways that people express their grief, just as it is an influence in the way that people deal with most other life situations. It is important to recognize that each individual may express his or her grief uniquely and it is always wise to reserve judgment until we understand the cultural context of behavior. Chapter 8 addresses the influence of culture and spirituality in more depth and will help to better prepare you for culturally sensitive practice. Despite limitations, the information that has been gathered by researchers and grief therapists and the theories they have constructed can help to guide us in understanding

people whose grief reactions may require intervention and what type. A brief overview of some key theories and theorists is important in order to understand how the
concepts of "normal" and "complicated" grief are applied.

Early psychodynamic theories

Once again in this chapter, we draw upon theories and research based on bereavement
to understand grief reactions. There is still much research needed to understand grief in
reaction to symbolic losses, but understanding grief in reaction to death can help prepare us to support those coping with symbolic losses as well. Sigmund Freud was one
of the first psychiatrists credited with contributing to the theoretical understanding of
grief. His basic ideas were written in *Mourning and Melancholia,* which was published
in 1917. Subsequent theorists have elaborated on, and even disagreed with, what Freud
wrote, but his work still informs many grief therapists. Freud theorized that every human infant develops attachments to significant people through the process of cathexis.
This process of attaching emotionally is crucial to healthy development since it is
through these attachments with others that the infant learns to trust that basic needs (for
food, protection, and love) will be met. Freud also identified the process of decathexis,
or the process of "letting go" of the attachment, as an adaptive response to loss of the
significant object. The process involves both intellectually and emotionally letting go.

John Bowlby is another important theorist who elaborated on the ideas that Freud
developed about human attachment and loss. Bowlby (1973) proposed that attachment behavior toward caregivers in human infants helps to establish and maintain a
sense of security. He observed that infants and children react with searching behaviors
when separation from a significant person occurs (in his era defined most often as the
mother). The infant searches in an attempt to reestablish the bond and the sense of security that the presence of the mother/primary caregiver provides. According to Bowlby's
theory, *grief* is the reaction of the bereaved to the loss of a significant other. Bowlby
noted that, just like the infant who continues to search for the significant other, a grieving individual may try to avoid or deny the reality of separation that death imposes.
However, Bowlby posited that the bereaved individual must cease investing his or her
emotional energy (referred to as *libido* by both Freud and Bowlby) in the deceased in
order to reinvest it in other relationships. Both Freud and Bowlby believed that with the
passage of time, grieving individuals could-on their own or with help-both intellectually
and emotionally achieve *decathexis*, or withdraw energy (libido) from the deceased.
These psychoanalytically oriented theorists agreed that failure to eventually do this-to
free oneself from the clinging attachment-resulted in emotional or psychological difficulty, often described as depression. Many grief experts still use these basic concepts to
explain why mourning is considered a normal process in reaction to loss.

Eric Lindemann (1943) conducted research that supported much of what Freud
and Bowlby postulated about grief. Lindemann became very interested in studying
grief reactions after a major tragedy in Boston, the Coconut Grove nightclub fire, took
the lives of 492 people, many of whom were college students celebrating the football
victory of Holy Cross College over Boston College in the overcrowded nightclub in
November 1942. Lindemann studied the grieving survivors to learn more about how
people react to the death of a significant other. He found that common reactions in

the acute period following the death included physical or bodily distress, preoccupation with the image of the person who had died, anger or hostility, guilt, and impaired functioning in work or family roles. He also identified tasks that grievers appeared to complete that resulted in a diminishment of these symptoms. The tasks included (a) acknowledging the reality of the death, (b) adjusting to life without the deceased person, and (c) forming new relationships. Lindemann's task model has informed later grief theorists as well as therapists.

Elisabeth Kubler-Ross

The person whose name is probably most closely linked with grief in many people's minds is Elisabeth Kubler-Ross, a physician who worked extensively with dying patients. Kubler-Ross made major contributions to our understanding of anticipatory grief, the reactions of people who are dying, in her pioneering publications in the 1960s and 1970s that described her stage model of adjustment to death. She proposed that people who have been told they will die from a terminal illness go through five stages:

- Denial
- Anger
- Bargaining
- Sadness
- Acceptance

Many subsequent writers and practitioners have applied her model to those who are grieving, suggesting that individuals who are grieving the death of a significant other also experience the reactions that Kubler-Ross described in patients who are dying. Even grief experts who apply Kubler-Ross's model to those who are dying and/or those who are grieving someone else's death note that not all patients who are diagnosed with life-limiting illness evidence all of the stages identified in Kubler-Ross's model or, even if they do, that they do not move through these stages sequentially.

Theories of contemporary grief practitioners and researchers

Grief counselors such as Therese Rando (1984, 1993) and J. William Worden (2009) and more contemporary researchers have expanded on earlier theories in order to provide practical guidance to professionals working with those who are grieving. Rando, a grief counselor who has authored many books on grief and loss, suggests that many clients who seek psychotherapy for problems such as depression or anxiety often present issues of unresolved loss-either symbolic or actual. She and many other mental health specialists suggest that a wide variety of losses, not just the death of a loved one, can precipitate a grief reaction. *Symbolic losses*, as discussed in Chapter 2, may include the loss of the family life one dreamed of when divorce occurs, the loss of the type of future one imagined for a child if the child is born with, or acquires, a severe disabling condition, and the symbolic loss of one's biological family after adoption or foster care placement. When assessing normal and complicated grief reactions, it is useful to remember that acknowledgment and support of an individual or a family can help a person to cope with both loss through death and symbolic loss.

Thinking about what reactions represent "normal" and "complicated" grief has continued to evolve as more research has been conducted with more diverse populations. Klass, Silverman, and Nickman (1996) have contributed a new understanding of the "continuing bonds" bereaved individuals maintain with those who have died. While earlier theorists hypothesized that it is necessary for a grieving individual to sever his or her attachment to the deceased in order to invest in new relationships, Klass and colleagues suggest that it is possible to maintain the attachment as well as invest in new relationships. Thus, when grieving teens report that they "talk" to a deceased parent, depending on the other adaptive behaviors they are using to integrate the loss, this does not represent an impediment to healthy adjustment. Stroebe and Schut (2001) have constructed a model for understanding grief reactions that they have identified as a "dual process," based on their findings that most bereaved people oscillate between episodes of intense pining for the lost person (loss orientation) and periods during which they can plan and carry out forward-looking activities that help them adjust to the secondary losses that often result from a death (restoration orientation). These theories inform our understanding of normal and complicated grief so that we can more effectively identify those individuals and families who are at risk for health and mental health problems related to loss and to offer effective interventions for those who can benefit from them.

COMMON REACTIONS IN "NORMAL" GRIEF

It is now well recognized that individuals manifest a wide spectrum of grief reactions that vary according to cultural backgrounds, social support networks, age, gender, and socioeconomic status as well as psychological health and the circumstances of loss. Many people who experience the loss of a significant other do not require professional intervention to help them cope with their grief. Most often, the social and emotional support that is provided by friends, families, and communities assists the grieving individual or family: helping them through acknowledging their loss, sharing the pain, supporting their adjustment to the new situation, and memorializing the loved one. Children, adolescents, and adults all benefit from this kind of social support.

It is important to understand the wide range of behaviors that are considered to be a part of normal grieving because grieving individuals may experience them as frightening or disturbing and need reassurance that these are part of an expectable reaction.

- Sadness, anger, guilt, anxiety, loneliness, fatigue, helplessness, numbness, shock, and even relief (in cases such as a prolonged illness) are all feelings that are normal and expectable following a significant loss.
- Tightness in the chest or throat, lack of energy, and stomach distress are physical sensations that are common in response to loss.
- Confusion, inability to concentrate or remember details, and auditory or visual experiences that mimic hallucinations such as seeing an image of the deceased person or hearing their voice are not uncommon in the weeks or months following loss.
- Sleep disturbance, loss of appetite, and restlessness are also very common reactions.

Over the course of time, with average social support and the opportunity to participate in grieving rituals within a cultural or spiritual community, most individuals will gradually experience a diminishment of these feelings, behaviors, and sensations. While there is no definitive time period by which this happens, if an individual or members of a family continue to experience distress intensely or for a prolonged period-or even unexpectedly years after a loss-they may benefit from treatment for complicated grief.

COMPLICATED GRIEF

In some situations, an individual may have difficulty coping with loss and manifests either pronounced difficulty, or prolonged distress, long after the loss has occurred. This can occur even when environmental or social support has been strong. A history of depression, anxiety, or difficult adjustment to previous losses may be contributing factors. It is important to be attuned to this reaction, often described as *complicated grief* or *complicated mourning*, because counseling may help the grieving individual or family to work through the painful feelings of loss.

Drawing from Bowlby's, Lindemann's, and Rando's work as well as his own research, grief therapist J. William Worden (2009) has identified four tasks that he considers a necessary part of the mourning process. These tasks include:

I. Accepting the loss
II. Experiencing the pain of grief
III. Adjusting to the new environment without the deceased
IV. Finding an enduring connection with the deceased in the midst of embarking on a new life (p. 50)

Worden emphasizes that these tasks must be completed in order for an individual to adapt to the loss of a significant other. Failure to eventually complete these tasks, according to his theory, results in several types of complicated mourning. Delayed grief occurs when a loss is insufficiently mourned, often because the loss is not acknowledged or the grief is not supported by others. The delayed grief then appears later in the individual's life. When grief is absent immediately after a loss but appears later in the form of a medical or psychiatric problem, it is referred to as masked grief. When a normal grief reaction, such as depressed mood or anxiousness, goes beyond normal grief to a clinical level of depression or anxiety, it is referred to as exaggerated grief. Chronic grief is when the mourner is stuck, sometimes for many years, in the grief process. Worden (2009) recommends grief therapy for complicated grief.

Who is at risk for complicated grief?

There are many factors that influence how grieving individuals cope with loss and that may contribute to complicated grief reactions. Individuals and families experiencing complicated grief will be encountered in many different settings, so it is important to be familiar with risk factors.

1. *The circumstances surrounding a loss* influence individuals' reactions
Disenfranchised losses are those accompanied by stigma resulting in loss of support or acknowledgment for grieving survivors. The execution of a prisoner,

losses associated with AIDS, and the death of a drunk driver following a fatal DUI accident are examples of these types of losses. Many people close to a person who has died by suicide feel a complex mix of guilt and isolation that can make acknowledgment and acceptance of the loss more complicated. Grieving family members sometimes hope to avoid stigma, so they may not let others know of their loss or feelings about it. Sometimes the loss is not acknowledged by others who could provide support, because they are unsure about how to express their condolences. Many adoption and foster care workers as well as graduates of the foster care system report that the symbolic loss inherent in removal from one's biological family precipitates a grief reaction that is insufficiently acknowledged or formally addressed in the formal child welfare system. Grieving loved ones experiencing disenfranchised grief may carry their complicated and unacknowledged feelings for many years. The following journal entry is illustrative of this kind of loss and grief reaction.

> In some of the clients I have worked with at the jail, especially some imprisoned for dealing drugs, the violence and ongoing losses from their neighborhoods, that happen while they are incarcerated shows up sometimes as flat affect and numbness, and they appear to be reliving the losses in their heads. In groups and one on one clients are opening up and sharing some of what may be happening. Clients' behaviors change: Sometimes, they act out, become aggressive, have sleeping problems, withdraw, isolate, and use substances. These men also experience symbolic loss because of being separated from their families, especially their children. The children who experience these losses seem to act out a great deal during their time at our after-school program. The emotions are usually consistent with most children. Some children express their anger by becoming very defiant, and disrespectful to staff. There are often times when children display some suicidal behaviors either verbally or physically. The behaviors are usually a continuation from school, and escalate once they arrive at the program.
>
> In reaction to their incarcerated parent, they either become very angry or very sad. The children's anger usually manifests through aggression toward another child or to themselves. Sadness can be manifested through other observable behaviors: isolating themselves from the group, not participating in activities, tantrums, and in many cases, trying to run off the premises. In regard to the incarcerated men, their anger or sadness usually manifests into regret and humility. When discussing their separation from their children and the loss they have suffered because they will probably never have a relationship with them, they become overwhelmed with sadness. Because of the setting they are in, they are unable to display their real emotions in a group setting. They seem to abide by some "jail code" of maintaining silence. This is unfortunate because individuals who suffer symbolic loss usually do not receive the same support or are

unable to grieve in the same way as someone who loses a loved one to death. This coupled with the inability to openly express emotions in jail leads to bottling all that emotion, a risk for complicated grief. (Preston, 2010)

Some losses are so unique that they can be expected to produce intense grief reactions that are profound and last a very long time. Among these is the death of a child. When one's child dies, it is perceived to be out of the normal sequence of life events. Parents expect their children to outlive them and to carry on the family heritage. Research indicates that the grief of parents for a deceased child is particularly severe, when compared with other types of bereavement (Rando, 1984). For parents, the process of mourning for one's child involves not only dealing with the loss of a child, but with the symbolic loss of parts of oneself, since parental attachment consists both of love for the child and self-love. It also may involve a loss or lessening of perceived social support. Many parents whose children have died report that others do not know how to support them in this unique type of loss and thus may avoid the grieving parents or avoid discussing their painful feelings with them. This can result in a sense of social isolation that can magnify the loss. Strategies for assisting individuals and families at high risk will be discussed at the end of this as well as other chapters, but in this case, as well as other situations in which social isolation complicates grief, peer support can be most helpful and can be enhanced through referral to a grieving parents support group or organization.

CASE EXAMPLE: CHEREEN AND MIKE

Chereen and Mike are parents whose only child, Kyle, died precipitously from meningitis while attending college. Although equally devastated, they were coping differently with the loss and strain had developed in their marriage. Mike mostly expressed anger and guilt, questioning the medical procedures that led to the late diagnosis and treatment and isolating himself from friends and family. Chereen more frequently expressed intense sadness, crying and talking about Mike Jr. with family and friends and finding comfort in being with her extended family, which included a nephew and several nieces. Chereen's coworkers in a local real estate office were concerned as they listened to her worry about Mike's anger and his tendency toward isolation. Mike's coworkers in an elementary school were concerned because he seemed withdrawn, didn't speak about Mike Jr., and they felt uncomfortable approaching him. Through a notice posted in the school's parent newsletter, Mike read about a meeting of a group for parents who had lost a child sponsored by an organization called Compassionate Friends. Although he wasn't eager to attend any group, he and Chereen agreed that this group might be a place to meet people who really understood what it was like for them. In the first group meeting, Mike and Chereen heard from other parents that their reactions were very normal and understood. Other couples in the group spoke about how, as individuals, they grieved differently too. They also talked about ways they had found to gain sustenance from each other, even though the pain was intense. Mike and Chereen were surprised to hear that other parents had found a way to gain meaning and even some hope, even though they all had experienced a devastating tragedy. They attended the group regularly for about a year and became active supporters of other couples whose young adult children had died.

2. Perceived lack of social support: Other types of losses can be expected to result in a difficult mourning process, partly because of perceived or actual lack of social support. Suicide, as noted earlier, is a most difficult loss to sustain because of the social stigma associated with it and survivors often perceive a lack of social support. Older adults who have already sustained the loss of many members of their primary support network-including friends, siblings, and adult children-may have very limited social support to help them adjust and to fill the void when someone important in their life dies. An example of such a situation is the nursing home resident whose roommate dies. Partners in gay and lesbian relationships, especially among elders whose relationships may not be publicly acknowledged, report feeling isolated in a way that heterosexual partners may not. Often, symbolic losses are not acknowledged in the way that loss from death is acknowledged. Since there are no shared public rituals to assist the individual or family that has sustained a symbolic loss, such as loss sustained through divorce or placement in foster care, there may be no formal way for the difficult feelings of sadness or anger to be acknowledged or support provided. This is illustrated in the following case example:

I have worked in child protection for just over a year now. One of the things I see often is right after we take a child out of the home. Whereas this is a symbolic loss, very frequently we see changes in the child's behaviors. Currently on my caseload is a family which I will refer to as the S family. Mrs. S is the single mother of 2 children, a son who is 9 and a daughter who is 14. Mrs. S. has a diagnosis of a bipolar mood disorder. She stops taking her medications about twice a year, resulting in psychiatric hospitalization and foster care placement of her children. In the last year alone, the children have been removed three times. The most recent time, we were unable to keep the children together. So in addition to their grieving the loss of their mother, they are also grieving the loss of each other. Unfortunately, while Mrs. S. is hospitalized the children receive limited visitation with her. However, the agency does do visits between the two children once a week.

Since being placed in their current foster homes, the 9-year-old is experiencing encopresis. And the 14-year-old has exhibited aggressive behaviors, stealing from the foster parents, and an increase in sexualized behaviors (due to a past trauma of sexual abuse).

When the children are removed, they do not cry and they seem to be exhibiting masked grief. They have come to see this as a normal routine in their life. Occasionally they will cry at the end of a visit with their mother. However, when the children have gone a few weeks without seeing their mother, their behaviors tend to settle down in the foster homes.

One of the things we have done is have the children involved in steady individual therapy. The agency stays in communication with the therapists to ensure that the agency is doing the very best in the interests of these children. Every time their mother is released from her hospitalizations, the family participates in family therapy sessions before the children return home.

In this particular case, there is a lot more going on and a lot has happened over the span of 5 years in which this case has been open with us, including procedures to change the goal to adoption and termination of parental rights. As this process begins to unfold, the needs of the children will change and it is highly likely that their behaviors will increase because in the past the children have always returned home (Miller, 2009).

As in this case of children in foster care, when an individual experiences perceived or actual lack of social support after a loss, professionals can provide much-needed support through active listening as well as referrals to support groups and organizations that provide information and peer exchange in addition to individual and family therapy. In addition, professionals as well as foster parents and other community members can provide essential models of adults who care when other attachment figures are absent (Kagan, 2004). More about these strategies is discussed in Chapter 10.

3. High-profile losses: Lack of social support is not a problem in some very high-profile losses, but instead intense media coverage and public attention may overwhelm members of a family. Many survivors of the terrorist attacks of 9/11 and of public losses such as a police officer's death in the line of duty have acknowledged that lack of privacy and frequent inquiries about or exposure to the details of the loss make it difficult to obtain needed respite. Prolonged and intensified grief can result when graphic details of the death are repeatedly encountered by survivors who are often subjected to insensitive reporting and unrelenting public exposure. Some survivors and trauma specialists believe that it can actually add to survivors' distress when too much attention is focused on the loss, particularly the traumatic details, or when survivors are urged to talk about the trauma repeatedly (Bonanno, 2009). Some report that distress is relieved more successfully through taking action; forming task groups to influence policy or obtaining resources for survivor families and communities. In situations of complicated grief that can result from high-profile tragedies, however, peer support and professionally led programs are reported to be very helpful (COPS, 2003; Kirby, 1999).

4. Multiple stressors: Unfortunately, many losses are accompanied by additional stressors such as reduced income or unexpected bills, loss of important roles, and even loss of a job or health insurance. Single parenting is often perceived as an additional stressor in situations where an active partner in parenting dies or leaves the family. It is important for professionals to be aware that these will often intensify the grief reaction or make it more difficult for individuals to complete the necessary tasks of grieving, since they may be preoccupied by these challenges and unable to achieve relief from the pain of loss. When learning that someone has sustained a loss, we can be attuned to the possible additional strains they may be experiencing and inquire about these so needed help can be obtained.

It is important to be familiar with factors that might predict if an individual or a family is at risk for complicated bereavement. A study by Kelly and colleagues (1999) looked at predictors of bereavement outcome among family caregivers of cancer patients. They discovered that families with the greatest distress in bereavement had suffered a greater number of adverse life events, had prior losses or separations in their lives, had more troubled relationships with the patient, and the patient was more severely ill at the time of palliative care referral. Further, being psychologically distressed prior to the patient's death predicted greater distress for the family caregiver following the death.

Kissane and colleagues (1998) classified five types of family responses to a death and labeled maladaptive responses as those involving hostile or sullen reactions, which were characterized by high family conflict, low expressiveness, and poor expressiveness. The use of a 12-item Family Relationships Index was found to be an effective screening tool to identify families at risk.

INTERVENTIONS FOR NORMAL AND COMPLICATED GRIEF

Why and how can a referral to a mental health professional or grief therapist help?

The Diagnostic and Statistical Manual of Mental Disorders, published by the American Psychiatric Association, is the primary tool that mental health professionals (including social workers, psychologists, psychiatrists and counselors) use to make an accurate assessment of symptoms that may be indicative of either normal bereavement or a more serious depression. The current version of the manual *(DSM IV-TR)* notes that depressive symptoms are a *normal and expectable reaction* to the death of a loved one and that sadness, diminished interest in daily activities, weight loss, and diminished ability to concentrate may all be evident in *uncomplicated bereavement*, which does not represent a mental disorder. In the *DSM*, uncomplicated bereavement, like other problems that are a focus of treatment but may not represent a mental disorder, is categorized as a V. Code. As noted earlier, people are usually able to cope with bereavement with the support of family, friends, and often a spiritual community. However, when risk factors are present or when individuals are evidencing signs of complicated grief, they may require specialized grief intervention.

According to the current *DSM IV*, bereavement is considered to be complicated by a major depressive episode *if* the depressive symptoms are accompanied by morbid preoccupation with worthlessness, suicidal ideation, and/or marked functional impairment or psychomotor retardation of prolonged duration. However, a new version of the *DSM (V)* is scheduled for publication in 2013. Each edition of the manual involves revisions and additions, and a major addition that is proposed for the new version is the inclusion of a diagnosis for complicated grief (Lichtenthal, Cruess, & Prigerson, 2004; Prigerson, Vanderwerker, & Maciejewski, 2007).

The creation of this diagnosis is expected (as is the intent of all diagnoses) to aid mental health practitioners in accurately assessing and identifying a problem or set of symptoms that may be treatable with specific interventions. Some of the criteria that are being considered for the diagnosis (among many others) include:

- Feeling that part of oneself has died
- A shattered worldview (e.g., lost sense of security, trust, control)
- Excessive irritability, bitterness, or anger related to the death

The symptoms must endure for at least 6 months and cause clinically significant impairment in social, occupational, or other important areas of functioning.

Whether or not a separate diagnosis is created for complicated grief, individuals experiencing prolonged or immobilizing grief, and symptoms like those described earlier, often benefit most from grief therapy (Schut, Stroebe, Van Den Bout, & Terheggen, 2001, Neimeyer & Currier, 2009). "Both complicated grief and grief-related major depression can be persistent and gravely disabling, can dramatically interfere with function and quality of life, and may even be life threatening in the absence of treatment." (Zisook & Shear, 2010). Although this quote came from an article written for psychiatrists, it is important for all helping professionals to refer to mental health specialists those clients whose functioning is impaired and who might be at serious risk as a result of complicated grief. Specific interventions will be discussed in Chapters 10–12, and it may be useful to understand different models that are used for different types of grief and different populations.

Professionals who provide these specialized grief interventions can be identified through a local hospital, hospice organization, or mental health agency. Many professional organizations with state or national offices, such as the Association for Death Education (ADEC) and the National Association of Social Workers, can also be a source of information about how to obtain professional help. Once potential sources have been identified, it may take repeated efforts to actually link the distressed individual or family to the appropriate source. For some it may suffice to simply pass the information along, but usually specific information or a specific name, with details on why or how that resource can help, will help insure that the referral is successful.

SUMMARY

Our understanding of "normal," or expectable, grief responses and those considered to be "complicated" grief reactions comes from many sources. There is still debate among researchers and practitioners about whether complicated grief is a valid construct since so many grieving individuals appear to reestablish equilibrium and experience less distress over time. Also many reactions that are considered a natural part of a culturally prescribed grief reaction in one cultural group may seem highly unusual, even distressing, to members of another cultural group. The current edition of the *Diagnostic and Statistical Manual of Mental Disorders (DSM)* does not have a diagnosis for complicated grief, although it is being proposed for the 2013 edition *(DSM V)*. Helping professionals should be acquainted with the biological and psychological experiences of normal grief in order to support individuals and families they work with. These include sadness, anger, guilt, and anxiety in the psychological realm, tightness in the chest, fatigue, and stomach distress in the physical realm, and confusion and lack of ability to concentrate in the cognitive realm. Symptoms such as feeling that one has lost a part of oneself and excessive anger about the death that last for more than 6 months and cause clinically significant impairment in social, occupational, or other important areas of functioning are under consideration as diagnostic criteria for complicated grief. These reactions may be considered expectable for certain kinds of losses such as the death of a child, however. Most individuals and families reestablish equilibrium through a normal grief process. Current research suggests that those who experience complicated grief gain the most benefit from grief therapy provided by specialists.

CHAPTER 8

Cultural and Spiritual Influences

CHAPTER OUTLINE

Expect to have hope rekindled. Expect your prayers to be answered in wondrous ways. The dry seasons in life do not last. The spring rains will come again.

Sara Ban Breathnach

THE INFLUENCE OF CULTURE AND SPIRITUALITY IN COPING WITH LOSS AND GRIEF

As part of the self-assessment exercise recommended in Chapter 3, you were asked to think back to experiences related to loss in your own life. There is a good chance that in doing this, you described ways of coping with loss that were significantly influenced by your cultural and spiritual background. When I have assigned this exercise to students in my classes, the memories that frequently stand out are those of religious or spiritual practices, such as a wake or memorial service that they attended as young children, and many of these spiritual practices are recollected in the context of culture.

For example, in a class discussion a student reflected on her experiences:

> I am part Native American (Cherokee) and part African American. I have roots in South Carolina. Our traditions and food are southern in distinction. Typically each person visiting a family who has recently suffered a loss would bring a dish of their best effort. Religion in the south is just as fun and light as any social event up north would be. It is an inherently natural way of holding the family together. It fosters common and traditional values and mores for the community and the family. My upbringing included religion, and holidays were for bringing out the tablecloth and my mother's best effort at southern cooking. My mother can cook, and make cakes from scratch like you would not believe. My tradition includes the return to the church for spiritual guidance and fellowship, and the typical black funeral with song and reading, with a gathering at the home afterward. Funerals and wakes were sad during the service but after the service ended it was clear that the fun and socialization at the home of the decedent was for a more lively presentation. It is not uncommon for the family to have libation and laughter, just like a party at some homes. My family usually just has good food and good stories. (Butler-Jones, 2002)

Culture and spirituality are discussed together in this chapter because they are often intertwined and sometimes inseparable. Even though your own cultural and spiritual experiences may be very distinct or different, and they may be for many of the people you find yourself assisting, it is important to understand how they both can influence our own and others' reactions to loss.

CULTURE

Culture is a complex concept. For this discussion, the description used by the National Association of Social Workers is helpful. "The word *culture . . . implies the integrated pattern of human behavior that includes thoughts, communications, actions, customs, beliefs, values and institutions of a racial, ethnic, religious or social group. Culture is often referred to as the totality of ways that are passed down from one generation to another*" (NASW, 2000, p. 61).

Other professional disciplines may use slightly different definitions of culture but share the same principle that it is essential to understand the influence that cultural beliefs and practices have on the individuals, families, and communities we serve.

In addition, it is helpful to know that some people define their cultural group through identification communities, the members of which share common experiences. Examples are individuals who identify with the deaf culture, or individuals who identify themselves with gay culture in addition to cultural groups based on ethnicity such as Mexican American. Awareness of the cultural group with which an individual or a family identifies is very important for professionals who want to assist with grief because the beliefs, values, and behavioral norms to which their clients have been socialized will most likely have influence on their responses to loss. Culture may also influence how an individual or a family regards professionals and their offers of help. For example, a French Canadian member of our interdisciplinary hospice team acknowledged that in her family of origin self-sufficiency is highly valued and accepting help from those outside the immediate family is sometimes difficult because it is viewed as contradictory to this value. Her perspective was helpful to other members of the team in better understanding the meaning of accepting a hospice referral to a family in our community who shared this background.

CULTURAL AWARENESS, SENSITIVITY, AND COMPETENCE

Most professional training programs now emphasize cultural competence, or at least cultural sensitivity, in preparing professionals for practice in a multicultural society.

In your professional training you have most likely already begun to study and practice within this framework. For the purposes of this discussion of grief, *cultural sensitivity* is used to describe an awareness of, and appreciation for, the differences in values, beliefs, and norms of people from different cultural and spiritual backgrounds. *Cultural competence* implies that the professional practices with this awareness and appreciation for differences but is also able to engage and interact effectively with people from diverse cultural backgrounds. Transcultural Nursing, an organization devoted to preparing nurses for practice with diverse populations, encourages nurses to understand their own worldviews and those of their patients. This can be done by obtaining cultural information and then applying that information.

Awareness of cultural norms can aid us in providing assistance that demonstrates respect and understanding. Failure to understand and acknowledge these differences can be perceived as disrespect and may impede our ability to be helpful.

A school counselor wrote,

> I came to the United States from Portugal when I was an elementary school student. When I first attended a funeral in the U.S. that was not for a Portuguese person, I couldn't believe the differences from my own culture, from beginning to end. For example, something as simple as attire can be viewed in extremely different ways . . . . For example, in my culture one always wears black out of respect for the mourners regardless of whether you are family or not. When my neighbor's son died, she wore clothing with colors to the funeral and I was shocked. Coming from my frame of reference, that symbolized disrespect and lack of feeling. At home, after the funeral, she changed into a housedress that was multicolored with very vibrant colors. I know that the color you wear outside has nothing to do with feelings of loss (or the color one may feel on the inside) yet it was culturally shocking to me.
>
> I have also found the funerals for Americans that I have attended to be more reserved. In Portugal, in my experience, one witnesses the arrival of the casket into the church being carried by close friends or family, and you then escort the casket to the burial ground (cemetery) and witness its descent into the ground while mourners sob and scream. Here in the U.S. (at least at the funerals I have attended), the family is more likely to grieve and mourn in private; there is less public display. It is important to

be aware that everyone handles death in a very different way and one cannot judge how someone else feels or infer how someone feels by looking
at them or their behavior from the outside." (Silva, 2003)

Lack of awareness of different cultural groups' responses to loss can lead us to:

- Misinterpret an individual's or a family's reactions,
- Fail to offer support or assistance that might be perceived as helpful,
- Offend the grieving person(s) and create a barrier to their receiving care and
  support.

There is perhaps no better illustration of this kind of error than the situation
described in Anne Fadiman's (1998) *The Spirit Catches You and You Fall Down*.
Fadiman recounts how the many professionals involved in caring for a 3-year-old
Hmong child with epilepsy did so without understanding her family's cultural beliefs
and practices. Everyone suffered as a result. The parents were deprived of the understanding and support they sought and the medical providers felt frustrated at their
inability to intervene and prolong the child's life. Yet, it is reasonable to question how
any individual or team can possibly expect to become knowledgeable about the literally hundreds of cultural groups whose members they may encounter in their work.

It is also important to recognize that knowledge of a particular *group* does not
necessarily equip us to adequately understand an *individual*, who may not subscribe
to the beliefs or norms of the group. Even if we are from a cultural background that
is similar, we cannot assume that our own perspective applies to someone else. Some
members of the same cultural group, for example, have different spiritual practices or
subscribe to different norms based on factors such as socioeconomic status or multiple group memberships.

Therefore, most experts in cross-cultural practice suggest that the best approach
to working with individuals with diverse backgrounds is to ask them what values, beliefs, and practices are important to them. Expression of sorrow for a person's loss is
almost always appropriate, followed by a general statement such as, "I would like to
help in any way that I can. Perhaps you can tell me what you or your family would
prefer." If you are planning to attend a memorial or visit with a grieving person, it is
usually helpful to find out about how to best show respect or what kind of behavior
is expected in mourners with their background, but be aware that there may be other
expectations that you can't anticipate. To learn as much as you can, Koenig and Gates-
Williams (1995) recommend making use of available resources, including community
or religious leaders, family members, and language translators. Another member of
your staff who is familiar with cultural norms may also be able to give you information.

As a beginning social worker, I was fortunate to have spent the first 2 years of
my career working in a Jewish rehabilitation hospital, even though I was raised in
the Roman Catholic faith. Shabbat services were held every Friday at sundown and a
Kosher menu was provided for residents and their visiting family members. My first
supervisor, along with the hospital's rabbi and the families I worked with, was instrumental in helping me to learn about Shiva and the mourning rituals that take place for
seven days following a death. During this time, family members mourn at home and
visitors bring food and comfort to them. Orthodox families covered the mirrors in the

home, wore black clothing, and observed other practices that were very different from those I had observed in my own childhood. Acknowledging my lack of information enabled me to learn about this and the many other rituals related to death so that I could show respect and assist grieving residents and families, despite our differences.

Over the years I have learned a great deal from my colleagues with diverse backgrounds who have shared their experiences related to grief and mourning. For example, one colleague shared that in her family's small village in the Philippines, when her grandfather died, the whole community came together, rubbed the body with oils, dressed his body in linens, made a crown of flowers, and paraded around the small community. Following this there was a celebration with food, singing, storytelling, dancing, and prayer.

Another colleague wrote:

> My experience with death has been affected by cultural attitudes. In my Latino culture the response to death is an intense one. When a person has died in the Puerto Rican culture we can expect overwhelming responses by family and the Hispanic community. The visual I have of Puerto Rican funerals is of women standing around the deceased in an emotional uproar and of ambulances on standby outside the funeral parlor. My eight year old was so affected by the emotional responses of the Latina women in our family when her father's brother died that we made the choice not to have her participate in any of the funerary rituals. My experience also has been that the more tragic the death the more intense the response will be by family and loved ones. Intense grief reactions by individuals around me make the experience of death for me unpleasant. (Elias, 2001)

A student in a class discussion shared a very different perspective after attending a funeral in which intense emotion was expressed following a tragic death:

> Every aspect of this funeral was unlike any other that I have attended. There were over 1,500 people in attendance. Prior to the service the family had been there to view the body and there was time after that for others to view. As the service started the family of about 150 extended members paraded down the aisle to reserved seats in the front. There was a very large choir that sang, several friends gave speeches, and there was a lot of dancing involved. I do not remember what religion the family was, but the focus of the service was on eternal life and the preacher focused on celebration rather than mourning. There were nurses present because people got so in touch with the "holy spirit" that they would pass out. I have never been to such a ceremony/celebration before. It was unreal, the spirit in the room over someone that had died. The service lasted about 4 hours and following was a reception with all kinds of food sponsored by my agency. It was a beautiful commemoration. (Hildreth, 2002)

A colleague who attended the funeral of a Mashantucket Pequot tribal elder shared her observations. This elder was buried in her full Native American tribal dress. There were pastors from various churches who each spoke about her and her life and the things she had done to help others. The funeral was a celebration of her life and called a "Homegoing" or a celebration of her transition from the natural life on earth to a spiritual life in heaven with God. The funeral had lively music with singing and dancing.

Yet another student informed me about Buddhist practices. She explained that in the Buddhist tradition, death is seen as an inevitable part of a larger process of nature's cycles of which human manifestation is but a small part. Prayer is not offered to a being outside oneself, but the ritual of chanting is used as a tool for cleansing one's consciousness. Beliefs of life after death include the teaching that one's thoughts, words, and actions leave an imprint on one's consciousness, and that rebirth (life after death) is a manifestation of the energies related to those imprints. It is believed that the spirit hovers over the body for 3 days after death so the body is not moved for 3 days. It is also believed that touching the body (except for cleansing) could disturb the spirit. Chanting is believed to liberate the spirit and may continue for long periods.

Learning about these different practices, and learning more about what is unfamiliar to me, has been essential in my own professional development. The Internet also now offers many excellent sources of information. Many diverse cultural groups and professional organizations provide information and guidance on their Web sites. Some of these are listed in the Internet Resources for this chapter. Professional organizations are also developing standards for culturally competent practice or cross-cultural practice to guide their members. The National Association of Social Workers, for example, has published Standards for Cultural Competence on its Web site. Many medical organizations publish both standards of practice and information about different cultural practices related to grief, since health care professionals interact frequently with diverse populations and grief is commonly experienced in health care settings. A universal set of standards has been developed by the U.S. government's Office of Minority Health to guide all health professionals in cultural competence. Web sites like EthnoMed and others listed in the Internet Resources for this chapter provide specific information about different cultural groups that include mourning practices.

GENDER AND MEDIA INFLUENCES

Before more specifically addressing spirituality, it is important to discuss one more aspect of culture and its influence on grieving individuals. A male colleague alluded to the influence of our contemporary "American" culture in the perspective he offered on gender and grief. He noted that for men in America it is often difficult to grieve a loss in the same way that women do, because many men are taught from an early age not to show emotions such as sadness, loneliness, or depression. He noted that many men he has worked with, when faced with the overwhelming feelings of loss of a loved one, are unable to cope with the feeling they are experiencing and may not have healthy outlets to express their emotions. This perspective also reminds us that cultural messages are transmitted in many ways, not only through direct family communication or interaction. Many grief experts note that the mass media in America has a tremendous influence on our ideas about how to react in the face of loss. The way the media commonly focuses on violent death in the news, in movies, and in television programs generally omits presentation of the long-term effects on survivors or healthy longer-term mourning practices following loss are believed by some to contribute to a "grief denying" culture.

Many students, when reflecting on the influence of the media on their own perceptions of death and loss, acknowledge that they may have learned to avoid the topic of grief, partly as a result of their exposure to mass media. Cartoons, for example, often show characters undergoing traumatic injuries only to reappear, unscathed, in the next scene or episode. Similarly, in television programs and computer games, people are annihilated with no reference to the grief experienced by survivors. There are some movies that have depicted both realistic and positive models of grieving individuals and families with diverse backgrounds. A few of these, such as *Smoke Signals,* are included as suggestions for this chapter's exercise, which is located in MySocialWorkLab for *Advancing Core Competencies* under Resources in the "Grief and Loss" section). It involves viewing one of a number of popular movies addressing loss in the context of culture.

One other very important point that has been underscored by many of my students and colleagues is that too many children in America as well as in other countries grow up in a "culture of violence" in which actual death and loss are a constant part of daily life. One student articulately expressed her concern that our current grief theories and textbooks, and many professionals working with children and families, do not effectively address this issue. In a class discussion, a student voiced her thoughts and feelings about this very assertively and gave all of us in the class much food for thought. She said that there was a gap for her in the theories of grief we had been studying and said there is *nothing* she would like and appreciate more than for grief experts to explain to her the culture of poverty as it relates to the ghetto and the pain of waking up and living another day, facing an endless accumulation of losses. She asked the instructor and the class if we could help her to understand how and why there is so much news coverage about violence in a foreign country, but so little coverage about the culture of violence in our own country, cities, neighborhoods, communities, homes. She added that it frightens her that people can ignore such pain, loss, and suffering. Who are we fooling? The pain and suffering exist but they are addressed only when they spread (e.g., school shootings) to more affluent communities. She asked those of us in the class to please not take this personally but suggested that we all need to start understanding what it is like to feel worthless, hopeless, and very, very *angry* about poverty and violence in our society.

This student and many others who live and work in communities where poverty, violence, and multiple losses are very prevalent have made me increasingly aware of how little attention the grief of vulnerable populations is given.

This is an area where much more work is needed including needs assessments, research, and program development. For those of us working with children and families exposed to daily and often traumatic losses, we can begin by acknowledging these losses. We must also raise our voices to advocate for, and participate in, community action and change to prevent this injustice from continuing in our society.

SPIRITUALITY

In an interview about integrating spirituality into medical interviews, Christina Puchalski (1999), a physician who has developed the FICA spiritual assessment tool, explains why spirituality became important to her, as a member of the helping professions. She reports that her parents were very spiritual and they had drawn upon their spirituality when experiencing multiple losses during World War II. She had a model for utilizing spiritual beliefs to help cope and to find meaning in life. She herself did not embrace her parents Catholic religion but instead explored Judaism and Hinduism along with other spiritual beliefs and practices. Based on this interest in spirituality, and several significant deaths in her own life, she became interested in integrating a spiritual history into the medical interview. Her tool, the FICA, is available online and can easily be used in medical, social service, and mental health settings.

An American student's observations about the way that people in Ecuador acknowledge death serve as an example of how culture and spirituality are both important in grief reactions and are often intertwined. In a class discussion, she shared that she had spent 2 months in Ecuador and attended a university course for Americans on Ecuadoran culture. She learned that families in Ecuador celebrate death by having a picnic on the grave of the deceased loved one, making a plate for the deceased individual, and leaving it as an offering. It was explained to the American students that the family members are celebrating life and feeding the soul of their loved one who has gone on to the next life. Every year, Ecuadorians celebrate The Day of the Dead, when they have another picnic on the grave of their loved ones and continue the feeding of the soul. She remarked that it is interesting how we Americans think of death in very negative aspects but this culture celebrates it.

It is now recognized that spirituality and religion are very important influences in peoples' lives, particularly in coping with death and loss. Rabbi Earl Grollman has written that when unexpected crises occur, people of all faiths often ask the same questions: "Is it God's will? If God's will is for Life, why did this terrible death occur?"(Grollman, 1996, p. 2). Yet, professionals and laypersons alike have some difficulty defining the concepts of both spirituality and religion. Until recently, the two terms were sometimes used interchangeably and few professional training programs emphasized religion or spirituality. In the last two decades, however, both the popular media and the professional literature have paid a great deal more attention to religion and the broader concept of spirituality.

While the term *spirituality* has been used in different ways, many training programs now use a broad, inclusive definition such as *that which gives meaning to one's life and draws one to transcend oneself. Religion*, on the other hand, is defined more narrowly as a *communal* or *institutional expression* or *practice of faith*.

Practitioners may find it most helpful to view spirituality as a broader concept than religion, and religion as one expression of spirituality. In addition to the many formal religions that serve as expressions of spirituality, others include prayer, meditation, interactions with others or nature, and a relationship with God or a higher power. Spirituality, in whatever way it is expressed by the individual, is considered by many to be important in helping both those who are dying and those who are grieving a loss to make meaning of life (Highfield, 2000; Koenig, 2002; Doka & Morgan, 1999).

The Gallup Poll has been asking the American public about the role of religion in their lives since 1952. In more recent polls, questions about spirituality have been asked as well. In a 2007 poll, 56% of those sampled reported religion to be very important and only 17% reported not very important. In a January 2002 poll, 50% of Americans described themselves as "religious," while another 33% said they are "spiritual but not religious" (11% said neither and 4% said both). When respondents to a 1999 Gallup survey were asked to define "spirituality," almost a third defined it without reference to God or a higher authority: "a calmness in my life," "something you really put your heart into," or "living the life you feel is pleasing" (Gallup, 2002).

It is therefore very important to take into consideration, and be informed about, religion and spirituality when assisting individuals, families, and communities in coping with grief and loss. A Vietnamese student wrote:

> I remember the first time that I experienced death more than ten years ago when I was a young teenager and one of my best friends died in an accident. I still remember the feeling of pain that I felt inside of me when I attended her funeral. I cried for many days after her death, and I asked myself what did she do to deserve death? Because we were prohibited in my family from discussing the topics of death or dying, I didn't get any advice or what to do to cope with her death. After her death, I felt more appreciative of what I had in life right then and still do at this moment. I believe in reincarnation, and I hope that I could be reunited with my best friend in our next lives. (Tran, 2002)

An African American from the southern region of the United States wrote:

> In our southern African American culture, a funeral service is held and is called a "Home Going." The Church affiliates, the Pastor and friends provide support in many ways. They bring over food, they listen and talk-whatever is needed. The ceremony is religious in nature. Within this tradition, Christians live on in spirit and it is believed that their souls go on to be with the Almighty according to the King James Version of the Bible. The activity that takes place before the actual burial is what is called a processional. All immediate family members walk into the church to view the body in an open casket (optional, but usual). The family members walk through, almost as in a parade, where grief is displayed publicly. At this service, people are asked to share a few words about the deceased, a song, usually a solo, is sung and the Minister or Pastor speaks to the family about the deceased and offers condolences thereafter. The body is then taken to the burial place and a parade of cars with their lights on follows closely behind. The body is placed in the ground and flowers laid over it. (DeVeux, 2002)

Yet another student shared her experiences with a range of different spiritually based funerary ceremonies.

I have attended a range of services/ceremonies marking the rite of passage from death to life. Services have been held in the Native American, Jewish, Catholic, and Protestant traditions. The one I found the most powerful and healing occurred eight months ago when a fellow supervisor died in a car crash. His family conducted a private ceremony in Utah, and my agency conducted a Native American memorial service based on his form of spirituality. It began with a native mourning song, which, though in native language, invoked strong feelings of sadness, putting mourners in touch with their feelings. Following the song, a Native American prayer was read which symbolized the spiritual journey, the return to Mother Earth, and the concept of acceptance. Another co-worker played a native song on his guitar, which stirred feelings of comfort and connectedness. Mourners who consisted of colleagues, friends and clients were given an opportunity to speak in his remembrance. Most powerful were the words of his clients whose lives he had so deeply touched. A final ritual was offered which involved dropping a stone into a large round clay pot of water and through the rippling effect meditating on how we had each been affected by his presence, as well as our overall interconnectedness with each other. (Davis, 2002)

It is not uncommon, however, for members of a family to practice religion or express their spirituality differently from other family members. While spirituality/religion and culture are often closely intertwined and are often shared by families, as was discussed in Chapters 2 and 3, other factors also influence individual differences that may cause a grieving individual or even an observer to respond differently than those around them. These differences can be disconcerting and each individual may need validation for his or her own way of dealing with loss.

In the African American church culture that I grew up in, we celebrate the life of the person through a ritual of a funeral. In the black church, specifically the Pentecostal movement, if one dies in the faith (meaning they have accepted that Jesus Christ born, lived and died for the sins of the world), they have lived a life believing and hearing that death is a part of living but death is not final. Death is viewed as "sleeping" and the service is called a "homegoing," for it is a celebration of the life of the deceased. Services are a wonderful way of bringing closure to death, or at least is a beginning of closure. When my grandmother died, her last wishes were that she be cremated. She was a Jehovah's Witness and we did not worship or celebrate death the same way. At her service, we were made to feel that we shouldn't grieve. My family was told that we shouldn't grieve because my grandmother wouldn't want us to cry. This concept was foreign to me as I am used to openly grieving. I think that it may be this way for others who look at my culture and the ways in which we grieve and may find it foreign and weird. One thing is for sure; I grieve at all funerals. Even if I didn't know the person well, just seeing others grieve makes me cry. All in all, I believe that it is very necessary for some form of ritual to take place when death occurs. (Gatling, 2001)

A colleague shared the following:

Once I went to a funeral of a mutual friend with a friend. The deceased was a Jehovah's Witness and they conduct memorial services instead of funerals with a body and sermon as is customary in some other cultures. Well after we were seated, the person that I went to the funeral with asked me where was the body because she had never been to a service where there was no body and people were not crying and becoming very emotional. I politely said to her as I pointed toward an urn on a pedestal (the body is in that vase). She almost fainted and it was all I could do to contain myself and not burst out laughing (I know that I shouldn't have, but you had to have seen her face). Afterwards she began to laugh because she now realized that there are different strokes for different people. This person is my best friend and we still laugh about the day she found out what it was like to attend a memorial service at a Kingdom Hall. (Walker, 2002)

Many counselors, teachers, and rehabilitation specialists today include spirituality in their assessments and interventions. Just as individual helpers cannot be expected to be competent in the multitude of cultural groups found in most practice settings, not all helpers are expected to be experts in spirituality. However, it is useful to be aware of diverse religious and spiritual practices in order to better understand their significance to those we are helping. Inclusive language that uses a variety of religious and spiritual references is important in conveying understanding and acceptance in exploring coping. For example, using open-ended questions that acknowledge differences are more helpful than closed-ended questions such as "Are you planning to hold a funeral?" An example of an open-ended question is: "Is there a specific spiritual or religious practice that you or your family has found helpful in the past?" This question conveys understanding that there is wide variation in the practices or beliefs of individuals and families. Familiarity with a broad range of practices and belief systems enables you to better use inclusive language. However, even more important than specific knowledge is the awareness of differences and the willingness to acknowledge our own limitations.

It is also important to attend to verbal and nonverbal signals that might indicate the importance of religion or spirituality. The presence of religious or spiritual articles such as clothing, medals, or books might indicate they are a resource to be drawn upon. When concern about religion or spirituality is expressed by someone facing loss, there may be a need for further exploration or referral to a spiritual resource. There are a number of tools that are used by psychologists, social workers, and pastoral care counselors to assess spirituality. One tool, FICA, is named for the acronym that identifies the four areas of questions about spirituality that it addresses. These include F: faith or beliefs (what faith or beliefs are important to you?), I: importance and influence (how much importance do they have in your life and how do they influence you in times of distress or celebration?), C: community (is there a religious or spiritual community that you belong to?), and A: address (how can we best address your spiritual or religious needs?) (Puchalski & Romer, 2000).

Requests for spiritual counseling or expression of existential doubt may be verbal indications of spiritual needs. Sometimes, a referral to the hospital chaplain or a resource in your community for pastoral or spiritual counseling is helpful. Many grieving people have already established relationships with pastors or a spiritual practitioner to whom they can turn in times of distress. Just as in the case of culture, it is also important when it comes to spirituality not to make assumptions but rather to listen carefully to what an individual or a family is expressing, use inclusive language when inquiring about what they find helpful and be ready to support them, even if the practice may be unfamiliar to you. Ramos (2003) notes that there are wide variations across groups but that many cultural beliefs do not separate spiritual or emotional from physical causes of illness and health care and other helping professionals need to be aware of this.

This respect and appreciation of the spiritual and cultural practices of clients is referenced frequently in contemporary training programs and textbooks. Spiritually competent practice is also addressed in many professional ethical codes. For example, the NASW Code of Ethics states that social workers should strive to exhibit sensitivity to clients' religion in at least two of its standards. Spiritually competent practice also requires that as helpers, we be aware of how our own beliefs or practices influence us as practitioners. A variety of studies indicate that practitioners in many disciplines report that their own spiritual practice is important to them. In one study of family physicians, for example, 74% of the surveyed physicians reported at least weekly or monthly spiritual or religious service attendance, and 79% reported a strong religious or spiritual orientation (Daaleman & Frey, 1999). Recent studies indicate that there is increasing recognition that the spiritual well-being of helping professionals is important and can contribute to effective management of stress related to working with vulnerable populations (Fisher & Brumley, 2008).

SUMMARY

Culture and spirituality are discussed together in this chapter because they are often intertwined, particularly when it comes to observing mourning rituals and beliefs about death. Culture is a complex concept that is defined slightly differently by different disciplines. It is generally defined as a pattern of behaviors that includes customs, beliefs, and values. It is imperative for professional helpers be aware of culture and spirituality when working with grieving individuals and families, since the beliefs, values, and behavioral norms to which they have been socialized will most likely have influence on their responses to loss as well as to our offers of help following a loss. One of the most practical and efficient ways to demonstrate cultural sensitivity is to ask about cultural beliefs and practices when discussing loss with an individual or a family. This is particularly important when it comes to mourning practices and burial or memorial rituals.

Spiritual beliefs and practices are also very significant when it comes to mourning. *Spirituality* and *religion* are sometimes confused, but they are separate terms that refer to related concepts. A serviceable definition of *spirituality* is "that which gives meaning to one's life and draws one to transcend oneself." *Religion*, on the other hand, is defined more narrowly as a *communal* or *institutional expression* or *practice of faith*. Like culturally sensitive practice, sensitivity to spiritual beliefs and practices is essential in order to engage with and respond to grieving clients effectively. This does not mean we must have direct knowledge of every religious or spiritual community and specific practices but it does mean that we need to demonstrate our understanding that spirituality or religion may play a significant role in an individual's or a family's life. The FICA is a useful tool for conducting a spiritual assessment in the context of death but simply asking a family about their spiritual beliefs and practices also demonstrates spiritual sensitivity. Training programs are now recognizing that spirituality is not only an important influence on clients but also serves an important function in the lives of many helping professionals, assisting them in coping with the loss and grief they encounter in working with vulnerable populations.

CHAPTER 9

Grief in the Context of Anticipated Loss

CHAPTER OUTLINE

*Some people come into our lives and quickly go. Some
people move our souls to dance. They awaken us to new
understanding with the passing whisper of their wisdom.
Some people make the sky more beautiful to gaze upon. They
stay in our lives for awhile, leave footprints on our hearts,
and we are never ever the same.*

Flavia Weedn

ANTICIPATED LOSS IN DIVERSE PRACTICE SETTINGS

My professional colleagues in oncology nursing, social work, and medicine and I
have often talked about the clients we have worked with who have impacted us most,
professionally and personally. One example is the bone marrow transplant survivor
who contacted me via Facebook to tell me that now, 24 years after her transplant for
lymphoma, she is happily married and the proud mother of two college students. It
is a tremendous privilege to have this kind of joy shared with us. It is also a tremendous privilege to work with individuals and families who give us an opportunity to

listen and learn when treatments are not able to achieve remission or cure. Ruth Van Gerpen, a nursing colleague, talked with me about what it is like to witness family discussions related to anticipatory grief in her work as an oncology nurse. She shared the following example:

> Becki was diagnosed with colorectal cancer at the age of 39. Surgery, chemotherapy, and radiation were successful-no evidence of disease in her scans or her blood tests. However, at her 5-year-check, her tumor markers were elevated and a CT scan showed disease in her lungs. Her colorectal cancer was back. She resumed chemotherapy, but after six months of treatment, tests showed her cancer was not responding. A different chemotherapy regimen was started, but it caused significant side effects and she discovered her cancer had spread to her bones. At that point, she knew the cancer was not going away. She had lost both of her parents, just months apart, to cancer—so she knew what lie ahead. At the point, she decided she was going to die her way—with dignity.
>
> Along with her husband and two children—a daughter, 18 and a son, 15-she lived each day as if it could be her last. Her motto was "plan for the worst, hope for the best." She told people what they meant to her and said things that otherwise would have gone unsaid. They had a family portrait taken. They held Christmas in July with all their extended family. She took a special trip with her son to celebrate his junior year of high school—one year early. She bought a special gift for her daughter when she eventually gets married. She bought a special card for her husband's 50th birthday—in two years. She wrote letters to her children letting them know what they meant to her and to tell them all the things she hadn't taught them yet. And the family attended a grief program designed for children—she wanted to begin the process of helping her family prepare for when she would no longer be with them in person.
>
> Becki died four months after she decided to stop treatment for the cancer and instead focus on making the most of every moment. At the funeral, her husband commented that she lived her final months exactly as she wanted to. (Ruth Van Gerpen, 2011)

This example highlights end-of-life care, a context in which death is anticipated. The topic of grief in the context of anticipated loss has been added to the second edition of this text because so many readers of the previous edition expressed a need for knowledge and skill in this area. As discussed in the preface of this text, every one of us, no matter what our practice setting, will encounter people who are grieving. Similarly, it is highly likely that no matter what our professional role, in every practice setting we are also likely to encounter individuals with life-limiting illnesses or their caregivers who are anticipating death. We may find ourselves working with a child with cancer in a school, family members caring for a dying loved one in a mental health clinic, or a husband and wife with life-threatening pulmonary and heart conditions in a senior services center. In child and family protective services we might encounter any of these but also individuals and families anticipating a significant symbolic loss, such as the loss of permanent custody of one's children. And while we may not be the professionals directly responsible for helping patients and families with the emotional responses to these situations, understanding that grief is a part of anticipated loss enables us to better support these individuals and families.

"ANTICIPATORY GRIEF"

I first encountered "anticipatory grief" as a clinical social worker in a brand new bone marrow transplant unit of the Dana Farber Cancer Institute in Boston in 1978. On my first day, our charge nurse asked me to visit Ms. C., a 36-year-old woman who had advanced ovarian cancer who was crying in her room. After I introduced myself as a social worker and asked if there were any emotional or practical concerns I might help with, she looked up at me and asked, through her tears, "How do I tell my nine-year-old daughter her mommy is going to die?" Her grief was palpable and encompassed all of the reactions we associate with normal grief, including both deep sadness at the thought of not being able to see her daughter grow up and intense anger at the cancer that was taking her life.

One of the first comprehensive discussions of "anticipatory grief" I encountered was in Therese Rando's (1984) now seminal book *Grief, Dying and Death*. As I was seeking guidance about how to be supportive to the many individuals and families I was meeting, her description was most useful. She noted that a form of normal grief occurs in anticipation of a future loss, and called this *anticipatory grief*. She noted that anticipatory grief included many of the symptoms and processes of grief that follows a loss. Rando also noted that depending on the situation, anticipatory grief could be either helpful, enabling sharing of feelings that promote intimacy and connection, or unhelpful, particularly if it results in distancing between family members.

In the hundreds of families I have worked with since that first 36-year-old mother, much of the focus of support has been on helping individuals in the family to remain connected to each other in positive ways, even in the face of ultimate or permanent separation. At times this means helping an individual to identify feelings and find constructive ways to express them. After much discussion and rehearsal, Ms. C found a way to tell her daughter that although her doctors had tried everything they could, she was going to die someday, and that day could be soon. She was able to say how sad she was but how lucky she felt to have her as a daughter and how confident she was that her daughter would grow up to be a wonderful woman, always loved and cared for by her father and other family members. She also wrote letters for her daughter to open at key events in her life.

Some families may need more help or support in identifying and expressing the normal feelings that result from an anticipated loss. This is often the case in the face of life-limiting illness when death, like Mrs. C's, is anticipated but the timeline is uncertain and focus is centered on treating the illness or providing palliation for symptoms. In some families communication may be inhibited for a variety of reasons, including cultural norms that discourage direct expression of feelings among family members. For some families, family conferences or conversations with professional health or mental health providers help to foster communication. Individual members may also seek out or receive counseling or conversations with providers as they anticipate loss. They may benefit from the opportunity to express their feelings and concerns about adjustment even if not directly expressing them to significant others until death is pending or has taken place. This is particularly true when there have been long-standing conflicts in the relationship or when powerful negative feelings have created distance. Intervention when loss is anticipated can prevent problems from developing later (Rando, 1984). Since Kubler-Ross and Rando wrote their pioneering works, research has continued to investigate what is helpful and when, in terms of anticipated death, and a wealth of information has been created to assist both those who are directly anticipating loss and those of us who are assisting them.

END-OF-LIFE AND PALLIATIVE CARE

Competence in supporting individuals and families anticipating loss is not restricted to, or only important for, professionals directly providing physical or mental health services. An organization called the Supportive Care Coalition (SCC) has prepared a variety of tools to assess competence in end-of-life (EOL) care that include the emotional realm of care for both professionals and organizations. According to SCC, competence in the emotional aspects of care includes supporting patient and family expression of emotional needs, including listening actively, supporting as appropriate and referring to support groups, other patients, and families with similar conditions, and/or professionals with expertise in this area. Open-ended questions such as "How are you doing? How are things going in your life? What, if anything, are you feeling anxious about?" are examples of this competence that every helping professional should be able to demonstrate.

Several professional organizations have also begun to develop resources to enhance professionals' knowledge and skills in EOL care. The End of Life Physicians Education Resource Center (EPERC)'s http://www.eperc.mcw.edu/ is a very useful Web site for all professionals working with those who are anticipating death. Anyone can register for free to use the Web site and its Fast Fact sheets offer guidelines on a variety of topics that can assist professionals in providing effective care.

Another very useful tool available through the American Association of Family Physicians is a cultural competence self-assessment tool. Developed for physicians, it is also relevant for other professional caregivers. Cultural competence is relevant in addressing anticipatory loss, just as it is in addressing grief following loss, since views about sharing information and feelings in general, and EOL issues in specific, vary significantly. For example, in the family retreat program that I help to facilitate for families facing cancer, many Puerto Rican American mothers subscribe to cultural norms of not disclosing their diagnosis of cancer to their children. Establishing a relationship with them and their children has been possible only through respecting this belief. In this retreat, participation in a workshop for parents entitled "Helping Children Cope When a Parent Has Cancer" has afforded parents of both genders and diverse cultures an opportunity to hear how others handle communication with their children, spouses, and family members. In many instances, when fears and concerns about forcing a conversation or increasing family distress have been alleviated, parents make their own choice to communicate differently and seek support in doing so from their peers and the workshop facilitators.

Helping individuals

As discussed in Chapter 7, Elisabeth Kubler-Ross generated her stage model while working with individuals who were facing their own imminent deaths. While this sequential stage model has been challenged, the various reactions described by Kubler-Ross—denial, depression, anger—are commonly manifested in individuals who are facing death and other significant losses. Like the student in the first case example of this chapter, many professional helpers feel initial discomfort when approaching a client about an impending loss or death. We may feel relieved if persons with a life-limiting illness or injury do not directly bring up the topic of death during our contact with them. But more often than not, if we listen carefully, they do. In their text, *Final Gifts*, hospice nurses Maggie Callanan and Patricia Kelley (1997) share examples of the many ways that people communicate with family and caretakers when they are approaching death and the comfort that can come from this kind of communication—for both dying individuals and the person caring for them.

One of the most public examples of this is Randy Pausch (2008), a computer science professor at Carnegie Mellon University, who not only communicated what he needed to in his "Last Lecture" but also in the book of the same title. He opens the lecture, which can be viewed online, stating that his dad always taught him if there's an elephant in the room, introduce him, and then shows a slide showing the ten cancerous tumors in his liver, which his doctors have told him mean he has 3–6 months of good health left. In the book he recounts a session with the psychotherapist he and his wife saw during his life-limiting illness with pancreatic cancer and the conversation they had about his need to deliver his last lecture. He said that Dr. Reiss saw, in him, a man not yet ready to climb into his deathbed, and he told her he wanted to do the lecture because it was a chance to think about what really mattered to him, to influence how people would remember him and to achieve some "good" before his death. Later in the book he writes about the hurt he feels because his children will grow up without their father. This hurt is the grief reaction to anticipating loss. In addition to communicating what he needed to in the lecture and the book, he notes that the therapist had seen him and his wife many times holding each other in tears, a small but essential acknowledgment of the feelings that accompany the knowledge that death is approaching.

It is important to develop the capacity to sit with those tears and to listen to what needs to be expressed and/or what need not be expressed. We need not be a trained grief therapist to do this. However, therapists trained to provide the specialized counseling that may be needed when distress is intense are an important resource. There are relatively few documented studies or evidence-based models to guide us specifically in counseling those who are facing impending death and even fewer for those facing impending significant losses of other types.

In a review of treatment approaches, Crunkilton and Rubins (2009) identify three: a client-centered, supportive, emotionally expressive and strengths-based approach that includes life review and an exploration of the patient and family's fears and concerns, an 8-week experiential group therapy focused on sustaining a sense of meaning in terminally ill patients, and dignity therapy (Chochinov et al., 2005), which is a single-session approach, designed to enhance a sense of meaning and facilitate dignified closure. In dignity therapy, the practitioner transcribes the session and returns it to the patient, which provides a tangible record of what the client believes is most important and meaningful about his or her life, in much the same way that Randy Pauch's "The Last Lecture" did for him and his family.

"The Last Lecture" Web site and many other Web-based resources listed in the Internet Resources for this chapter provide additional guidance to both clients facing loss and professionals who wish to equip themselves to be more effective helpers in this arena.

Helping families

In some ways, every family member facing the death of, or permanent separation from, a loved one is at risk for emotional distress, due to the strong emotions and the changes in family structure and functioning that accompany anticipated or actual loss. Family members' responses to the life-limiting illness and death of a family member are influenced by a wide variety of variables including age, gender, cultural background, and relationship with the ill family member. The relationship of the individual to the person he or she is losing has a significant influence on how the individual is affected by impending loss. The more dependent the family member is, the more they will be affected by changes in roles and functioning that a life-limiting illness or the dissolution of a relationship imposes. An older adult spouse, for example, who has depended on the ill spouse to manage the household, may experience significant anxiety regarding his or her own well-being in the face of losing that partner. Similarly, a spouse caring for young children or teens, or child of a single parent may be overwhelmed by the prospect of the responsibility he or she will face after losing that partner or parent.

While many families cope effectively with the major life transitions that occur with the end of life, some do not. Some come to the end of life with histories of difficult family relationships and ongoing conflicts that may be exacerbated by the impending death (Coyle, Ingham, & Altilio, 1999). Family therapy may be needed to assist those families who are at greater risk. Those with preexisting difficulties such as substance abuse, domestic violence, and major mental disorders in members will often be involved with, or will need to be referred to, agencies where appropriate services can be provided.

Structural family therapy, developed by Salvador Minuchin, is particularly useful in single-parent families or in families in which children or teens may be carrying too many adult roles and responsibilities. Family therapists using structural techniques focus on strengthening family boundaries between the adult and child subsystems. Murray Bowen's model of systemic family therapy emphasizes the patterns that are passed from one generation to another that may need to be recognized and modified for the family to interact effectively with current problems. The Genogram, a family assessment tool, is commonly used in this second model and can help to identify previously unresolved losses that may be impacting current reactions to impending loss (Nichols, 2010).

There are many other models of family therapy, including postmodern models such as solution-focused and narrative therapy that offer different opportunities for families to resolve difficulties and establish healthier and more effective interactions. In one of the few studies of grief in caregivers prior to a loved one's death, Tomarken et al. (2008) used a caregiver version of the predeath inventory of complicated grief to identify caregivers at risk for complicated grief. Their results indicate that caregivers who think pessimistically and who are experiencing stressful life events beyond the loved one's illness are at most risk and can benefit from preventive intervention. If you are working with a family or family members who present these risk factors, and are well informed about the programs, resources, and professionals in your area that are available to help families, you will be better able to make successful referrals. This can be an extraordinary gift to families who are struggling, in addition to the support and care you provide.

ADVANCE DIRECTIVES

This chapter on grief in the context of anticipated loss has been added to the text, as noted, because students expressed a need. When I added EOL and palliative care to my grief and loss course, I asked students if they thought advance directives belonged in the course and received a resounding *yes* as an answer. Many students, in class discussions, mentioned the Terry Schiavo case—a case of a young woman in a coma that was widely publicized because of the family conflict that arose around decision-making and life support. Often, after our class discussions, students began to view advance directives as a means to prevent the conflict and distress that can result when an individual has not expressed his or her wishes in writing before becoming incapacitated. While many initially believe that advance directive discussions belong only in medical settings, students come to realize that they are important in a wide range of settings where illness, injury, or death can occur to our clients unexpectedly.

Professionals who work in correctional facilities, mental health, and substance dependence treatment programs as well as those who work with foster grandparents or seniors in senior services centers and nursing homes have recognized the need for providing clients with information about advance directives. Many, however, acknowledge that they have not completed their own advance directives and that they are uncomfortable bringing the subject up unless a client asks them. Some students acknowledge not knowing what advance directives are, exactly.

Advance directives are the legal mechanisms through which individuals can specify what kind of care they do and do not want, in the event that they become critically ill or injured and cannot make decisions themselves. Each state in the United States has its own laws regarding advance directives, so it is important to be aware of what they are in the state in which you practice. Since every one of us will die at some point, and some of us without warning, it is useful for every one of us to complete an advance directive. Many state laws require that a proxy, an agent or a designated legal representative be identified as part of the advance directive and recommend discussions be held between the proxy and the individual designating him or her in order to have clarity and agreement about preferences.

Caring Connections, a Web-based program of the National Hospice and Palliative Care Organization, provides a link through which the advance directives for every state can be downloaded; this site also acts as a vehicle for online storage of the completed forms. Durable power of attorney, designation of a health care proxy, and a living will are all examples of advance directives that may be identified in a particular state.

Because many deaths occur in institutions and because advances in technology have made medical care very complicated, patients and families with life-limiting injuries and illnesses face a multitude of decisions that can significantly influence not only the quality but also the quantity of life they will have. Offering information on decision-making and advance directives can be instructive and can also open the door to the kinds of discussions that both facilitate decision-making and underscore the important relationships in our lives.

In the "Planning Ahead" chapter of the *Handbook for Mortals*, Drs. Joanne Lynn and Joan Harrold recommend this kind of discussion long before decisions have to be made. They call it "what if" planning, which might be uncomfortable at first but can help individuals feel more in control. These authors suggest that it can also be a gift to family and loved ones, who can be spared the burden of making choices without knowing what is most important to the individual in the event that a decision must be made.

While it may take practice and rehearsal to feel comfortable discussing EOL concerns and the feelings related to anticipated loss, it can be a most rewarding experience to assist our clients with issues many others avoid. In my experience, there is often a sense of relief and gratitude that clients express following these conversations. Dr. Ruth Livingston, a psychotherapist, poignantly recounted her experience in this arena in a recent *New York Times* article. In it she described the courage her client displayed in facing and talking about her feelings related to her own death; she also wrote that she learned a great deal from her client about courage and honesty and depth and that their work together during the final days of her client's life had a profound impact on her own life. The title of the article identifies what many of us have come to appreciate about addressing EOL issues and working with clients who are dying: "In Talks With Dying Patient, Affirming Life."[1]

SUMMARY

Every one of us, as helping professionals, no matter what our practice setting, will encounter people who are grieving. Similarly it is highly likely that no matter what our professional role, in every practice setting we are also likely to encounter individuals with life-limiting illnesses or their caregivers who are anticipating death. Therese Rando was one of the first mental health practitioners to identify anticipatory grief in her seminal text *Grief, Dying and Death* (1984). *Anticipatory grief* is a controversial term and has been described by some as helpful, when it enables sharing of feelings that promote intimacy and connection in anticipation of a loss, and by others as unhelpful, particularly if it results in distancing between family members. The feelings of sadness and anger that are part of normal grief reactions following a loss are also what people often express when they are anticipating a loss.

---

[1]Retrieved from http://www.nytimes.com/2009/06/02/health/02case.html

Conversations with individuals and families who are anticipating loss can involve the expression of these feelings as well as foster meaning-making in the face of loss through life review. Identifying and assisting clients who are anticipating a loss and experiencing intense feelings of distress, particularly those who have problematic histories or stressors beyond the loss of a significant person, can help to prevent complicated mourning reactions after a death. Family conflict can occur in the absence of discussion about end of life decisions and treatment preferences. Providing information and opportunities for discussion of advance directives can help to prevent problems like those that arose in the Terry Schiavo case.

CHAPTER 10

What Can We Do to Help Individuals and Families?

CHAPTER OUTLINE

Do what you can, with what you have, where you are

Teddy Roosevelt

MISCONCEPTIONS ABOUT GRIEF

Depending on our own experiences with loss, the cultural norms we have grown up with, and factors such as our relationship with the person who is grieving, we, as professionals, may feel less or more comfortable acknowledging a loss and listening to others talk about their feelings. But because grief results from many different types of losses, not only from death, and because many different situations can remind people of their losses and trigger a grief reaction, we are highly likely to encounter people who are experiencing grief in our everyday work lives. Many of us wonder how best to be helpful and acknowledge loss and grief, especially when we are uncertain about the affected person's comfort level or potential reaction to our outreach.

One student expressed this in a journal for a class on grief and loss.

A situation which causes me discomfort, and that I need to work on, is feeling like I am prying when I try to encourage someone to talk to me about their feelings. I have such a strong sense of personal privacy and personal space that I naturally assume others have that sense and therefore I often feel that asking personal questions is intruding. I realize from reading about grief that often people will not talk about loss and death without encouragement from another person, and even are relieved when someone else brings it up. But it still feels like a risk to bring up difficult issues and encourage those who are grieving to explore their feelings. (Kaiser, 2002)

There are many common misconceptions about grief that can inhibit our reaching out to those who are grieving. Not knowing what to do or say, people often avoid acknowledging or talking about a loss to an affected individual or family. Unfortunately, this can lead to a grieving person feeling isolated and alone. The following list includes common misconceptions about grief and provides helpful ways to support yourself and others to make the transition from grief to healing.

- *Misconception # 1:* Time heals all wounds
     Time alone does not heal. It is what people do over time that matters. To facilitate healing, people need to be able to acknowledge their loss, express their feelings, and feel a sense of connection with others who care.
- *Misconception # 2:* People find it too painful to talk about their loss
     Many people coping with grief have expressed that even though it can be painful at times, they also find it comforting and healing to have opportunities to express and share their feelings in a safe and nurturing environment. This connection provides a source of comfort and strength, creating a foundation for healing to begin.
- *Misconception # 3:* Crying indicates that someone is not coping well
     We sometimes feel that tears or other expressions of feelings are signs of weakness or a reflection that we are not handling things well. However, these expressions are a normal and healthy response to loss. Friends and interested others can help by being supportive listeners and by encouraging survivors when they feel ready to share these heartfelt emotions.
- *Misconception # 4:* The grieving process should last about 1 year
     There is no designated timeline for how long the grieving process should last. There are no "shoulds" with grieving. It is important that people process and work through their grief in a way that feels comfortable to them.
- *Misconception # 5:* Quickly putting grieving behind speeds the process of healing for every grieving individual
     Each individual grieves in his or her own unique way. For some, blocking out or repressing feelings can actually serve as a barrier to healing and for others dwelling in grief, even in the first few months, may not help either. We can help by supporting grieving individuals and families through actively listening to their thoughts and feelings and supporting both their need to experience the pain of loss and restorative activities and experiences.

It may be helpful to know that the literature on grief includes many more reports of people feeling upset that their loss was not acknowledged by others than reports about their losses being too frequently acknowledged. (An exception is very public or high-profile losses, such as those related to 9/11. In very public losses, individuals and families may feel there is more acknowledgment, often through media, than they can respond to. This kind of public reaction will be discussed in Chapter 11.)

When a loss is not acknowledged and support is not offered, however, survivors may experience "disenfranchised grief," a cause of complicated grieving that was discussed in Chapter 7. It is even often important to acknowledge an impending loss, as discussed in Chapter 9, since individuals or families affected by a life-limiting illness may be experiencing "anticipatory" grief and will benefit from support.

A caseworker for children and adolescents in foster care writes,

> A huge part of the treatment with children in foster care setting is helping them to process their feelings around being separated from their loved ones and supporting them around these feelings. In many ways it's like grief work around loss through death. Many of the emotions expressed by children in out of home placements are anger, frustration, sadness, anxiety, confusion, disbelief, mistrust . . . all of the same emotions that a child would express if they were experiencing bereavement. Rando (1984) points out that it is important to provide children with constructive ways to address their grief. Doing this will also facilitate a working relationship with these children. Validation is a big part of the work that I do. I try my best to identify their feelings and validate them whenever possible. It is also important in this type of work that all providers are on the same page. The therapist, the psychiatrist, the outreach mentor, the school staff, the after-school program, the foster family, the birth family, and the case worker all need to communicate regularly and share information. Whenever there is a dilemma involving the client in any facet of his/her treatment, it is vital for all providers to be aware. Intervention and structure needs to remain consistent for trust and a healthy working relationship with the child. (Hildreth, 2002)

EMPATHIC COMMUNICATION

Most experts in both the fields of therapeutic communication and grief encourage the use of basic empathic communication skills in acknowledging a distressing situation and providing support. These skills are important in all helping situations but are especially important to practice in the context of grief, when discomfort in one or both parties may impede the connection.

Rando (1984) describes therapeutic communication in the context of loss as communication that expresses respect, maintains realistic hope, and offers appropriate reassurance and support through statements of comprehension and empathy. Empathy involves our trying to put ourselves in the other person's shoes and responding in the way that helps *him* or *her* to feel comfortable, *not* necessarily with what makes *us* feel comfortable.

Key skills of empathic communication include active listening and communication facilitation.

Active listening involves attending behavior that indicates we are listening, including:

- Appropriate eye contact;
- Attentive body language such as slightly leaning forward;
- Verbal following (nodding and verbal statements such as "I see" indicate that you are following what the person is saying and interested in hearing it)

Communication facilitation includes:

- Reflection of feeling ("It sounds like you're feeling really sad")
- Paraphrasing (summarizing or repeating in shortened form what was said)
- Use of minimal encouragers ("Can you tell me a little more?")
- Use of open-ended questions ("How are these first few weeks going?")
- Therapeutic silence (allowing silence and space in the conversation for thoughts or feelings to emerge)

The art of reflecting involves restating your understanding of the emotional content of what the person you are listening to is saying, not just his or her words. In general, in communicating with someone who has experienced a loss, it is helpful to *avoid* the following:

- Saying "I know how you feel" or "I understand"
- Talking about your own losses (me-too-ism)
- Parroting (repeating the speaker's exact words). Try, instead, to respond to the actual content expressed
- Thinking about or planning your own responses instead of listening to what is being said
- Giving unsolicited advice
- Breaking silences too quickly or filling in before the speaker has finished speaking
- Expressing judgments about what the speaker is saying, like commenting that he or she is wise
- Using clichés
- Challenging the other person's perception of the situation or feelings

CASE EXAMPLE: A SPECIAL EDUCATION STUDENT

An intuitive special education teacher recently recounted her experience with a child that illustrates the importance of empathic communication. She teaches in a resource room in a large urban magnet school serving grades 1–4. She had been hearing from the second-grade teacher about an eight-year-old who was exhibiting defiant behavior in the classroom and who had been involved in several altercations with other children in the class. While he had been a student in the school since kindergarten and had performed well academically in the past, he had recently been placed in foster care due to his mother's inability to care for him. Her health was rapidly failing due to AIDS and while two younger siblings were placed together in a preadoptive home, he was placed in temporary foster care. One day, not long after hearing about this child's classroom behavior, the special education teacher saw him sitting angrily in the principal's office where he had been sent for disciplinary action.

Since the principal was not available, the teacher offered to allow him to wait in her resource room during her lunch break. A simple inquiry, "It sounds like you've been having some pretty rough times" unleashed a rush of emotions—anger and tears all mixed together. He was angry about being taken from his mother's home and the separation from his siblings and even more furious about moving to a different house each night. Simply reflecting his feelings, "that sounds like it's really hard" lead to an outpouring of grief. With hot tears he reported that he could take care of his mother and his little sisters and he was really worried that his mom could die because he knew she was really sick. Due to the unavailability of a longer-term foster home, he was being housed each night in a different emergency foster home, each with its own rules, demands, and stresses.

As was discussed earlier, complicated grief can result when loss is not acknowledged and the individual experiencing the loss does not have an opportunity to grieve. It is likely that the empathic listening that this attuned teacher displayed was a key intervention that allowed this overwhelmed little boy to express his acute feelings of grief. The next step would be to alert the school adjustment counselor as well as the protective worker to the intense grief needs he was expressing. This could lead to any number of therapeutic interventions, including individual counseling or play therapy, participation in a peer-support group, and the opportunity to participate in art or journaling activities to allow him to express his feelings.

INTERVENTIONS FOR NORMAL AND COMPLICATED GRIEF

Grieving individuals

A variety of programs, interventions, and resources to address the distinctive needs of grieving individuals have been developed over the past three decades. Most of these are designed to assist those who are grieving a death, and there is still much to be learned about interventions that are most effective for those grieving symbolic losses. Many bereaved people adjust to the loss of a loved one with the support of their natural helping networks and complete the tasks of grieving without specific grief intervention (Konigsberg, 2011).

> Grief interventions that have been developed can be viewed as addressing needs along a continuum, from normal bereavement to complicated bereavement. It is important, when considering interventions to assist the bereaved, to match the level and type of service to need. This ensures that those whose bereavement is more complicated receive the care that will best address their needs. (Walsh-Burke, 2000)

The continuum of bereavement interventions includes:

- Preventive interventions (anticipatory grieving, support)
- Monitoring, with social support
- Bereavement support groups (including online and telephone groups)
- Bereavement counseling
- Grief therapy (individual, couple, family)

Preventive interventions

Anticipatory grief, and support to those anticipating a loss, was discussed in Chapter 9. Many individuals and families, however, do not receive professional support in advance of a loss, particularly if the loss was unanticipated (as in a suicide, a sudden death, or sudden dissolution/termination of a relationship). However, when a loss occurs, either unanticipated or anticipated, educational interventions can help to normalize the grief experience and social support can help reduce the isolation or loneliness that grieving individuals often report is challenging after a loss. Bibliotherapy, or therapeutic reading, can be most useful to grieving individuals and families. Many of my clients have asked for Web resources or reading materials that offer guidance in specific types of loss situations both for themselves and for their family members or friends. Appendix A includes an annotated list of Web sites that have been recommended for each chapter. Links to these can also be found in MySocialWorkLab for Advancing Core Competencies under Resources in the "Grief and Loss" section. Appendix C is an annotated bibliography of books that are listed for each specific age group, very young children, school-aged children, teens, and adults. These along with some of the resources already discussed for different age groups, including the PBS series for children, *Talk, Listen, Connect* and fact sheets about grief included in Appendixes D and E of this text, can be useful to provide to clients in your practice.

Monitoring, with social support

In some hospitals and most hospices, routine telephone contacts with surviving family are made within a specified time period. Hospice bereavement protocols call for these contacts every 3 months for a year following a death. These contacts are usually welcomed by the bereaved. The contacts provide social support from someone who understands the grieving process and provides the opportunity to monitor whether "bereavement is proceeding normally or if complications have arisen" (Blum, 1993). Engagement of the bereaved family member in further counseling or a referral for grief therapy can then be provided if needed.

BEREAVEMENT COUNSELING

Bereavement counseling is provided to assist a mourner in completing the tasks of grieving. This kind of help can be provided by a variety of trained counselors, including peer counselors, pastoral care counselors, psychologists, and social workers. While most people are able to complete the tasks of grieving without bereavement counseling, at times the nature of the loss or the social situation of the affected individual can make adjustment difficult. Bereavement counseling often consists of

- Encouraging the bereaved to tell his or her story and share memories
- Acknowledging and giving permission to express feelings
- Identifying strategies to cope with the effects of grief, such as relaxation training
- Helping the bereaved person to plan for his or her life without the deceased

The bereavement counselor can help the survivor in a variety of ways. Telling the story can help the survivor come to grips with the loss, since sharing the details can make the loss experience more "real." The counselor's support during the telling of the story and the expression of feelings can help to reinforce the mourner's coping efforts through identification of previously effective strategies and teaching of new strategies. In the counseling, the survivor is also helped to identify and express feelings such as anger and helplessness that are more difficult for many people to express. Many survivors also express feelings of guilt and the counselor can help with reality testing when the survivor may have difficulty seeing the situation rationally. Sadness and anxiety are other feelings needing expression.

Perhaps the best endorsement for the healing power of expressing emotions related to grief comes from Morrie Schwartz, the retired Brandeis University professor, immortalized in Mitch Albom's best selling book, *Tuesdays With Morrie* (1997). In his narratives to Mitch, Morrie discourages holding back on emotions, noting that if you don't allow yourself to go through them, you may remain afraid of them. He encourages throwing yourself into the emotions and says that by allowing yourself to dive all the way into them, you experience them fully and completely. Through knowing what pain is, knowing what love is, knowing what grief is, according to Morrie, you can allow yourself finally to detach from them (Albom, 1997).

Some techniques used by bereavement counselors, in addition to verbal counseling, include writing letters of farewell. This can be especially helpful when the grieving individual did not have an opportunity to say goodbye in person. Poetry and journal writing are useful techniques, along with drawing, role-playing, and relaxation training. Pennebaker, Zech, and Rime (2001) cite a number of studies that support the effectiveness of writing about emotional upheavals in improving physical and psychological health. The research identifies those who are not able to naturally talk to others about their emotional experiences as those most likely to benefit from this intervention. Expressive therapy and play therapy techniques can be especially effective for children and adolescents or individuals who have less verbal facility. An example of a child's letter to her deceased cousin is included in Appendix E.

In addition to providing support and utilizing these techniques for facilitating completion of the tasks of grieving, the bereavement counselor can help to interpret the experiences of the bereaved person, provide reassurance about the "normalcy" of the grief process, and assess the coping and adjustment of the bereaved. If the grieving person is unable to cope effectively with the support of counseling or manifests complicated grief, the bereavement counselor may make a referral for grief therapy.

It is important to note that the same kind of supportive counseling that can be helpful to bereaved individuals can also be helpful to children, adolescents, and adults who are grieving symbolic losses such as divorce and foster care placement. While individuals grieving a death may have sufficient support through natural helping networks and not need any type of counseling, those grieving symbolic losses may experience less support for their grieving from their natural social networks and benefit even more from the counseling process.

GRIEF THERAPY

Complicated grief may require grief therapy, which is more intensive than bereavement counseling. While bereavement counseling is sometimes provided by peers and mental health professionals who encounter the bereaved in community service settings, grief therapy is generally provided by specialized mental health practitioners who have expertise in therapy models that address trauma and complicated grief. Many grief therapists use psychodynamic therapy models to help clients gain insight into the source of their distress regarding attachment and loss. Interpersonal therapy and Bowenian therapy are also models used in helping individuals and families deal with complicated bereavement, which often involves unresolved past losses and intense feelings of depression, guilt, and melancholy. More and more researchers are investigating the effectiveness of various models of grief therapy, recognizing that these may be more effective than previous psychotherapy models that include, but are not designed specifically for, targeting complicated grief. It is encouraging that more research is being conducted in this important arena of care, although students of evidence-based practice know that it often takes many years to determine the effectiveness of a particular model or intervention; there is much still to learn.

One example of evidence-based intervention is described in an article in the *Journal of the American Medical Association (JAMA)*. Shear et al (2005) developed an intervention to treat bereaved individuals who met the criteria for complicated grief, a diagnosis under consideration for inclusion in the *DSM V* for grief that is beyond normal bereavement. This 16-session intervention utilizes interpersonal therapy and is based on treatment for posttraumatic stress disorder that includes reliving the moment of the death, saying goodbye to the deceased, and using in vivo exposure to situations the bereaved person had been avoiding since the death (such as the cemetery). Many other studies are currently underway and this research should yield more models to inform practitioners and those who wish to refer clients for treatment of complicated grief.

Noting the family's primary role in caring for the terminally ill, Kissane et al. (1998, 2006) have developed and tested a model of family grief therapy for complicated grief. At-risk families who have experienced a death are identified through screening and offered a focused, time-limited intervention that runs for six to eight sessions (1.5 hours each), which span about 6 months. The goals are to increase cohesion, conflict resolution, and expression of thoughts and feelings. According to the authors, this therapy progresses through five phases: (a) assessment, (b) identification of relevant issues emerging from the initial phase of grief, (c) focused treatment, (d) consolidation of coping skills, and (e) ending. Most of the therapists are social workers who are carefully trained in the model. The results of a randomized clinical trial of this model indicate that family-focused grief therapy may aid in preventing pathological grief. The benefit is greatest for families with intermediate family functioning and "sullen" families. The authors suggest that care is needed to avoid increasing conflict in hostile families while providing bereavement intervention.

Neimeyer and Currier (2009), after an extensive review of evidence-based interventions, identified common components of effective grief therapy that include re-telling of the grief narrative with help provided to the client in taking perspective that is healing, guided encounters with the deceased such as through letter writing, and promoting "restoration-oriented" coping and development of new goals. They conclude that while much has been learned about the value of addressing traumatic imagery related to loss, fostering hope, and addressing practical readjustments in grief therapy, much is still to be learned about how to make it most effective.

Most helping professionals will primarily provide support to grieving individuals and will refer those clients who are coping with complicated or traumatic grief to specialists for grief therapy. It is therefore very useful to know the difference between supportive counseling and grief therapy and to know which practitioners in your community provide these services so that explanations can be given to clients about the different treatment or support options and effective referrals can be made when needed.

COLLABORATING WITH OTHER HELPING PROFESSIONALS

Teamwork

The value of teamwork is emphasized in most professional training programs today, and is especially important in complex situations such as those involving grief. In most settings including schools, medical, correctional settings, and child and family service agencies, members of an interdisciplinary team are responsible for helping to carry out educational or therapeutic goals. Whether formally "teaming" to construct an individualized educational plan (IEP) in a school setting, or informally consulting with other members of the team in a rehabilitation setting, team members are usually responsible for certain core functions related to goal attainment. These include:

- Completing a thorough assessment
- Contributing to the development of a comprehensive educational/treatment plan
- Participating as a member of the interdisciplinary team
- Implementing the components of the educational/treatment plan
- Evaluating progress
- Advocating

Each member of the interdisciplinary team has expertise that he or she brings to the assessment and planning process and each can play an important role in assisting with grief-related issues. Teachers often identify grief issues when they are reflected in their students' written assignments as well as behavior. The physician, physician's assistant, and nurse practitioner often identify unresolved or masked grief that may be expressed by a patient through somatic complaints or requests for "sleeping" or other medications. When a chaplain is a member of the team, he or she can carry out a spiritual assessment and treatment plan. The rehabilitation specialists on the team, including occupational and physical therapists and speech-language pathologists, carry out essential roles in helping to assess functional capacities and can make a significant contribution in referring those whose complicated grief reactions may be, whose complicated grief reactions may be exaggerated or chronic.

Functions of team members

Social workers, psychologists, and educational counselors are generally responsible for assessing psychosocial and emotional needs and recommending or carrying out treatment plans to address these, including supportive counseling to aid in adjustment to loss. An understanding of the risk factors and interventions associated with complicated and unresolved grief is a key contribution of these disciplines to the team. Another area of expertise that these team members contribute to the team is an understanding of *compassion fatigue* or *secondary trauma*. These terms describe the reactions that professional caregivers sometimes experience in the process of helping others with grief, loss, and trauma. Compassion fatigue may occur when a professional helper's own emotional resources become depleted. This can happen when we don't have an opportunity to process our own grief or when our exposure to grief and loss is prolonged. *Secondary trauma* refers to the trauma that professional caregivers can experience through listening to the details of trauma that others have experienced.

The same strategies that are useful in helping family members to cope with loss are also useful in helping professionals to cope effectively with the losses they experience in work. These strategies include expressing their feelings to others who can listen empathically and provide support. This sometimes takes place in team "debriefing" sessions, in individual supervision or consultation, or through staff support programs. Other strategies include routinely using stress management techniques and making sure there is a balance in our lives through exercising and taking vacation or respite when we are feeling fatigued or distressed.

Interdisciplinary team collaboration benefits everyone because members of each discipline contribute their specialized expertise to the treatment or education plan and team members can support each other as they work their way through losses. While some team members provide more direct counseling than others, each of us must also be prepared to understand and respond effectively to the various types of distress expressed by those to whom we provide service as well as those with whom we work. This is particularly true in situations involving grief when clients or students have a stronger relationship with a particular professional to whom they might feel more comfortable disclosing their feelings of sadness, anxiety, or anger as well as those situations in which feelings are being expressed indirectly. In other cases, a person who is grieving a loss may be receiving services for another identified problem but disclose his or her feelings related to the loss to the professional who is working with him or her most closely. Using basic empathic communication skills, each of us can listen supportively and help problem-solve when emotional distress is evident. We can also make significant contributions to individuals and families through providing support ourselves and making appropriate referrals when expertise is needed that is beyond our professional scope of practice. Margaret Drench provides many examples of this kind of effort by team members in her online continuing education course on loss, grief, and adjustment offered by the American Physical Therapy Association. In discussing situations such as a woman evidencing grief while participating in rehabilitation following a spinal cord injury and another woman whose movement is impaired due to Parkinson's Disease, she notes that while counseling is beyond the boundaries of a physical therapist's practice, physical therapists need to display a caring demeanor, use listening skills, and acknowledge the concerns, beliefs, and fears of patients. Pragmatic suggestions can also be offered that focus on outcomes of physical independence and self-esteem. This might diminish a patient's sense of isolation and help him or her adjust to losses (Drench, 2010).

The role of professional organizations

Like the American Physical Therapy Association, professional organizations in every discipline have developed information to help other professionals and the public to understand their areas of expertise. These organizations also provide resources and guidance to their members about specific areas of practice, such as EOL care or crisis intervention. The National Association of Social Workers, for example, has outlined the roles and functions of social workers in different arenas of practice and articulates the values of the profession in its Code of Ethics (www.naswdc.org). NASW has also recently developed Standards of Practice for social workers in End-of-Life EOL care. The American Academy of Physician's Assistants (AAPA) has published policy papers on various aspects of the physician's assistant role that include information on communicating around EOL issues. In addition, AAPA has developed clinical practice guidelines promoting the team approach because it enhances communication, efficiency, and patient care (AAPA, 2004). Other professional organizations include the American Occupational Therapy Association and the National Education Association (NEA), which is a professional organization for teachers. NEA offers several very useful resources for educators on its Web site including a crisis tool that is designed to assist teachers, administrators, and school personnel. The tool provides an overview of children's concepts of death as well as strategies for schools following a death.

The Web sites of these and other professional organizations offer a variety of publications and resources that can aid you, and the families you serve, in understanding and accessing the services these disciplines provide. An example is an article in *Society for Human Resource Management* entitled "Helping Employees Cope With Grief" (Tyler, 2003), published on the SHRM Web site. This article not only provides guidance for the human resource professional but also links to other organizations and Web articles on the topic of grief and loss.

SUMMARY

Many misconceptions about grief have contributed to confusion about how helping professionals can best assist those who have experienced a loss. The statement that "time heals all wounds" is not globally applicable, since many factors influence the grief process including the kind and quality of social support received during or following a loss. Professional helpers in every discipline can utilize empathic communication when working with individuals and families who following both an immediate loss and those that have occurred in the past. Empathic communication involves a set of skills including active listening and reflecting. Not every individual or family who has experienced loss will require specialized bereavement or grief intervention. Bereavement counseling can be beneficial for individuals who lack significant social support that is often provided through natural helping networks such as spiritual communities. Individual grief therapy has been found to be effective primarily for those with complicated or unresolved grief. A new model of family grief therapy has also been found to benefit specific families such as those with intermediate levels of family functioning. Grief specialists can often be found through hospices, community grief programs, or mental health agencies. Collaboration among interdisciplinary colleagues and community organizations is an important component of effectively supporting grieving individuals and families. Professional organizations are a source of valuable resources for their members and the public related to grief and grief education.

Helping Groups and Organizations

> *As the sun illuminates the moon and stars so let us*
> *illuminate each other.*
>
> Master Lui

GROUP MODELS

With increasing recognition of the impact of loss on individuals, more service organizations, schools, and health care providers have established programs to support grieving clients. In addition, many communities now house organizations that exist exclusively to provide grief-related services. Some of these offer resources and information nationally and internationally via Web sites as well as through grief camps, workshops, and retreats that are extended to clients well beyond their own communities.

There are three common group models through which grieving individuals are served.

- Support groups
- Psychoeducational groups
- Therapy groups

Groups are not for everyone, but they can serve an important function of helping to lessen the sense of isolation that individuals often experience after a loss. Groups can be tailored to focus on the needs of members who share a common experience and address specific types of losses such as parent, child, or partner death; divorce; unemployment; or adoption. Some groups are founded and facilitated by peers who have been through the experience, and others are professionally facilitated. Group services can be offered in person, by telephone and online and thus have the added utility of serving groups of individuals, like those living in rural areas, who might not otherwise have access to peers or professional counselors. Groups can be particularly effective with adolescents, for whom interaction with peers is very appealing (Corr, 2004).

When designing a group or referring clients to a group, it is important to be clear about the purpose and structure of the group.

A psycho-educational group is a group whose primary purpose is to provide education to group members. It is distinguished from a support or therapy group by its purpose and method. While a supportive environment is helpful in facilitating learning, the main purpose of a psycho-educational group is to provide education, not emotional support. This differs from a support group. It is very important to be clear with group participants about the purpose of your group. Misunderstanding may create disappointment or frustration. Most psycho-educational groups have a set number of sessions, a pre-determined time frame, and a clear agenda for each session, with topics to be covered. (Walsh & Marcusen, 2010)

This description of a psychoeducational group is from the facilitator's manual for the Cancer Survival Toolbox, a self-advocacy training program for people affected by cancer. There are many manuals and models available for facilitating groups, which is another advantage to them. A manualized group usually includes agendas, discussion topics, activities, and evaluation materials that have already been created; therefore, it may be more efficient to implement than creating one's own group. If you choose to implement a manualized group, it is also likely that you will be able to gather evaluation data about its usefulness with your client population, since it is possible to gather evidence from multiple groups and evaluate a program's efficacy with manualization and replication. A typical grief or bereavement group meets for eight sessions and might include the following topics:

- Introductions and confidentiality contract
- Normal grief reactions
- Sharing members' personal stories
- Tasks and phases of grief
- Coping with anxiety and depression
- Making meaning from loss
- Integrating loss and moving forward
- Identifying strengths and saying goodbye

These topics are applicable to grief resulting from death as well as to grief resulting from symbolic loss.

Children's groups

One of the greatest changes in the past 30 years of my own practice in the arena of illness and grief is the vast increase in research and programming related to children's bereavement. In the late 1970s it was rare to find a book for children on the topic of death, and even rarer to find a bereavement group for children. With the advent of hospice programs and a greater awareness of children's bereavement needs, a wide array of group services and programs are available today: some hospital or hospice based, some community based, and some Internet based. Many programs have incorporated children's bereavement or family bereavement groups. Often, these include the same topics and sequencing as adult groups, but with adaptations to suit children's development. For children's groups, activities are often included for each topic.

For example, in the introductory session of a children's group, participants can draw pictures of their families before and after the loss experience. For the session on normal grief reactions, children can complete a worksheet of a blank human face in which they can draw facial expressions to depict their feelings about the loss experience, or use a feelings chart to identify the variety of feelings that are experienced after a loss. They can bring in photographs or create scrapbooks to share along with their personal stories and can create a memory box when discussing integrating loss and moving forward. A variety of topics and activities for children's bereavement groups are included in Haasl and Marnocha's (2000) support group Leader Manual. Activities for teen groups, including writing a letter to the deceased, can be found in Wolfert's (2000) *Healing Your Grieving Heart for Teens* and Perschy's (1997) *Helping Teens Work Through Grief.*

IDENTIFYING AND DEVELOPING ORGANIZATIONAL RESOURCES

If you are reading this text, you may be a mental health professional or activities therapist who can assess the needs of the clients you serve and create bereavement programs and services to meet these needs. One of the first needs on the list may be to provide in-service education for staff in your agency or practice setting regarding grieving clients. When staff are attuned to actual and symbolic loss and the grief reactions accompanying them, they can become important sources of support and referral. If the focus of your work is not to directly address grief-related needs, you will want to identify who in your organization is able to do this. Schools, hospitals, and social service organizations all employ social workers, psychologists, or other counselors who may have expertise in grief counseling and who can be called upon for leadership and guidance when needed. Businesses often have Employee Assistance Programs (EAPs) that provide consultation to employees on a variety of issues, including grief. Referring clients to these resources, when needed, can be a key intervention.

As a supplement to direct intervention or referral, organizations can provide a valuable service to clients and staff alike through the provision of written or Internet-based information about loss and grief. Hospitals, social service agencies, and human resource offices may house a resource room where books, pamphlets, fact sheets, and computer access with a list of credible Web sites can be made available to those impacted by loss. Staff meetings, particularly following a death or loss within the agency, can also provide opportunities for sharing information and support.

If you or your agency does not offer groups or other direct services to grieving clients, familiarizing yourself with the practitioners and organizations that do offer these is important. Most hospices provide bereavement support groups to their own clients and members of the community at large. National organizations such as Compassionate Friends (for parents who have lost a child) offer specialized groups to community members experiencing specific types of losses. In some communities, bereavement organizations such as The Garden (http://hrymca.org/pages_general/thegarden.php) and camps such as Camp Sunshine (http://www.campsunshine.org/) offer groups and programs for children, adolescents, and parents. These specialized programs can be an exceptional source of direct service for grieving individuals in your organization, and they can provide expert consultation to supplement your organization's resources, if needed.

Some grief-related organizations and even individual practitioners now offer online consultation or support to individuals and groups who have experienced loss. Caution must be exercised in referring to any provider, particularly those with whom the only connection is through an Internet search. Grieving individuals may be very vulnerable. Evidence of professional training and appropriate licensure of staff should be listed in the credentials of reputable providers and organizations. Generally this training requires a master's degree, PhD, MD, or certificate from an accredited organization. Peer support can be invaluable but some evidence of professional consultation or supervision is generally a requirement for organizations that wish to protect as well as support clients in need. A list of links to organizations that have been carefully reviewed are included in the Internet Resources for this chapter.

Within every organization, events will inevitably occur that will impact all or many members of the organization. We and our coworkers will encounter situations in which we will need to join together to support one another, and those we serve, in coping with loss. You have most likely heard about, or even participated in, such efforts already in your career. You may, in the future, find yourself taking a leadership role in helping your organization provide guidance and support to others. The situations discussed in the introduction to this book are examples.

The first example was of a faculty member in a college who died just before the close of the school year. The department head called together administrators from each area, along with a grief consultant, to create and implement a plan. In a larger organization such as a private corporation or public service agency, there are usually internal resources that can be utilized for this kind of consultation and planning. Counseling staff, school guidance professionals, and employee assistance personnel often have expertise in grief. In an academic setting, the college chaplain is usually a source of support and guidance. There may be faculty in college and university departments who have expertise they can share, and students and staff who have experience in this area or who are motivated can help to gather information and resources.

ESTABLISHING A BEREAVEMENT PROTOCOL: INTERDISCIPLINARY AND INTERORGANIZATIONAL COLLABORATION

Identifying potential members of a grief response team is the first step that an organization can take to prepare to address anticipated or unanticipated grief effectively. Usually all that is needed to put this kind of team together is one individual with initiative who takes responsibility for contacting administrative personnel from the relevant departments or employee groups and someone with expertise on grief responses, either within the organization or in the surrounding community.

An initial organizing meeting can bring interested response team members together. Next, a protocol, or a series of steps, is established that can be implemented any time a death or major loss occurs. Establishing the protocol involves identifying who will carry out the steps (e.g., who will contact members of the response team after a death has occurred), how the steps will be carried out, and when they will be carried out. The protocol can be written and published within the employee handbook or other organizationwide communications and discussed during employee orientation.

These are steps that organizations can take to help those affected following a loss:

1. Notifying members of the response team so that the protocol can be initiated
2. Communicating the news to all the members of the organization who might be impacted by the death

This is often done through electronic bulletin boards, written letters distributed in mail boxes, and personalized phone calls (especially to those who may have a close connection). A sensitively worded statement can be made such as "It is with deep sadness that we inform you of the death of one of our community members . . . ." This serves to inform people of the death and can also be a vehicle for disseminating information about funeral or memorial services. It may be important to provide the contact number for the counseling service, chaplain, or a crisis service in this message for those who may need to talk with someone personally. Additional actions include:

1. *Providing guidance to key personnel.*   These personnel include department heads, or in a school setting, teachers, who should receive guidance in about how to communicate and offer support to staff or students in their areas who may have reactions.
2. *Identifying concrete ways for people to express their caring and concern.*   In many organizational and academic settings, students and staff have spontaneously created memorials by placing flowers, pictures, poems, and notes of remembrance in a foyer or outside an office. These notes often describe memorable moments in the classroom or office or significant interactions with the person who has died. These recollections might then be collected and recorded in the time leading up to a memorial service where the life and contributions of the faculty member, student, or staff member are honored.
3. *Acknowledging the loss.*   Whether it's in meetings or classes, publishing an article in the school or organization's newsletter, including content on grief and loss in classroom instruction or in-service education programs, and providing

small group sessions for anyone wishing to talk about the loss are all possible strategies that may be considered important life lessons. A similar protocol might be used following tragedies that affect whole communities, like those that occurred on 9/11.

In the second example in the introduction to this text, a counselor in an alternative high school died after being stabbed in a classroom in front of his students. Students from our social work program who were interning at the school took a leadership role in creating a giant mural dedicated to this man and posting it along a central corridor of the school. The mural was quickly filled with hundreds of messages from students and staff. Some chose to write memories, some wrote words of encouragement to his family and others suffering from his loss. The interns and other counselors were positioned close by and were available to provide support and crisis intervention to those who needed it throughout the week and months following the tragedy. School administrators and counseling staff communicated with teachers, students, and their families and made arrangements with the school bus transport company so that every student and staff member who wished to could attend the memorial service. Classroom discussions and assignments also provided students with opportunities to express their thoughts and feelings and to memorialize this important person in their lives.

In a local elementary school, a memorial tree was painted on mural paper and affixed to the wall outside the school office for a month after the death of a beloved school secretary. Students, staff, and parents were invited to write their thoughts on sticky notes and post the notes on the tree, which was later given to her family. Teachers offered students time to write poems or draw pictures of the staff member or anyone else who had died that they wanted to remember, and the school social workers and guidance counselors visited classrooms to acknowledge the loss. Those who expressed distress or appeared to need help coping with the loss were offered small group or individual opportunities to talk.

Another example was provided by a local high school in the community where I reside. An automobile accident took the life of a teenager in the junior class late in the afternoon just 2 days before the senior class graduation. The school administration responded immediately by communicating with one another, the family, and key members of the school community who knew the student. By the time school opened the following morning, they had implemented a plan. A memorial display was created in the entrance foyer and school personnel greeted all students entering the building with the news and an invitation to view and contribute to the memorial display. They also announced that a memorial service would be held in the school that evening and students interested in participating were encouraged to speak with their guidance counselor. Counseling staff were available throughout the day and evening to provide support to students, and many teachers provided students with opportunities to talk about their reactions during classes.

School and community groups in which the student had participated were actively engaged in planning the memorial service and a program was quickly put together that included readings and presentations by members of each of these groups, including a performing arts group and the school's chorus. Songs, prayers, and remembrances were created and shared by many different members of the school community. All of these activities served to bring together the members of the school and community to support one another. The service also provided a tribute that the student's parents could share in and remember. The timing of this memorial was important as it allowed the loss of his life to be acknowledged and honored before the school community proceeded with graduation. More information on memorial rituals and services is included in Chapter 12.

Each of these is an example of how a small group of committed professionals in a school or organization, with the right support and resources, can take a leadership role in organizing and carrying out an appropriate ritual of remembrance. Each example is also illustrative of how teamwork can work very effectively, even if the members of the team do not have grief expertise. What is most often required is a pooling of resources and areas of strength and a commitment to helping each other in the face of tragedy. One organization that has developed model resources in this arena is the National Center for School Crisis and Bereavement (NCSCB [www.NCSCB. org]) There are excellent resources, including downloadable fact sheets about grief and templates for developing a bereavement protocol, available through this Web link and a variety of credible Internet sites that are provided on the MySocialWorkLab Web site under grief resources.

SUMMARY

Support, psychoeducational and therapy groups are three common group models through which grieving individuals are served. Groups can serve the important function of helping to lessen the sense of isolation that individuals often experience after a loss. They can be tailored to meet the specific needs of members and are especially appealing to teens. There are many manualized models available for bereavement groups and these can be adapted to address symbolic losses such as divorce or foster care placement. Activities can be incorporated for children's groups that utilize expressive therapy techniques. Whether or not the provision of treatment groups or other direct services to grieving individuals is the focus of your agency's work, staff education regarding grief and loss can help to attune staff to the needs of grieving clients. Mental health providers within an agency can take a leadership role in assessing needs and developing resources within an organization to address these. Referrals can be made to carefully screened community and Web-based resources if needed. Every agency can benefit from a bereavement protocol, which identifies personnel and procedures for notification and addressing grief-related needs following a significant loss within an agency. Guidelines for developing a bereavement protocol are included in the exercise for this chapter.

CHAPTER **12**

Communities and Traumatic Grief

CHAPTER OUTLINE

Trauma
Posttraumatic Stress Disorder
When Communities Experience
    Trauma and Grief

When communities grieve
Creating Remembrances and
    Memorials
Summary

> *Grief knits two hearts in closer bonds than happiness ever*
> *can; and common sufferings are far stronger links than*
> *common joys.*
>
> Alphonse de Lamartine

TRAUMA

Trauma and grief in reaction to traumatic loss have become topics of increasing interest in a number of practice arenas including the military, schools, correctional facilities, and mental health agencies. This is unfortunately because so many deaths and symbolic losses occur in the context of traumatic events such as wars, natural disasters, and domestic as well as community violence. It is rare today that anyone escapes exposure to these events, particularly with the attention devoted to them through print and telecommunications media. I have been struck, as I have taught my course in grief and loss and conducted trainings in the past decade, how rare it is to encounter a professional helper or student in training who has not experienced trauma. Some acknowledge that they have sought training, in part, to gain a greater understanding of their own experience as well as to gain knowledge and skills to help others. One such student has generously given me permission to include her reflective journal entry in this text. While her experience of war-related trauma is unique, it is illustrative of the many traumatic experiences that can motivate us to become professionals in order to help others master the most challenging of life circumstances and events.

My country of origin Burundi has been known by its unrest and on and off wars since 1965. But the 1993 one really affected me. Maybe because I was old enough to understand what was going on and mostly because some of my friends were killed, wounded or just flew the country. On October 21, 1993, Burundi's first democratically elected Hutu president, Melchior Ndadaye and most of his colleagues, mostly Hutus, were assassinated by Tutsi extremist army. As a result of the murder, violence broke out between the two groups, and an estimated 50,000 to 100,000 people died within a year (according to the 1996 UN report). Since that day, the country's situation rapidly declined as Hutu peasants began to rise up and massacre their neighbor Tutsis. In acts of brutal retribution, the Tutsi army and Tutsi armed militia groups preceded around the country to round up thousands of Hutu and kill them. At 24 years old in 1995 I got engaged, 3 months later I got married and 2 days after the wedding my husband flew the country because the situation in the country worsened. The reason why I am talking about this year, it's because I was supposed to celebrate the greatest event of my life but that year became the year when I really understood what "war, Hutu and Tutsi" meant. I was lucky 1 month after my husband left the country I joined him. That was the saddest day of my entire life. I left behind my family, friends, neighbors. I remember looking at their faces; the fear of knowing that they can get killed any second just broke my heart. I can't count how many times I cried just for thinking about innocent people being killed.

On Sunday, 11 June 1995, 3 weeks after my departure, a party was being held at the Jesuit College of Holy-Esprit, in Kamenge, where Hutu and Tutsi students who studied together were enjoying the party. At around 5 PM, while the party was coming to an end, a gunman traveling in a vehicle forced his way into the college compound and shot four young men, 2 Hutus and 2 Tutsis. My best friend, A.A.N, a Hutu and former student at that college, suddenly was surrounded and severely beaten by Tutsis militia who threatened to kill him. Gendarmes arrived moments later. A.A.N. tried to escape but gendarmes soon found him hiding in a toilet. He came out hands in the air and bleeding all over his body. He was arrested by the gendarmes, beaten and put in jail. That same day, the violence at the Holy Spirit College sparked off the killing of at least 15 unarmed Hutu students by their Tutsi colleagues at the University of Burundi in Bujumbura. That night, I lost a friend A.N and other students I knew. A.N was killed by Tutsi students using knives and iron bars. Tutsi students then went on the rampage attacking their Hutu classmates using weapons such as machetes and knives, grenades and guns. Some Hutu students were taken to Nyakabiga one of the towns in the capital and a Tutsi stronghold, where they were killed and buried in a mass grave. Some bodies of the victims were reportedly found in the

Ntahangwa River. Some sources in Burundi have said that as many as 98 Hutu students were killed. Months later due to international pressure my friend A.A.N was released, he then flew the country. These students were just regular students who didn't deserve to die that day. Those incidents changed my life completely. They were my friends, people I knew, most of them my age, and what happened to them could happen to me too. I was not in Burundi when that happened, but the news was all over the place. The Internet material I was able to find helped me to understand why I always feel guilt for what happened to my friends I left behind. According to the material, it's a normal feeling but, for me I still feel like that I abandoned them, and maybe I should speak up about the danger young people were facing in my country as soon as I flew the country, or just do something to prevent the killings, I really still don't know, and am still thinking about the whole thing. (*Ndikunkiko,* 2009)

POSTTRAUMATIC STRESS DISORDER

Posttraumatic stress disorder (PTSD) is a relatively recent diagnosis that first appeared in the third edition of the *DSM* (1980). Initially it was applied to those who had witnessed death, such as combat soldiers, or whose lives had been threatened. In the fourth edition of the *DSM-TR*, it is recognized that symptoms of PTSD can develop in response to witnessing or experiencing a threat to bodily integrity. These include combat and sexual and physical assault; being held hostage or imprisoned; terrorism, torture, natural and man-made disasters, accidents, and receiving a diagnosis of a life-threatening illness. Learning about unexpected or violent death, serious harm, or threat of death or injury experienced by a family member or other close associate is also included as a precipitant of PTSD in the *DSM IV-TR*. PTSD can be acute when it is experienced in proximity to the event, chronic when it continues for more than 3 months and delayed when it begins more than 6 months after. In my own therapy practice I see many individuals and family members who have experienced the symptoms of PTSD. Many of these clients have experienced early childhood trauma through physical or sexual assault, trauma as a result of diagnosis and treatment of the life-threatening illness of cancer, and clients who were, or whose family members were, in New York City on September 11, 2001.

Not all individuals who experience trauma develop symptoms that meet the full diagnostic criteria for PTSD, but they may evidence some of the symptoms. Symptoms can include recurrent and intrusive distressing recollections of the event, markedly diminished interest or participation in significant activities, feeling of detachment or estrangement from others, restricted range of affect (e.g., unable to have loving feelings), sense of a foreshortened future, difficulty falling or staying asleep, irritability or outbursts of anger, persistent anxiety, difficulty concentrating, and hypervigilance or high arousal (American Psychiatric Association, 2000). Examples from my own practice include a 40-year-old teacher with chronic insomnia that began following the terrorist attacks in New York where her family lived close to the towers, the mother of a child who died after 3 years of multiple and grueling treatments for acute leukemia, an adult who was one of the very earliest survivors (since 1958) of childhood leukemia who had been treated for more than 10 years of aggressive chemotherapy and witnessed most of his fellow patients dying, and a large group of adult survivors of complex cumulative trauma from long-term childhood sexual abuse combined with domestic violence.

WHEN COMMUNITIES EXPERIENCE TRAUMA AND GRIEF

Loss is almost always associated with trauma, and can include loss of the sense that the world is a safe place in addition to actual losses such as the death of a close associate or the destruction of one's home. I live near both Springfield and South Hadley, Massachusetts, and work with colleagues whose children attend school in both communities. In 2010, both communities were in the national news when a child in each of their schools died from suicide attributed to bullying. Not only my colleagues' children but also my colleagues were traumatized by the deaths and the public debates that ensued about the prevalence of peer aggression in their school systems. Everyone felt a loss of security.

Countless stories have been shared about similar losses that have resulted from school and workplace shootings, mining, and other occupational disasters, and no one who travels by air in the United States can escape the routine reminders of terrorist attacks when going through airport security. These are man-made disasters that might immediately affect only certain communities but, like natural disasters that destroy lives and property, can have a global impact.

Whaley (2009) identifies trauma and loss as the main results of natural disasters like Hurricane Katrina. Included are the obvious physical traumas of injury and loss due to death from the floods, flying debris, and unstable structures as well as the psychological losses, including the void created by the death of significant others and the destruction of property (p. 469). Grief that is associated with traumatic loss is not universally defined by the term *traumatic grief*, but the term is increasingly seen in the literature on the impact of trauma. As was discussed in Chapter 7, some researchers and practitioners have suggested that the term *traumatic grief* be used to identify a variety of complicated grief reactions, but others have disagreed. Pomeroy and Garcia (2009) have noted the lack of agreement and have suggested that the term *complex grief* be used to describe a grief process complicated by internal or external factors that interfere with the process of expected grief. They note that complex grief needs to be addressed appropriately to prevent "life-depleting" responses. Until the debate is settled, it seems most important for us as professional helpers to be able to identify when and how support is needed and how it can effectively be provided to those who have experienced trauma and loss.

This includes being aware of traumatic events that have occurred in the lives of our clients (such as past history of sexual abuse or sudden death in the family) and events that occur in our communities or global community, as these all potentially have an impact on our clients as well as on us. This awareness is very important, particularly because traumatic memories and grief reactions can be triggered by sights, smells, sounds, dates, and other stimuli associated with the trauma, sometimes without awareness on the part of the survivor(s). In the case of high-profile community disasters where media is involved, it is important to remember that anniversaries of the disaster or traumatic event can remind survivors of their losses. The event date each month can trigger grief reactions but can be especially strong on the yearly anniversary of the event (SAMHSA, 2005).

When communities grieve

Prior to 9/11/2001 researchers and practitioners were developing new models for understanding and treating trauma in both children and adults. Following 9/11/2001, information and training has been much more widely disseminated on both treating trauma and treating grief associated with traumatic events. Multiple organizations, networks, and coalitions have developed resources for both those directly impacted by trauma and loss and those of us who work with them. Some of these, like the Center for School Crisis, have been discussed in previous chapters. These organizations can be an invaluable resource when we are working with individuals experiencing trauma and grief or when a traumatic event occurs in our community.

The National Institute for Trauma and Loss in Children has published useful concept maps that differentiate between the types of normal bereavement reactions that occur in the context of death and grief reactions that cause impairment in reaction to trauma. This training and education resource includes a Parent Resource Center with online materials on trauma and grief in English, Spanish, and Arabic that professionals and parents can download and distribute. From its online Self-Esteem Bookstore, therapeutic books, like *When Something Terrible Happens: Children Can Learn to Cope With Grief"* by Marge Heegaard, can be ordered. The Center for Traumatic Stress in Children and Adolescents identifies traumatic grief as grief that occurs as a result of a traumatic loss in which the child is "stuck" and cannot complete the tasks of grieving. The Center has developed an evidence-based model of Cognitive-Behavioral Therapy for Traumatic Grief (CBT-TG) that focuses on teaching children coping skills, helping them to tell the story of the traumatic death, rethinking confused or distorted thoughts, sharing the trauma narrative with parents, and then using grief-focused sessions to grieve what has been lost. (http://pittsburghchildtrauma.org/articles_1.html). Information about this model as well as an exceptional online training program for continuing education credits can be accessed through the Web site. Government organizations have also increasingly recognized the need for understanding and treating trauma and loss in both children and adults. The U.S. Department of Health and Human Resources has established a National Center for Trauma Informed Care on its Substance Abuse and Mental Health Services Administration (SAMHSA) site. A wealth of downloadable materials, videos made by individuals who have experienced mental health problems, and links to resources such as the National Veterans Suicide Prevention Hotline can be found on this site.

The U.S. Department of Veteran's Affairs has also established a National Center for PTSD. Videos on PTSD and effective treatment approaches, self-help information for veterans and families with diverse cultural backgrounds, and an online book entitled *Iraq War Clinician Guide* can be accessed through this site (Pilvar, 2010, p. 75).

Pilvar identifies the close bonds that occur in combat units and the violent deaths of comrades in chaotic situations that combat soldiers' experience. She describes one study of Vietnam veterans that detected grief reactions at very high levels of intensity 30 years after the combat losses had occurred. The study results indicated that bonding and attachment to the unit may result in some protection against subsequent development of PTSD, but also that unresolved bereavement may be expected to be associated with increased distress over the life span unless these losses are acknowledged and grief symptoms treated on a timely basis (p. 75). Military family members and their communities can also be expected to experience grief reactions when members of these close combat units die, particularly with the repeated deployments of military personnel in the most recent wars. Children of all ages of military personnel can be considered at risk. Special resources for military children and families have been developed by a number of programs, including the PBS Sesame Street Bilingual Outreach Initiative for Military Families, which is part of the larger Talk, Listen, Connect program on grief available online through PBS.

When we as helping professionals encounter individuals, families, and communities who are impacted by trauma and loss, we can use the same empathic listening techniques and other interventions discussed in previous chapters. It is important to know, however, that a number of researchers and practitioners emphasize caution when intervening with victims of trauma in the immediate aftermath. There is significant support for the idea that early encouragement to identify and express affective reactions to trauma may have a detrimental effect. The initial focus in many trauma intervention models is on cognitive behavioral approaches that facilitate coping and restore a sense of self-efficacy before exploring emotional reactions (Dass-Brailsford, 2007). Training is available from the American Red Cross and other relief organizations for those interested in immediate disaster intervention.

While we may not all be skilled in the area of trauma intervention, and the best we might do as an individual is to listen empathically and provide practical assistance, we can all be aware of resources that survivors can be referred to. We can all also be effective leaders in our organizations and communities in developing and promoting programs and interventions to assist those who are grieving.

Although horrific tragedies such as the terrorist attacks on September 11, 2001, and Hurricane Katrina were devastating on multiple levels, positive lessons were learned and a wealth of resources were produced in response to these events. There are more sources of culturally sensitive information and support available now than ever before to assist those who are trying to cope with grief and loss. As with each of the other chapters in this text, an exercise is provided for this chapter in MySocialWorkLab for Advancing Core Competencies. This exercise involves developing your own notebook or file of resources to keep on hand for future reference if your organization does not already have this available. This includes building on the grief protocol you developed in Chapter 11, adding an index of national organizations and programs, and including tip sheets and other downloadable materials and videos you have located through this text and the web links that are provided. You can then refer to this directory when you, or someone with whom you work, needs assistance. In addition, the Internet resources for this and other chapters are excellent sources of information for both professional helpers and those who are grieving. National organizations like the Compassionate Friends (a support organization for parents who have lost a child) or COPS (an organization assisting survivors of police who die in the line of duty) can be especially helpful to those in rural areas or whose unique losses may not be as common in one's local community.

CREATING REMEMBRANCES AND MEMORIALS

Grief experts identify many ways in which memorial ceremonies, rituals, and activities assist those who are grieving (Worden, 2009). Funerals and memorial activities validate the lives of the deceased and can strengthen the connections of those who survive losses. Family and friends are reminded of the importance of every life—the deceased's as well as their own-during funerals and commemorative activities. As discussed in earlier chapters, issues related to grief and loss are present not only in cases of death but also in many other types of losses. Many people have developed rituals and ceremonies to grieve symbolic losses such as divorces or moving from one's place of origin. Harry Close, a pastoral counselor, has published *Ceremonies for Healing and Growth* that includes a ritual of transition for leaving one's home for a nursing home, and a ceremony for divorce. In the divorce ceremony, he—a pastoral counselor—acknowledges the grief that accompanies divorce as well as the need for support in the anxious time of transition and rebuilding that are necessary following divorce. Like all ceremonies and rituals, these ceremonies for special situations assist those who are grieving by providing an opportunity for the acknowledgment and expression of feelings related to the loss. Providing practical and emotional support before, during, and after these activities is a way that members of a support network or community can express their caring. Sometimes, a ritual of remembrance or a memorial ceremony can help bring closure and convey support for losses that have been unresolved from the past.

Throughout this text, we have discussed the fact that if attuned to unresolved loss, most helping professionals can identify loss-related needs in every aspect of our work. The many types of losses that children, teens, and adults experience, and that we will encounter through our interactions with them, present both challenges and opportunities to us to be helpful. We can make a significant difference through a variety of helpful responses.

- Empathic communication, discussed in Chapter 9, is always indicated.
- Sometimes a referral to a support group, a bereavement counselor, or another community provider is the best type of help we can provide, and is essential for those experiencing complicated or traumatic grief.
- Attending a funeral or planning a memorial service can serve as an expression of support to surviving family and community members and can also assist us, as professional helpers, to cope with our own grief in reaction to a loss.
- Offering to be present with or "companioning" those who are grieving.

Just as it is important to assess our own motives and skill when addressing grief that we suspect is causing distress, it is also important to assess our motives as well as the impact our actions will have on the person who is grieving when we are deciding whether or not to attend a funeral or memorial service. In many instances clients or students are comforted by the presence of familiar professionals at important public ceremonies of remembrance. Some helping professionals have also attended funerals or memorials to both show their respect to the family of the person who has died and acknowledge their own grief. A medical social worker wrote,

> Both Therese Rando (1984) and William Worden (2002) speak to the benefits accorded an individual through the funeral ritual. Because there are varying degrees of involvement that I have with each patient and family member I see, I would not, nor would I feel the need to, attend the service of every patient who dies. There are, however, patients, for whatever reason, that I become close with, who touch my heart, who teach me and who I am better for having known. For those patients, the grief I feel at their death is very real. In a hospital environment where one often needs to be readily available to go from one situation to the next, feelings about the losses that occur have to be put on hold and remain there for some time to come. The funeral ritual provides for me a place to reflect upon and grieve the loss, pay tribute to the individual, acknowledge the importance of the loss to the family and let the family know their loved one made a difference in my life. (Jaycox, 2003)

While professionals' attendance at memorials can be very helpful to family members, depending on the relationship, there are also times when a professional helper's presence might be uncomfortable for the individual or family who has sustained a loss. As with other grief interventions, the decision to attend a service or ceremony planned by a grieving family should always be based on an assessment of how it will meet the grieving individual's or family's needs rather than our own. Except in very large public ceremonies or services, such as a citywide memorial service for a public servant killed in the line of duty, we should always think carefully about why we should or should not attend and if it will serve the needs of the client for us to remain absent; there are many other ways to attend to our own grief reactions, including debriefing or processing in a team meeting or agency-sponsored memorial.

As a grief counselor, I have often been inspired by the creative and caring rituals that families, communities, and organizations have used to honor and remember loved ones. One group of friends created a memorial cookbook, using the recipes that their dear friend, who was an avid cook, had served to them before she died. At her memorial service, these dishes were prepared and served, accompanied by little notes recalling the events and celebrations during which their friend had served them.

A family with whom I am acquainted gathered at a park where their father had enjoyed his daily walks, walked the perimeter together, recalling stories of his life, and decided on a site overlooking a pond on which to locate a memorial bench, which they donated to the park. Another family I know, who owns their own small business, has planted ornamental shrubs on the business property, with small plaques honoring employees who have died and who will be remembered. Many families choose to donate the organs of a deceased family member as a "living tribute" to a loved one. The gratitude and appreciation of life expressed by many recipients during and after a memorial can offer a source of comfort and hope in the face of overwhelming grief.

In the Unity camp program for families affected by AIDS, an annual ritual consists of each family constructing together, from what they find in the natural environment, a memorial boat which is launched in an evening ceremony. Stories and memories are shared as the family members gather sticks, leaves, bark, and nut shells to decorate their boats which symbolize the "passing on" of their loved ones. Later in the evening, just after sunset, each family lights a candle, places it on their boat, and "launches" the boat onto the lake before gathering around a campfire for shared gospel music (Schmucker & Laughlin, 1999).

Many hospitals, churches, and community organizations now host an annual memorial service to honor staff and members of the communities they serve who have died. Each year thousands of people walk in the American Cancer Society's Relay for Life to raise money for cancer research and programs. The Relay includes a "luminaria" lap during which individuals and families light candles in decorated luminaria bags and walk in memory of their loved ones. Many similar events sponsored by other organizations offer a therapeutic means to remember one's loved one and make a meaningful contribution to organizations that help others. December 5 has been established as an annual night of remembrance worldwide for parents who have lost a child. Many communities sponsor a gathering for these grieving parents to come together on this night to light candles together and remember their children. The public show of support and acknowledgment that these events provide can be invaluable in helping individuals or families to connect with one another, acknowledge their feelings, and make meaning of one of life's most difficult experiences—the death of someone important.

While many people rely exclusively on clergy or spiritual community leaders to plan memorial services or events, many books and Web sites now provide guidelines and resources that aid in planning and carrying out these kinds of events and activities as well as information about how to become involved in those that already exist. Musical selections appropriate to the occasion, inspirational readings and quotations, art work for printed programs, and even guidelines for obituaries and eulogies can now be found quite easily, using the resources listed for this chapter. In addition, a sample program for a memorial service is included in the Internet Resources for the text.

Internet-based memorials are becoming a major vehicle for remembering those who have died and honoring their memories as well as connecting those who experience a common loss. This is particularly true for adolescents and young adults who increasingly use their social networking sites to solicit and receive information and support. In discussing the suicide of their son-in-law with an elder couple in my therapy practice recently, they noted that their 15-year-granddaughter had posted a notice on her Facebook page the night of his death and had been communicating with her peers as well as extended family members throughout the week immediately following, even late at night when she had been unable to sleep. Funeral homes often offer families an Internet memorial page along with other funeral services where friends and acquaintances can memorialize the loved one through sharing memories and anecdotes as well as pictures, music, and video.

Service activities represent another arena of memorial interventions that can help to facilitate healthy adaptation after a loss. Sometimes grieving individuals and communities, particularly those who are affected by public tragedies, gain a sense of empowerment and hope after devastating loss through actions that help others in some way. Each year hundreds of thousands of individuals throughout the United States raise funds in memory of loved ones in events like the American Cancer Society's Relay for Life, the Leukemia and Lymphoma Society's Light the Night walk, the Susan G. Komen Foundation's Race for the Cure. "For the Love of Ali" (Waldsmith, 2000) recounts how Anna Ling Pierce has gained hope and provided inspiration through Ali and Dad's Army, an organization that raises funds for a pediatric cancer treatment center at the University of Massachusetts in honor of her daughter and husband. Ann Pierce's daughter Ali died of cancer at age 13 in 1995. Ann's husband, Ali's dad John, created a fundraising organization called Ali's Army to raise money in her memory and set a goal of raising $500,000 over 5 years. In October 1997, just 11 months after Ali's death, John, age 50, died of a heart attack while training with Ali's Army to run and raise money in the Boston Marathon. Ann, while shattered by the loss of her husband and daughter, has found meaning and comfort through continuing Ali and Dad's Army and reaching the $500,000 goal in just 1 year. She says that she now wakes each day with a crystal clear purpose and feels like she has a family of hundreds of people who have joined her in raising money for this memorial fund.

While not every family or community will choose to carry out this kind of service activity following loss, as helping professionals we need to remember that there are many ways to acknowledge and express both grief and caring. Fortunately, there are many routes and resources to support a diverse array of needs.

Just as we can be leaders in designing and implementing interventions and programs to address the specific needs of those who are grieving, we can be leaders in designing and promoting memorial services and ceremonies as well as rituals that provide support and acknowledgment to members of our communities grieving many kinds of losses. We can also promote the empowerment of the vulnerable grieving populations we serve when we encourage and assist them in designing and implementing the memorials, ceremonies, rituals, and practices that best serve their unique needs.

SUMMARY

Too many deaths and symbolic losses today occur in the context of traumatic events such as wars, natural disasters, and domestic as well as community violence. Not all, but some individuals who experience traumatic events such as combat, rape or sexual abuse, or witness a life-threatening event, develop symptoms of posttraumatic stress disorder (PTSD). In the most current edition of the *Diagnostic and Statistical Manual of Mental Disorders*, it is also recognized that learning about unexpected or violent death, serious harm, or threat of death or injury experienced by a family member or other close associate can be a precipitant of PTSD. Loss is almost always associated with trauma, and can include loss of the sense that the world is a safe place in addition to actual losses such as the death of a close associate or the loss of one's home. While there is not agreement among grief experts about whether the term *traumatic grief* applies in these situations, grief reactions can be expected in response to these losses and normal grieving may be complicated by trauma. It is important for helping professionals to be attuned to the kind of traumatic events our clients may have experienced and aware that PTSD symptoms and grief reactions can be triggered by smells, sounds, and anniversaries associated with these events. Even those in communities not directly impacted by traumatic events can experience reactions. Although horrific tragedies such as the terrorist attacks on September 11, 2001, and Hurricane Katrina were devastating on multiple levels, positive lessons were learned and a wealth of resources were produced in response to these events. There are now myriad resources available that can be utilized, along with empathic communication and other interventions discussed in this text, to assist us and our clients with grief and loss related to trauma. Some of these include resources to plan and carry out ceremonies, rituals, and memorial activities that can facilitate the grieving process.

CHAPTER 13

Self-Care: Sustaining Hope, Helpfulness, and Competence in Working With Grief

CHAPTER OUTLINE

Continuing Education and
    Professional Development
Self-Care

Professional Support Systems
Summary

*The source of all abundance is not outside you. It is a part
of who you are. However, start by acknowledging and
recognizing abundance without. See the fullness of life all
around you.*

Eckhart Tolle

CONTINUING EDUCATION AND PROFESSIONAL DEVELOPMENT

Professional development encompasses not only the education and training that prepares us for our work with others, but also the ongoing development of knowledge and skills to carry out our work effectively in an ever-changing environment. You may be reading this text as part of a professional training program, and if so, you will be better prepared to identify and address grief-related issues as they arise in your work. It will always be important, however, to regularly evaluate your knowledge and skills and to participate in continuing education to expand your capacity and remain current.

Most professionals find continuing education to be essential for many reasons. Continuing education helps to infuse our practice or teaching with new information and methods. Acquiring new knowledge and skills, especially through interaction and contact with other professionals, provides a mechanism for capacity building, consultation, and even support for many who work with challenging and vulnerable populations. Professional licensing and certification boards recognize the importance of continuing education (CE) and require that professionals participate in CE programs in order to gain, or maintain, licenses or other credentials that ensure competence. There are many methods for continuing education and advancing professional knowledge and skills. Now that you have read this basic text and acclimated yourself to basic theories and skills related to grief and loss, you can avail yourself of the rich array of continuing education and professional development offerings that will increase your competence in areas specific to your own professional practice.

There are conferences and courses offered by grief-specific organizations such as the Association for Death Education. Most academic training programs based in colleges and universities offer courses, advanced degree programs, or lectures to their alumnae and surrounding professional communities in topic areas of specific interest to their disciplines. It is helpful to be aware of these programs while you are still a student so that you can take advantage of them after you complete your basic professional training. Government agencies such as the Veteran's Administration and SAMHSA (the Substance Abuse and Mental Health Services Administration, which houses among other resources, the National Center for Trauma Informed Care) not only provide excellent Web-based educational resources but also sponsor conferences and trainings on a wide range of topics related to grief and grief intervention models.

Professional organizations also offer a wide variety of continuing education options to members as well as the public. Many offer continuing education credits for interdisciplinary colleagues as well as members of their own discipline, and participation in interdisciplinary CE programs can enhance the richness of the learning experience. However, membership in a professional organization is highly recommended because it will link you to important resources beyond continuing education. The Association of Oncology Social Work, for example, has been a major resource for me over the past 25 years, providing annual conferences for education and networking, an Internet listserv for consultation and support, a monthly newsletter and a professional journal in which research and practice articles are published, and connection with colleagues around the world who are interested in and committed to sharing best practices and advocacy for programs and services that address the needs of clients as well as professionals who serve them.

What has been most encouraging, since the publication of the first edition of this text, is the vast increase in professional development resources and methods that the Internet has provided. Distance learning offerings that include video-streamed case examples make continuing professional development accessible in ways that were impossible until this century. The opportunity to participate interactively with panelists during Webinars and teleconferences also enriches discussion and learning among diverse participants from different geographic areas and practice settings that is increasing our knowledge exponentially. More and more professionals are also using the Internet to connect in peer supervision groups as well as for individual supervision and mentoring, and this can be a vital resource for busy professionals in demanding work environments. The Internet Resources for this text include a select sample of these.

SELF-CARE

Self-care is also an essential component of ongoing professional development that can sustain us and contribute to professional resilience. The changing terminology, research, and conceptualization that has emerged in the helping professions related to self-care in the last decade is testimony to the increased attention to, and understanding of, this arena of practice. Early studies of the impact of stress on professional helpers used the term *burnout* to describe the physical and emotional reactions that impeded effective practice. "Burnout refers to physical, emotional and psychological exhaustion accompanied by a sense of demoralization and diminished caring, creativity and professional accomplishment" (Hooyman & Kramer, 2006, p. 352).

Compassion fatigue is a term that followed *burnout* in the literature and is used to describe "the emotional depletion that professional caregivers may experience when an imbalance occurs in self-care and care for others" (Pfifferling & Gilley, 2000). A clue to compassion fatigue is when a previously caring and compassionate professional expresses a lack of concern, understanding, or compassion for others who are distressed. A professional who is experiencing compassion fatigue may

- Be irritable
- Express anger when asked to help
- Make disdainful or negative remarks about a client's distress or
- Avoid discussing another person's painful feelings because he or she can't hear one more painful story

Even when we are very well prepared educationally, are self-aware, and have addressed our own past issues with death and loss, we can experience compassion fatigue in working with others who are grieving. Continuous assessment of one's own levels of distress and practice of self-care can help to contribute to the ability to practice effectively and derive sustained meaning and reward from intimate connection with those in distress.

These and other self-care strategies that help to create balance in our lives and gain support for ourselves as we provide support to others are essential to professional resilience. Yet for many, this is easier said than done. For most professionals regular time off is essential, and yet we often find it difficult to get or take vacation or "mental health" days. Creative expression through art, music, or dance can also be very helpful; yet in a recent training for teachers and school guidance personnel, most of the seasoned participants lamented that they are so exhausted at the end of the day or work week that they simply can't find the energy or time to meet their own needs for creative expression. It is a recognized limitation in many of our professional training programs and contemporary workplaces that professionals' own self-care needs are neglected.

Organizations that employ professional helpers may not offer the formal support or structures to facilitate the grieving process for staff. In one of the first publications to address professional self-care in the context of grief, Therese Rando (1984) acknowledged that organizational attitudes and policies often contradict what we know contributes to effective practice. She noted that the lack of organizational support in human service systems is a source of stress and points out that explicit recognition of the need to address staff needs would help to reduce staff stress and provide staff with vehicles for processing their grief.

Similarly, Durfee (1997), who has written about grief related to child abuse and death due to family violence, speaks to the lack of organizational policies and programs that address the grief of child protection and emergency care workers who assist children and families after a case of severe abuse or violent death. He points out that there is a lack of intervention for professional and volunteer service providers who are affected by this kind of death. He recommends critical incident debriefing within an agency or in supervision that can enable workers to feel competent, while attending to their need for empathy and protection.

While peer support is generally considered helpful, there is not always time or structure allocated by agencies for this and protocols are not always established for provision of staff support or attendance at funerals. Both Rando and Durfee recommend that organizations take steps to meet the grief-related needs of professional caregivers that include opportunities for debriefing and time off as well as provide education on the grief-related needs of clients and workers. Dale Larsen, in his book *The Helper's Journey* (1993), suggests that, because workplace stress can impact one's personal life and stress in one's personal life can impact work, professional caregivers compartmentalize work and personal life, keeping them separate if possible. Berendson (2011) in a recent article entitled "Staying Passionate: Five Keys for Keeping the Soul in Our Work" recommends accepting disappointment and disillusionment while building safety nets and retaining a sense of humor.

Progress can be seen in the arena of professional self-care if we look at the increase in publications like these across the helping disciplines. There has also been an increase in research and educational programs focused on professional sustainment that has occurred in the past decade, particularly in the wake of traumatic events such as September 11, 2001, when professional helpers suffered not only emotional but physical harm through their efforts to rescue others. More researchers and organizations are focusing on learning more about ways to promote professional resilience, and more professionals are becoming aware that they must take care of themselves if they are to take care of others.

The term *professional resilience* has come into more common use in the literature on professional stress and coping. Fink-Samnick (2010) defines it as a professional's "commitment to achieve balance between occupational stressors and life challenges, while fostering professional values and career sustainability." Some organizations are providing guidelines and formal mechanisms to support staff in achieving this balance over the long haul in demanding work environments. There is now also a term for those workplaces that foster worker resilience: workplace resilience. Adrian Van Breda (2011) has identified several characteristics of such organizations including their supportive networks, collaborative problem-solving, positive appraisal and harmony or balance between work and personal life. Both attending to one's own self-care and helping to make one's workplace one that fosters resilience are important to all of our careers when we are in close proximity to grief.

The National Center for Trauma Informed Care (NCTIC) identifies the need for self-care in its Tips for Emergency Response Professionals, which is available for downloading on its Web site. This organization recognizes that while emergency response work is rewarding, it also has the potential to affect workers in ways that may be harmful to their health and well-being. Because the work is demanding and the hours are long, it can deplete energy, but it also includes exposure, as many helping professional roles do, to human suffering. The tip sheet includes steps that can be taken to counteract the stress and replenish one's energy, including taking time to process experiences with a peer or colleague.

Time off, debriefing, and opportunities for creative expression related to professional caregiver grief are only a few of the many strategies that can help sustain us in our work and help us to be most effective. Many professionals find that their own spiritual practices enable them to find hope and make meaning in the face of loss. And, of course, it is important to practice what we preach; get regular physical exercise and adequate sleep, and follow a nutritionally sound diet.

While this chapter may give you ideas about how the organizations you work for can more effectively support you in your work, you may also want to implement your own program for self-care. There are many ways to do this, including the use of personal retreats in which you allocate time and space for utilization of the strategies that work best for you (Louden, 1977). The following list of self-care strategies has been generated over the years by students in my classes, whose ages span from 23 through 56; who come from a variety of ethnic, cultural, and racial backgrounds; who are both males and females; and who practice in a diverse array of settings. They identified these strategies:

- Spend more time with friends and family
- Enjoy evenings full of laughter, ice cream, and good times
- Exercise regularly
- Eat healthy food
- Take a bubble bath
- Paint
- Go to the beach
- Play in the water with children until your hands look like a prune
- Watch a sunset
- Read for leisure
- Take pleasure in life outside of work
- Gardening
- Go kayaking or canoeing
- Do snowmobiling
- Keep up on the latest research and findings
- Hug someone
- Listen to music (singing along with the radio in the car works wonders)
- See movies (save the heavy dramas for when your life isn't already full of drama)
- Talk to a friend
- Go for a walk
- Dance
- Get a good night's sleep every night
- Eat one piece of chocolate
- Reduce clutter

- Get more organized, so that the details of everyday life don't add to your stress
- Take a weekend retreat
- Do yoga-active relaxation
- Do Tai chi'
- Take a vacation
- Take a day trip
- Listen to soft music in combination with some deep breathing exercises
- Listen to a guided imagery tape
- Meditate
- Take at least 1–2 hours every week to do something you want to do
- Go bicycling
- Go hiking
- Take a ride in the car
- Listen to contemporary jazz or blues
- Have lunch with coworkers
- Go out to a nice restaurant with a girlfriend or boyfriend
- Go shopping for yourself
- Avoid junk food; eat something healthy
- Take time for appreciating or creating art
- Write in a journal
- Undergo psychotherapy
- Play rap really loud in the car
- Recognize what triggers negative stress and avoid it
- Spend time with people who know you well enough to call you on things
- Snuggle with a pet
- Laugh loudly
- Commune with nature
- Work on the 12 steps
- Get a massage
- Begin the day with gratitude and continue to practice it throughout the day
- Practice mindfulness
- Pray

It is important to remember that each of us, as professional helpers, copes in our own unique ways, just as our clients do. It is perhaps not so important *what* we do to maintain our well-being, but *that* we do it. Conscious attention to the activities and relationships, even the ways of thinking about our work that help us to feel fulfilled, will enable us not only to survive but to thrive and experience, in an ongoing way, the passion that initially brings most of us into our work.

PROFESSIONAL SUPPORT SYSTEMS

Taking time regularly to identify and utilize strategies or resources you can use through the different stages of your career will help you to maintain your own sense of balance and well-being. If we are self-aware, understand how our own beliefs and feelings are affecting us, and practice self-care, we are better able to be present with someone else, wherever he or she is in the process of adjustment to loss. If we do not do this, we put ourselves at risk for burnout or compassion fatigue as well as diminishing quality of work life (Hudnall-Stamm, 2009).

In the helping professions, there will always be times that challenge us. Work with vulnerable people has the potential to trigger unresolved loss in our own lives. We may experience "loss pileup," and in periods of great demand or in instances of traumatic loss, secondary trauma may be more than we can manage with our usual coping strategies. There are times when we may observe ourselves, or others, using maladaptive strategies in an effort to cope with powerful feelings or increased stress. These maladaptive strategies include

- Overworking
- Avoiding others
- Using substances
- Shutting down our emotions

These strategies are sometimes identified as symptoms of burnout. Whether or not we apply the label of burnout, maladaptive coping strategies are an indication of distress that needs to be addressed to prevent disservice to our clients and ourselves.

If we observe or experience these warning signs, it is time to seek help. Psychotherapy, pastoral counseling, grief or spiritual retreats led by experts, and/or treatment programs are not strategies of last resort, or exclusively for "others," but rather can be the lifeline that enables us, just as they enable those we work with, to carry out the essential process of grief and find ways to cope most effectively.

I have found it essential to utilize many approaches to professional development and self-care in my 33-year career. I continue to participate in my own ongoing therapy as well as a peer consultation and support group (Lesser et al., 2004). I maintain an active membership in professional organizations, including serving as president of the Association of Oncology Social Work, and spend as much time as possible with my most wonderful family and friends. I draw inexhaustible inspiration from my two amazing daughters and from the clients who have shared their lives with me. It has been a profound honor to do this work but it also cuts to the bone sometimes. Writing has been an essential vehicle for self-expression and restoration throughout my career and this text is the result of that commitment to professional writing that helps to sustain me. Creative writing provides me with a different type of self-expression and a way of making meaning from my work, as the following poem, written during a retreat week for Therapists in Mid-life, illustrates.

"Low Tide"

At low tide
You have to go through the muck
You have to look and feel carefully
For the dark sinkholes
But not let them stop you

At low tide
You have to bear witness to the

Vastness of the sea's litter
The shattered shells, the old bones
The broken creatures
Just a few hours ago, hidden
Now exposed

At low tide you must slog through
As the mud sucks at your feet
You have to slow yourself down
To move forward

And if you listen
You will hear the bubbling whispers
Of the clams and the oysters
Who have grown protective shells
That allow them to breathe but
Keep their tender parts safe

They will give you faith
That all this debris and the rivulets of receding tide
Will lead you to the quiet water
Where you can float and feel the warmth of life
Surround you

Where you can look back at the dark shore
From where you have come
And see the sun rising

Reading the creative work of others can also serve a restorative purpose and foster our professional resilience. Almost any poem by Mary Oliver can do this, but my number-one pick for professional helpers is "The Summer Day," a poem that begins with the question "Who made the world?" and ends with the question "Tell me, what is it you plan to do with your one wild and precious life?"

If you are reading this book, it is likely that you have already decided, or are in the process of deciding, to commit your life to helping those who are vulnerable, and therefore will experience loss. If so, I hope that you experience the tremendous rewards that I have experienced in more than 30 years since I embarked on my own career in oncology. This text concludes with the exhortation to all of us who choose to become professional helpers to be as empathically attuned, and attentive to, our own grief-related needs and our own need for restoration and renewal as we are to the clients who will inevitably need our help and professional wisdom in the future. While the study of the text is now coming to an end, I hope that it is only the beginning of a career as long and as satisfying as the one I have been privileged to experience. And because this is the beginning of the next chapter of your career, it seems important to conclude with the quotation we began with.

A journey of a thousand miles begins with the first step.

Chinese Proverb

SUMMARY

This chapter covers the very important topic of professional development and sustainment. It is extremely important for all professional helpers, but is particularly important for those who work with vulnerable populations and are destined, inevitably, to encounter loss and grief. Continuing education and participation in professional development activities such as conferences and workshops are important ways for professionals to maintain their competence and ability to practice effectively, no matter what the discipline. Professional organizations that sponsor these can also be an excellent source of support through list serves, informal and formal dialogues, and forums, in addition to customized education programs. The Internet has made these more accessible than ever, through distance learning and networking technologies that are affordable. A good deal of literature has been written about the vulnerability of helping professionals, particularly those who work closely with death and loss, to compassion fatigue and burnout. Some organizations that employ helping professionals have implemented formal policies and programs that support staff in processing their own grief and obtaining respite and renewal, but not all organizations do. Professional self-care strategies, in many forms, can help to promote professional resilience. Creative expression, spending time in nature, exploring our own spirituality, and a host of individual activities can provide a vehicle for dealing with our own grief and bring a sense of balance to each of us whose work and home demands can be depleting. The rewards of being attuned to grief and providing help to those who need it are profoundly satisfying and all the more so if we routinely seek support and renewal over the life of a career.

APPENDIX A
Common Losses Across the Lifespan

Childhood	Adolescence	Young Adulthood	Middle Adulthood	Later Adulthood
Death of parent	Any of the losses listed in childhood and/or	Any of the losses listed in childhood and adolescence and/or	Any of the losses listed in childhood, adolescence, and young adulthood and/or	Any of the losses listed in childhood, adolescence, young, and middle adulthood and/or
Separation from parent or primary caregiver	Loss of peers	Loss of partner	Loss of work/ career	Loss of support network
Death of grandparent	Loss of significant relationships	Loss of job	Divorce/loss of identity as spouse	Loss of mobility
Death of pet	Loss of connection to spiritual community	Loss of income	Loss of intact family	Retirement/loss of career
Loss of two-parent family		Loss of sobriety		Loss of memory
Moving from/ loss of familiar home	Loss of connection to parents	Loss of faith	Loss of health	Loss of independence
Loss of teachers, counselors, neighborhood	Loss of earlier identities	Incarceration/ loss of freedom	Launching of children/loss of role	Loss of home
Loss of friends	Loss of self-efficacy		Death of child	Sensory losses
Loss of innocence			Loss of vision or hearing	
Loss of sense of omnipotence			Loss of libido	

This list is based on several theories including life-span and attachment theories. While not every loss listed is *perceived* as a loss by individuals who experience them, and individuals in earlier stages of life may experience losses that are more common at later stages, these are some of the common experiences that may engender grief reactions. A tool that may be useful to you, as a developing professional, is to construct your own "lossography"—a list of losses you have experienced over your lifetime (DeSpelder et al., 2009).

APPENDIX B
Helpful Strategies for Coping With Grief

As a bereavement counselor and social worker, I have worked closely with many families and communities affected by loss. What I have found through my 30 years of experience is that many people feel confused or unsure about how to cope with their own grief or the grief of others. Not knowing what to do or say, people often mistakenly avoid talking about it or dealing with it altogether. Unfortunately, this can lead to further misunderstanding and leave people who need to be connected feeling isolated and alone. The following strategies can help you and those you care about through the grief process. It is also important to remember, however, that most people need periods of respite and renewal to balance active grieving so these strategies need to be selectively applied, according to need.

ACKNOWLEDGE THE LOSS

Time alone does not heal. It is what people do over time that matters. To facilitate healing, people need to be able to acknowledge their loss, express their feelings, and feel a sense of connection with the person who has died as well as with those who, in their support network, are still living.

EXPRESS AND SHARE FEELINGS

The period following a loss is a very sad and vulnerable time for people who are grieving. Yet many people coping with grief have expressed that even though it can be painful at times, they also find it comforting and healing to have opportunities to express and share their feelings in a safe and nurturing environment. This connection provides a source of comfort and strength creating a foundation for healing to begin.

ENCOURAGE SHARING AND OFFER TO LISTEN

We sometimes feel that tears or other expressions of feelings are signs of weakness or a reflection that we are not handling things well. However, these expressions are a normal and healthy response to loss. Friends and family can help by being supportive listeners and by encouraging survivors when they feel ready to share these heartfelt emotions.

ALLOW FOR DIFFERENCES IN THE NEEDS OF GRIEVING PEOPLE

There is no designated timeline for how long the grieving process should last. There are no "shoulds" with grieving. It is important that people process and work through their grief in a way that feels comfortable to them.

SHARE MEMORIES OF LOVED ONES TO HELP IN HEALING

Healing comes not from forgetting, but from remembering those who have died and the special times that were shared. One way people can do this is by creating a special ritual of remembrance such as candle lighting to honor and remember loved ones. Lighting the candle during times of personal reflection or at gatherings with family and friends can help to create a sense of peace and keep the memories of loved ones alive in our hearts.

APPENDIX C
Strategies for Professionals Helping Children and Families Cope With Traumatic Loss

In assisting families, organizations, or communities during or following traumatic events, keep in mind that:

1. **Natural human reactions to tragedy** range from:
   Anger to rage
   Anxiety to terror
   Sadness to intense grief
   Relief to guilt
   Despair to hope

2. These natural **feelings need to be acknowledged** and support offered. Just listening can be most helpful.
3. Children's, teens', and adults' **reactions will be partly influenced by their previous experiences** with trauma and loss.
4. **Children will understand and react differently**, depending on their stage of emotional and cognitive development. Information and support should be tailored to their developmental needs.
5. **Feelings of increased vulnerability** need to be acknowledged and reassurance provided.
6. **Reassurance should be provided** through statements such as "adults in authority are working very hard to be sure that everyone in our family and our communities will be safe and secure."
7. Families, groups, and communities **gain support and strength through gathering together** and acknowledging and expressing feelings of loss as well as hope. Helping people cope through such a gathering is important.
8. Parents and professionals can help families **establish plans and methods to be in touch with each other in the days and weeks following** the trauma to provide reassurance and support.
9. **Sharing memories** of those we have loved and lost helps with healing.

APPENDIX D
Remembrance Celebrations: Planning Your Own Memorial Service

That which is important can only be felt with the heart

Helen Keller

Life is no brief candle to me. It is a sort of splendid torch which I have got hold of for the moment, and I want to make it burn as brightly as possible before handing it on to future generations.

George Bernard Shaw

The inspiration for including this set of suggestions has come from many sources—mainly from the people I have known who have extended to me the privilege of knowing them, their sorrows, and their joys; and their accomplishments and the meaning they have made from life. In my work as a social worker I have come to know hundreds of people who let me share in their lives and the lives of their loved ones. One individual, in particular, had an extraordinary influence on me. Lisa was 46, the spirited mother of three teenagers, a daughter, sister, and wife. Together with her husband, she had accumulated a close circle of friends, was active in her synagogue, and was a highly respected and valued community member. Although we lived in the same community, I didn't meet her until she experienced a recurrence of cancer and called me for counseling. She explained that she was the sort of person who prided herself on "tackling problems" head on. While she had received life-extending treatment after her initial diagnosis and was continuing to make every effort to continue living, she was also determined to plan for the possibility that her life might be shortened. She wanted to be sure her family's needs were met, whether she survived or died. She therefore began to give some of her energy to reviewing her life and legacy, with her family, friends, and the important people in her life, and held a celebratory gathering in her home while she was still able to celebrate a lifetime of memories and meaningful relationships. While most people will not choose this type of memorial, the same activities and procedures can be very useful to include in a traditional (or nontraditional) memorial ceremony.

We live in a time and a place in which the occasions which mark beginnings—births, bat mitzvahs, marriages, graduations—are celebrated with rituals and ceremonies and free expression of feelings. We plan our celebrations with great care: being sure to invite important people; providing food we know those close to us will enjoy; and often incorporating music, toasts, and acknowledgment of the importance of relationships in our lives. Often we begin this planning process years in advance of the event, imagining what we will say, who we will include, and what our invitations will look like. Yet, when it comes to one of the most meaningful celebrations of our lives, very few of us plan our own funerals or memorial services. The following list includes resources that may be helpful to you or the people you are assisting in anticipating or planning a funeral or memorial.

Information Prior to Death

Organ Donation _____
Advance Directives _____
Health Care Proxy Designated _____
Preferred Funerary or Memorial Plan _____
Spiritual Connections or Practices _____

Information After Death

Personal Biographical Information (often included in the obituary in the newspaper)
Funeral Information (where and when it will take place)
Notification Checklist (who should be contacted and informed of the death)

For the Memorial/Funeral Service/Ritual

Program Designs
A small pamphlet or brochure to guide participants through the service/ritual is very helpful. It may include a listing of:

- What will take place during the service _____
- Who will lead the service/memorial _____
- Who else will speak or participate _____
- Musical selections _____
- Poetry or inspirations _____
- Pictures, artwork, or mementos _____
- Activities in which all can participate (e.g., visiting the cemetery following the service, placing flowers in a memorial vase, signing a guest book)

_____

QUOTATIONS   A list of inspirations can be found at http://www.comfortcandles.com under the Inspirations link. The following references listed also include some inspirations and quotations.

Helpful Organizations and Web Sites

http://www.AARP.org
   Association of Retired Person's site with Web links and advance directives info
http://www.partnershipforcaring.org/Advance/index.html
   Site with information on advance directives
http://www.aarp.org/confacts/lifeanswers/wrksheet-funeral.html
   Excellent funeral planning worksheet by AARP
http://www.beyondindigo.com/
   Funeral planning forms, information on grief and terminal illness

Helpful References:

Bennett, A., & Foley, B. (1997). *In Memoriam: A practical guide to planning a memorial service.* New York: A Fireside Book.

Doan, E. C. (1989). *Speaker's sourcebook II* (p.236). Grand Rapids, MI: Zondervan.

Sublette, K., & Flagg, M. (1992). *Final celebrations: A guide for personal and family funeral planning.* Ventura, CA: Pathfinder Publishing of California.

Lynn, J., & Harrold, J. (1999). *Handbook for mortals: Guidance for people facing serious illness.* NY: Oxford Press.

APPENDIX E
Expressive Techniques

Many people, professionals and nonprofessionals alike, find it very helpful to express their thoughts and feelings through the arts, writing, and other vehicles of communication. This can be especially true when the feelings and thoughts are very powerful, such as those connected to grief and loss.

WRITING

Journaling, poetry writing, scrapbooking, and participating in writing workshops can be very helpful in coping with grief and loss. These activities can be carried out independently or included in bereavement support groups, classes on loss and grief, and school assignments.

The following is an example of a letter that was written by daughter Jessy, when she was 8 years old, to her cousin Haley, after Haley's death from sudden infant death syndrome. It is illustrative of the therapeutic value of creative expression and I am grateful to her for allowing me to share it.

ART ACTIVITIES

Many people of all ages have given expression to their feelings through painting, drawing, and other artistic mediums. In our children's bereavement groups, we have used art activities such as making memorial boxes in which to store mementos, creating memory books, making candles, and lighting them in a memorial closing ceremony, and making picture frames in which to keep the picture of a loved one, a family home from which one has moved, or other important reminders. The Unity family camp program for families who have accumulated many losses from AIDS and HIV has created a lovely ritual for the closing evening of camp. Surviving family members collect from nature materials from which they construct a small boat to represent each family member who has died. After dark, small candles are lit on each boat and the boats are set out on the lake, their glimmering candles a reminder of the loved ones. Similar activities are often used in other bereavement camps and retreats.

DANCE AND THE PERFORMING ARTS

Physical forms of expression are easier for some individuals and groups than verbal expressions. Other physical activities such as focused breathing exercises, used often in conjunction with guided imagery, can be very helpful, especially when feelings are very powerful.

You may find some helpful suggestions for activities in Angela Hobday and Kate Ollier's (1999) book, *Creative Therapy With Children and Adolescents*. Impact Publishers, Inc.

APPENDIX F
Caregiver's Retreat Agenda and Sample Invitation Letter

Staff retreats or team development meetings can help to sustain hope and competence in professionals who frequently encounter grief. The sample agenda and invitation included here are examples of what can be sent to participants in advance of the retreat so they can be prepared. The retreats I have conducted with my own as well as other hospice staffs have been among the most rewarding endeavors of my 33-year career in this field. I hope they are for you as well.

SAMPLE AGENDA

9:00 a.m. Welcome and refreshments

As people gather together, each of the participants is asked to think about and respond to the following scenario:

The day is over. You're returning home, or have just returned to work. A trusted person (partner, friend, colleague) asks, "How was the team development session?" You respond, "It was one of the best sessions we could have had!" What would have happened during the day that would lead you to say this? Be as specific as possible!

Next, ask people to identify what items of significance they may have brought or thought about that help sustain them in their work. (As noted in the pre-retreat invitation, a thank-you letter, memento from a client or student, a picture, or a piece of music might be identified.) Participants can be invited to share their items just before or after each activity break in the day.

10 a.m. Icebreaker-getting acquainted exercise

Example: *Something in my pocket (book)*. In this activity, each participant is asked to find three items in their pocket or pocketbook that signify something about them and share the items with the group. (This provides information about multiple aspects of workers' lives and helps people get acquainted with what they have in common as well as unique differences.)

10:30 a.m. What brings you to this work?

Each participant is asked to share with the group what led them to working in their field and why they are interested in the topic of the retreat.

11:00 a.m. A window into feelings about our work

Each participant is given a piece of paper and is asked to draw four squares. Then they are asked to complete each square with a picture or a description in words of the following:

A loss that has been significant for you	An event that has occurred in your work that has significance for you
A personal goal for your future	Something you feel individually proud of regarding the work you've done with clients

Each participant is then asked to share two of the items he or she has written or drawn. If the group is large, it can be divided into smaller groups or pairs. The facilitator helps the group recap or summarize some of the key descriptions that were shared, noting common themes and unique experiences or expressions.

11:30 a.m. Providing positive feedback

Team members can be asked to identify strengths or contributions they have witnessed in other team members that make their work more manageable. This is very helpful for interdisciplinary or multidisciplinary teams who may not always articulate to each other what they appreciate.

12:00 p.m. Lunch

It is helpful to provide nutritious food that conveys caring and comfort. Music that creates an atmosphere of light and serenity is also helpful.

1:00 p.m. Sharing stories

Participants can be asked, if they have not done so already, to share items of significance they brought or that they keep in their offices, homes, or hearts. These items are often connected to powerful stories related to loss and hope from which all participants can gain understanding. Facilitators should be prepared to share a story, piece of music, or item of significance as well.

2:00 p.m. Writing exercise

The facilitator presents a box of random items (masking tape, band-aids, earplugs, candles, chocolates, sacred books, flashlight, etc.) that may serve as metaphors for the experiences of professional caregivers. Participants are asked to choose one and write about how the item symbolizes what they experience in their work. Music can be played while participants write for approximately 15 minutes. They can be encouraged to write a poem, essay, or in any form they choose. Participants are encouraged to share their work if they wish. Only positive feedback about the writing and what impressed the listener is encouraged.

3:00 p.m. Generating homework

Participants are each given a blank piece of stationary and an envelope and are asked to write their hopes and goals for their future work. They will be asked to seal the letter and put it in a safe place, to be opened 1 or 2 years later as a reminder of the work they did during the retreat.

3:45 p.m. Appreciation

Participants put their names on colorful pieces of paper and place them on their chairs. All participants are then given a colored pen or pencil. Each participant then moves around the room, writing a personalized positive statement of appreciation for every participant. Everyone is then asked to read his or her sheets silently. Then, in order to acknowledge the appreciation they received, participants read aloud to the group one or two of the statements written about them.

4:30 p.m. Closing exercise: A rose, a thorn, and a bud

With the participants gathered in a circle, the leader asks each person to think about the experience they had together and to think about sharing "a rose," " a "thorn," and a "bud." The rose represents a positive experience, the thorn represents something that caused discomfort or impeded enjoyment, and the bud represents a new idea to be used in the future. (An option: Participants can then be given a rose, to take home with them as a reminder of both the beauty and fullness of the work as well as of their final thoughts on the retreat.)

SAMPLE INVITATION TO STAFF RETREAT

[Date]

Dear Hospice Team Members,

I am very much looking forward to our team retreat on [date]. I have read the suggestions you generated for topics you would like to explore in our time together and appreciate your taking the time to do this.

In the time we spend together we will be working on team-building and communication activities that will draw on the many strengths and different abilities of team members, so please dress comfortably; sneakers or comfortable shoes and slacks or shorts will work well. In addition, please think about and bring with you an item that is a reminder to you of why you do the important work for hospice that you do. The items might be a thank-you note from a family, an inspirational poem, an article from a professional journal or book chapter that you used in your training, or a piece of music you like to listen to. The item should be representative of what gives you a sense of purpose or motivation. Please bring this item (a CD or tape with the musical piece if you have it would be helpful) with you to the retreat. This portion will constitute Session I, with a follow up later in the summer.

Again, I am very much looking forward to working with you and thank you for making the commitment to your team in this way. I will see you soon.

Best Wishes,

[retreat leader]

INTERNET RESOURCES

Chapter 1

The National Cancer Institute

http://www.cancer.gov/cancertopics/pdq/supportivecare/bereavement/Health Professional   Provides a comprehensive overview of grief, bereavement, and coping with loss. Specific topics included on the site, such as normal and complicated grief, anticipatory grief, and the influence of culture and bereavement interventions, are addressed throughout this textbook. There is a version for professionals and one for clients in English and Spanish.

The American Association of Retired Persons

http://www.aarp.org/relationships/grief-loss/   Provides information for older individuals and grieving families on a wide variety of topics including funeral planning, advance directives, normal grief responses, and spirituality and grief. The site hosts an unmoderated discussion group where individuals post their own responses on topics the group generates.

ARCH National Respite Network and Resource Center

http://www.archrespite.org/productspublications/arch-fact-sheets#FS_40   Provides many useful information sheets on a variety of topics that are downloadable. The Center encourages readers to copy and make use of them, but to credit the Network when doing so. A particularly useful fact sheet is entitled "Caregivers Grieve Too."

Chapter 2

The U.S. Department of Health and Human Services Child Welfare Information Gateway

http://www.childwelfare.gov/outofhome/casework/helping.cfm   Provides many useful articles relating to loss in foster care and adoption for both professional providers and foster parents. Topics include the effects of disruption and dissolution on children of different ages and strategies for helping toddlers transition to foster care. Links are provided to other educational resources, such as courses for foster and adoptive parenting.

ARCH National Respite Network and Resource Center

http://www.archrespite.org/images/docs/Factsheets/fs_40-caregivers_grieve. pdf   Provides respite and crisis services as well as many useful information sheets including supporting grieving children and caregiver grief. The Network encourages readers to copy and make use of them, but to credit the Network when doing so.

New York SCC

http://nysccc.org/fostercare/shared-parenting/going-home/helping-foster-parents-grieve/   The unique needs of grieving foster parents are discussed in this article, which is only one of the resources for foster and adoptive parents on this site. A recommended reading list includes a host of books and articles to inform and support foster parents.

U.S. Marine Corps.

http://www.usmc-mccs.org/leadersguide/Emotional/GriefLoss/symbolicloss.htm   The Leader's guide for Mananging Marines in Distress is an excellent resource that includes the topics of death and symbolic loss.

Chapter 3

Supportive Care of the Dying

http://www.careofdying.org   This site is geared to inform professionals who provide end-of-life care, including bereavement care. Competency standards assessments and other instruments can be downloaded from the Toolkit for Change provided on the site.

PBS Series: Bill Moyer's, On Our Own Terms

http://www.pbs.org/wnet/onourownterms/   This extraordinary Web site, created concurrently with the television series on the end of life, provides a wealth of resources including self-assessment tools for organizations and helping professionals as well as information for those facing the end of life. Included in the assessment instruments is a beliefs about death questionnaire that can be completed online with interpreted results that can inform professional helpers about their own biases and beliefs. Videotaped interviews with those who are dying are instructive and thought-provoking.

The Association of Death Educators

http://www.ADEC.org   Offers a variety of workshops, conferences, and continuing education programs related to death and grief to assist professionals in increasing their competence in providing bereavement support. There is also a section for the public that provides articles on a wide variety of topics such as animal companion loss.

Chapter 4

The National Cancer Institute

http://www.cancer.gov/cancertopics/pdq/supportivecare/bereavement/Patient/page9   Provides a comprehensive overview of children's grief reactions at different ages and information about grief reactions at different ages, including infancy, 2–3, 3–6, 6–9 years, 9 years, and older. Common questions that children might ask such as "Did I cause the death to happen?" are addressed along with treatment approaches. Information is provided in English and Spanish for patients and professionals.

Hospice Foundation of America and the National Hospice and Palliative Care Organization

http://www.hospicefoundation.org/pages/page.asp?page_id=78815 Provides a number of articles addressing children's grief by different grief experts. Topics include helping children cope with death; children, adolescents, and loss; and grief and the holidays. Practical guidance and information about myths related to grief are useful for clients as well as professionals.

Grieving Children and Their Families

Dougy Center: The National Center for Grieving Children and Families

http://www.dougy.org Provides information and support services to children and families onsite and through the Internet. Resources on the site include a search engine to locate grief support in local communities across the United States. Education and training for those who want to assist grieving families is also provided.

The Front Porch of Atlanta

http://www.remembertherainbows.org/Grief%20Resources.htm The Front Porch of Atlanta is a center that has programs and services that support children and families who are grieving. The reading room includes recommendations of books to assist children and families in the process of grieving. Kate's club is a support program for children and teens who have experienced the death of a sibling or parent.

The Garden: A Center for Grieving Children and Families

http://www.garden-cgc.org/ The Garden is an example of a community-based grief support center providing group services for children, teens, and families. This site also includes a recommended list of books to assist children at different ages and stages of development as well as an article on evidence-based practices to support grieving children.

Chapter 5

Journey of Hearts

http://www.journeyofhearts.org/jofh/grief/help2 This nonprofit Internet site offers information and support to people of all ages who are grieving. Some of the information is written by grief experts and some is not. Articles are posted on a variety of topics including grieving children and teens, the experience of parents with a disabled child, and inspirational stories. There are resources for professionals who are grieving losses as well, including "emergency pick me ups."

The Hospice Foundation of America

http://www.hospicefoundation.org/pages/page.asp?page_id=78811 Provides a wealth of resources on grief-related topics including articles on sudden loss, guilt after prolonged illness, holidays, and some written by survivors of loss. There is also a support group locator on this site for those seeking to refer a grieving individual.

Partnership for Parents

http://www.partnershipforparents.org/guide/grief.php   This site is the product of the Children's Hospice and Palliative Care Coalition and is designed for parents of children with serious illnesses or those who have lost a child to illness. The site is very user-friendly, offering a range of writings about illness, recovery, death, and grieving.

Caring Connections

http://www.caringinfo.org/i4a/pages/index.cfm?pageid=3367   Contains information about issues pertaining to aging, planning ahead, caring for someone, living with an illness, and multiple articles on grief as well as practical issues such as financial planning.

Grief's Journey

www.griefsjourney.com   This site describes its primary focus as "bereavement for the loss of a spouse and life partner," yet contains useful information for other types of loss and grief as well. The site is simple to understand and navigate, and the list of resources is extensive, encompassing a broad range of perspectives. Along with links to emotional and social supports, the site also addresses the practicalities of living alone by offering collections of resources devoted to finances, education, health, legal issues, and a do-it-yourself category that offers tips on topics like household maintenance and cooking.

Chapter 6

American Association of Retired Persons (AARP)

http://www.aarp.org/families/grief_loss/   Provides a wealth of information on loss and grief, including articles on practical aspects of death, such as funeral and financial planning and advance directives. This may be especially useful to older women whose partners may have managed household finances.

The Grief Blog

http://thegriefblog.com/grief-counseling/terminal-illness/   Provides a way to connect with other people around loss–to read their stories, thoughts, and fears, and to receive information. There is a section that recommends a new book every week on the topics of grief, loss, and terminal illness. It should be used with caution because there is no professional monitoring or facilitation.

The Fisher Center for Alzheimer's Research

http://www.alzinfo.org/alzheimers-grief-bereavement.asp   Provides useful information about Alzheimer's disease and dementia–treatment, diagnosis, resources, and research. The Alzheimer's Grief and Bereavement section covers topics such as coping with death, phases of coping, and the difference between grief, bereavement, and mourning. It also explains anticipatory grief and complicated grief in simple terms.

Blue Cross Blue Shield of Western New York

http://www.bcbswny.com/kbase/as/aa122313/what.htm   Provides information about older adults and how they grieve differently from young and middle-aged adults. Topics addressed include why older adults need help with grieving, how we can help them, and resources such as support groups.

Chapter 7

Boston Grief

http://www.bostongrief.com/id6.html   This is the site of a research-based program at Massachusetts General Hospital, currently investigating the efficacy of an intervention for complicated grief. On this site is a brief grief questionnaire to assess complicated grief.

The National Cancer Institute

http://www.cancer.gov/cancerinfo/pdq/supportivecare/bereavement/Health Professionals   Provides an overview of grief, loss, and bereavement, as well as information about complicated bereavement and grief at different stages of development. Information is written for professionals and patients and is available in English and Spanish.

The National Resource Center for Respite and Crisis Care Services

http://www.chtop.com/ARCH/archfs21.htm   Reviews normal and complicated grief.

Cancer Care

http://www.cancercare.org   Provides direct services in its New York and satellite offices as well as telephone and online bereavement support groups for family members and partners. Cancer Care also provides an online reading room with a wide range of publications that are downloadable for both consumers and providers on topics such as partner loss and grieving the loss of an adult child.

Concerns of Police Survivors

http://www.nationalcops.org/serv01.htm   Provides peer support and grief retreats to assist families of officers slain in the line of duty. This organization, described as a "lifeline" for survivors, also provides a peer mentor and counseling program as well as practical information on benefits and policies related to police homicide.

The Compassionate Friends

www.compassionatefriends.org   This national organization with local chapters provides grief support after the death of a child through a variety of methods including a worldwide candle lighting vigil, written materials, support groups, and a vehicle for creating a memorial Web site for a child who has died.

The End-of-Life Course

http://endoflife.stanford.edu/M21_bereave/vid_bereave1.html   Offered online by Stanford University, this course provides information for professionals on palliative and end-of-life care as well as bereavement. Several multimedia are utilized to deliver the content, including a videotaped interview with a grieving spouse and mother that illustrates an assessment interview.

Chapter 8

National Association of Social Work Standards for Cultural Competence

http://www.naswdc.org/practice/standards/NASWCulturalStandardsIndicators2006. pdf   NASW, like many other professional organizations, promotes culturally competent practice. This document identifies the standards for culturally competent social work practice including self-awareness and development of knowledge in the values, beliefs, and practices of the populations served.

Last Acts

http://lastacts.org/files/publications/Diversity1.15.02.pdf   Provides a useful document on diversity with case examples.

EthnoMed

http://www.ethnomed.org   Provides specific information on religious beliefs and practices, including those related to death, for many different ethnic groups. Information on various ethnic groups related to beliefs and values related to illness and health care is provided for professionals, and bereavement practices and health education materials in the languages of the different groups are included on the site.

The American Association of Family Physicians

http://www.aafp.org/fpm/20020600/39achi.html#6   Publishes several useful continuing education articles, including one that describes a cultural competence continuum and strategies for improvement of one's practice through the recruitment of diverse staff, training of staff, and provision of patient education materials that meet the needs of diverse patient populations.

The FICA Spiritual Assessment Tool

http://www2.edc.org/lastacts/archives/archivesNov99/assesstool.asp   Developed by Dr. Christina Puchalski, this tool is a simple way to assess the importance of spirituality and spiritual resources. The acronym stands for Faith, Interest, Community, and Address and allows for an individual or a family to let health care professionals know how health care professionals can address faith and spirituality in their care of a patient.

Passports

http://www.opb.org/education/minisites/culturalcompetence/teachers.html   A Web-based resource for culturally competent teachers that defines culture and cultural competence and provides guidelines for classrooms as well as lesson plans.

Transcultural Nursing Preparation

http://www.culturediversity.org/cultcomp.htm   This organization is devoted to improving nursing practice with diverse cultures and provides case examples from several diverse populations as well as written materials and Web links that enhance nurses' understanding of effective practice and barriers to care.

The Georgetown University Center for Child and Human Development

http://nccc.georgetown.edu/   Established national center for cultural competence with online courses and other resources, this organization provides specific self-assessment tools for professionals working in different settings including health, behavioral health, and education.

Chapter 9

American Association of Retired Persons

http://www.aarp.org/relationships/grief-loss/   On this site you can view a video on end-of-life conversations as well as read and watch videos on other topics related to grief and loss.

Principles for Care of Patients at the End Of Life: Emerging Consensus

http://www.milbank.org/endoflife/index.html   This document has been endorsed and accepted by a number of organizations including the American Medical Association. It includes 11 principles for end-of-life care, including respecting the right to refuse treatment and assessing and managing psychological, social, and spiritual/religious problems.

Supportive Care Coalition

http://www.supportivecarecoalition.org/   Provides a wide variety of resources to professionals and organizations involved in end-of-life care. It publishes several assessment instruments in its Tools for Excellence including an assessment questionnaire for use with bereaved individuals and organizational assessment tools such as a personnel competency assessment instrument.

Finding Our Way: Living With Dying in America

http://webpages.scu.edu/ftp/fow/   This free Web-based course, based on a series of 15 newspaper articles with patient stories, discussions, and resources, is useful for both professionals and those they serve. Participants in the course read materials, contribute responses to discussion questions, and can receive a certificate of completion following an online exam.

Handbook for Mortals

http://www.growthhouse.org/mortals/mor0.html   The free online version of this book is provided by the growthhouse organization. Designed to promote effective end-of-life care through educating consumers and professional providers, it includes subjects such as finding the help you need, living with serious illness, and finding meaning.

Caring Connections

http://caringinfo.org/i4a/pages/index.cfm?pageid=3289   Sponsored by the National Hospice and Palliative Care Organization, this Web site provides links for downloading state-specific advance directives and other useful resources for patients and professionals.

Chapter 10

American Hospice Foundation

http://www.hospicefoundation.org/pages/page.asp?page_id=86542   "Eight Myths About Grief" is just one of many informative articles available on the American Hospice Foundation Web site. This article stresses that grief occurs in reaction to all losses, not just deaths, and that all people affected by a loss, not only family members, grieve.

The American Physical Therapy Association

http://iweb.apta.org/Purchase/ProductDetail.aspx?Product_code=LMS-18   Offers a continuing education course on grief and loss; the course content is specific to physical therapists and the kind of loss experiences they encounter in their practice.

The American Occupational Therapy Association

http://www.aota.org   Provides its members with a number of articles discussing the role of occupational therapists in supporting clients who are experiencing grief in reaction to developmental disabilities, injuries, and in settings such as the neonatal intensive care unit.

National Education Association (and Affiliated State Teachers' Associations)

http://www.nea.org/crisis/Tool32.doc   Offers helpful information for teachers and school administrators including protocols for before, during, and after a crisis. Resources and lesson plans that can be used in the classroom are also provided.

PBS: Talk, Listen, Connect Initiative

http://www.sesamestreetfamilyconnections.org/grownups/grief/   A unique Web-based program for children and families that includes videos and materials for interactive activities to facilitate grieving, clips of the Sesame Street characters dealing with grief, and specialized resources for military families facing separation due to deployment and loss.

Chapter 11

National Education Association Health Information Network

http://www.neahin.org/crisisguide/   Provides steps for forming a crisis response team.

The Hospice Foundation of America

http://www.hospicefoundation.org/educate-yourself   Provides grief fact sheets that can be downloaded and distributed to those who are grieving, and guidance on finding support groups.

The American Association of Retired Persons

http://www.aarp.org/griefandloss/practical.html   Provides many resources related to grief and loss including information on funeral planning.

Chapter 12

National Child Traumatic Stress Network

www.nctsn.org   This site offers a wealth of resources on children and trauma including guidance, tools and links related to terrorism and disasters, an online educational community, and information to help professionals and the public understand traumatic stress in childhood.

Trauma Focused Cognitive Behavioral Therapy

http://tfcbt.musc.edu/   Online training for professionals in trauma-focused cognitive behavioral therapy for children, this free training includes a pretest and posttest and videotaped demonstrations of CBT techniques used with children.

National Institute for Trauma and Loss in Children

http://www.tlcinst.org   Provides a host of online courses on topics such as adolescents' responses to trauma, cyberbullying, trauma, and children of war. A fee is charged for the courses.

National Center for Trauma

http://www.samhsa.gov/nctic/trauma.asp   This site is sponsored by the Substance Abuse and Mental Health Services Administration and is devoted to providing information and resources for trauma-informed care. It includes information about and links to intervention models that have been utilized in a variety of organizations.

Federal Emergency Management Agency (FEMA)

http://www.ready.gov/kids/home.html   Provides a wide variety of resources including a planning kit for children to prepare for crisis in child friendly terms and formats.

FEMA

http://www.fema.gov/rebuild/recover/cope.shtm   This site is sponsored by the U.S. Department of Homeland Security and includes resources for disaster survivors, including information on recognizing and coping with disaster-related stress, coping with the emotional effects of disaster, and grief.

National Education Association Health Information Network

http://www.neahin.org/crisisguide/tools/p3_4.html   Provides information for schools on preparing for and coping with crises and disasters. It also provides a page devoted to helping guide school personnel through managing memorials following a death or multiple deaths.

Chapter 13

The New Social Worker Online

http://www.socialworker.com/home/   The New Social Worker is a free online journal that includes episodic articles addressing professional resilience. It is an example of a professional publication that can be a source of sustenance as well as professional development.

National Health Care for the Homeless Council

http://www.nhchc.org/shelterhealthguide.html   Guide book for essentials of care for people living in shelters. This online guide includes a wealth of information and resources for providers assisting clients living in shelters. A self-care self-assessment tool is included that may be very useful as an ongoing self-check for providers as well as clients.

SAMHSA

www.samhsa.gov/MentalHealth/Tips_ERWorkers.pdf   Provides tips for emergency room workers.

Journey of Hearts

http://www.journeyofhearts.org/jofh/grief/cope   Resources to aid the helping professional in coping with grief.

Center for Loss

http://www.centerforloss.com   Founded by a grief therapist, the Center for Loss site offers a variety of professional training workshops on grief and loss.

Hobart and William Smith Counseling Center

http://www.hws.edu/studentlife/counseling_relax.aspx   This college counseling site includes two downloadable recordings for progressive muscle relaxation and guided imagery that can be useful for professional caregivers as well as clients.

The Daily Motivator

http://greatday.com/   This site, created by Ralph Marston, offers inspirational slideshows with musical accompaniment. A nice pick-me-up and reminder of the meaning of our work.

American Public Media: Garrison Keillor's The Writer's Almanac

http://www.publicradio.org/tools/media/player/almanac/2008/06/30_wa   Recording of Keilor reading Mary Oliver's poem "The Summer Day."

ANNOTATED BIBLIOGRAPHY

Reading books can provide children with information as well as the comforting sense that others have experienced loss and found a way to cope with it. There are many books available on the topic of death and loss that can be found in your local library or bookstores. The following are listed just a few of those my clients and colleagues have found helpful. Some are nonfiction and address death and foster care placement and the feelings that are commonly experienced in reaction to these losses, and some are works of fiction that deal with these same subjects. Although there may not be a work of fiction that specifically matches the type of loss an individual child experiences, these books, in general, help to present death and loss as a part of life with which children can cope. It may be helpful for you to read a book first and then offer it to a child or family if you think it will meet their individual needs.

For Preschool-Aged Children:

Brown, M.W. (1958). *The dead bird*. Reading, MA: Addison Wesley. In simple words and pictures this book helps children understand the reactions of a group of children to the death of a bird. (Fiction)

De Paola, T. (1973). *Nana upstairs and Nana downstairs*. New York: Putnam. This story describes the death of a great-grandmother (Nana Upstairs) while grandmother (Nana Downstairs) and her grandson go on to remember her. (Fiction)

Gilman, J. L. (2008). Murphy's three homes. Magination Press. Murphy, a puppy, moves to a foster home but can't stay there and ultimately finds another home. (Fiction: Foster care)

Grollman, E. (1990). *Talking about Death: A dialogue between parent and child*. Boston, MA: Beacon Press. This book may be helpful to families with children of different ages who are coping with death. In simple language with pictures, it provides the framework for parents and children for discussion of the topic of death. (Nonfiction)

Lowry, D. (2001). *What can I do? A book for children of divorce*. Washington, D.C.: Magination/American Psychological Association. This workbook identifies the feelings of sadness, anger, and confusion that children experience with divorce and provides practical suggestions for dealing with these feelings. (Nonfiction: Divorce)

Oelschlager, V. (2010). *Porcupette finds a family*. Akron, Ohio: VanitaBooks. A book about a porcupine whose parent does not return and who finds a foster home. (Fiction: Foster care).

Wilgocki, J., & Kahn Wright, M. (2002). *Maybe days: A book for children in foster care*. Washington, D.C.: American Psychological Association. (Nonfiction: Foster care)

Ranson, J. F. (2000). *I don't want to talk about it: A story about divorce for young children*. Washington, D.C.: Magination/American Psychological Association. (Nonfiction: Divorce)

Stein, S. (1974). *About dying: An open family book for parents and children*. New York: Walker Books. This read-aloud book with pictures helps parents explain death to young children. (Nonfiction)

Viorst, J. (1971). *The tenth good thing about barney*. New York: Atheneum Publications. After Barney, a beloved pet dies, he is remembered for the good things about him while he lived and for helping flowers to grow where his body is buried. (Fiction)

Zolotow, C. (1974). *My grandson Lew*. New York: Harper & Row. In this book a young boy recalls his grandfather and learns to cope with his loss. (Fiction)

For School-Aged Children:

Alcott, L. M. (1969). *Little women*. New York: Macmillan. This timeless classic has provided many children with a first exposure to the death of a sibling. (Fiction)

Buscaglia, L. (1982). *The fall of Freddie the leaf*. New Jersey: Holt, Reinhart & Winston. In words and pictures this book addresses death as a part of the life of Freddie, a leaf, and his friends. (Fiction)

Caristio, M. A. (2010). *Black jack jetty: A boy's journey through grief*. Washington, D.C.: Magination/American Psychological Association. A young boy copes with his father's death and deals with his feelings of anger, anxiety, and guilt. (Fiction)

Coburn, J. (1964). *Anne and the Sand Dobbies*. New York: Seabury Press. A young boy learns what it means to die through the help of a friend and his fantasied Sand Dobbies. (Fiction)

Clifton, L. (1983). *Everett Anderson's goodbye*. New York: Henry Holt & Co. One of the few books with pictures depicting an African American boy whose father has died. This inspirational story of hope is a Coretta Scott King Award winner. (Fiction)

Fox, M. (1984). *Wilfrid Gordon McDonald Partridge* LaJolla, Ca: Kane/Miller Book Publishers. This story is about a young boy and his favorite person who was losing her memories. (Fiction)

Holmes, M. (2000). *A terrible thing happened: A story for children who have witnessed violence or trauma*. Washington, D.C.: Magination Press/American Psychological Association. (Fiction: Foster care)

Johnson, T. (1996). *Grandpa's Song*. London: Puffin Books. A story about Alzheimer's Disease. (Fiction)

Krasny, L., & Brown, M. (1998). *When dinosaurs die*. Boston: Little Brown & Company. This book receives high praise from many helping professionals. (Fiction)

Krementz, J. (1981). *How it feels when a parent dies*. New York: Alfred A. Knopf. Many grieving children of different ages have found this book very helpful. Children and teens from 7 to 18 share their personal experiences with the death of a parent and how they have coped. Photographs help to provide a sense of familiarity. (Nonfiction)

Levy, J. (2004). *Finding the right spot: When kids can't live with their parents*. Washington, D.C.: Magination/American Psychological Association. The narrator of this story is a school-aged girl who cannot depend on or live with her mother any longer as she adjusts to foster care. (Fiction: Foster care)

Mills, J. C. (2003). *Gentle Willow: A story for children about dying*. (2nd ed.). For children who may not survive their illness or children who know them, this book addresses feelings of disbelief, sadness, anger, as well as love and compassion. (Fiction)

Nelson, J. (2005). *Kids need to be safe: A book for children in foster care*. Minneapolis, MN: Free Spirit Press. This illustrated book explains why some children need to live in foster care and provides accurate information and support. (Nonfiction: Foster care)

Nelson, J. (2007). *Families change: A book for children experiencing the termination of parental rights*. Minneapolis, MN: Free Spirit Press. This illustrated book offers hope and support for children whose family situations are changing and promotes adjustment to foster care and adoption. (Nonfiction: Foster care)

Mann, P. (1977). *There are two kinds of terrible*. New York: Doubleday. After his mother dies, a young boy learns to cope with her loss as well as the difficulties of his grieving father. (Fiction)

Martin, A. M. (1986). *With you and without you*. New York: Scholastic, Inc. This book by the author of the popular Babysitters Club books is about the illness and death of Liza O'Hara's father and her family's coping. (Fiction)

Patterson, K. (1977). *Bridge to Terabithia.* New York: Corwell. An award-winning story of the close friendship of a boy and girl and the impact of her death. (Fiction)

Richter, E. (1986). *Losing someone you love: When a brother or sister dies.* New York: Putnam. Children share their own experiences about the death of a brother or sister. (Non-fiction)

Thomas, J. R. (1988). *Saying good-bye to Grandma.* New York: Clarion Books. A young girl describes her family's experience attending the funeral for her grandmother. (Fiction)

White, E. B. (1952). *Charlotte's web.* New York: Harper & Row. Another classic about the life and death of spider, Charlotte, with a hopeful ending about life continuing for survivors after a loss. (Fiction)

Williams, M. (1971). *The velveteen rabbit.* Garden City, New York: Doubleday. A beautifully written classic about serious illness and the meaning of life from a toy rabbit's perspective. (Fiction)

For Preadolescents and Adolescents:

Agee, J. (1959). *A death in the family.* New York: Avon. A classic which is sensitively written about how a family copes with the loss of a father. (Fiction)

Blume, J. (1981). *Tiger eyes.* New York: Dell. Fictitious story by a popular author about a girl who must cope with her father's murder. (Fiction)

Crane, S. (1951). *Red badge of courage.* New York: Random House. Another classic which deals with death from war through the personal reactions of a young civil war soldier. (Fiction)

Frank, A. (1963). *The diary of a young girl.* New York: Washington Square Press. The autobiography of a teenaged Jewish girl in hiding during the Holocaust. (Nonfiction)

Grollman, E. (1993). *Straight talk about death for teenagers: How to cope with losing someone you love.* Boston: Beacon Press. This book is written to teenagers and acknowledges the importance of their experiences of grief as well as addresses common feelings and how to cope with them. (Nonfiction)

Klein, N. (1974). *Sunshine.* New York: Avon. The life story of a nineteen year old girl who dies, based on her diary and tapes. (Nonfiction)

LeShan, E. (1976). *Learning to say goodbye.* New York: Macmillan. This is a very helpful resource, written to adolescents, about the experience of losing a parent to death. (Nonfiction)

McGregor, C. (2004). *The divorce helpbook for teens.* Atascadera, CA: Impact Publishers. Written for adolescents, this book addresses typical reactions to divorce and strategies for coping. (Nonfiction: Divorce)

Rofes, E. (1985). *The kid's book about death and dying.* Boston: Little, Brown. Eleven to 14-year-olds share their experiences with death. Written for teens by teens.(Nonfiction)

Schotter, R. (1979). *A matter of time.* New York: Philomel. A 16-year-old girl's mother dies and she is helped through the painful experience by a social worker. Helpful for teens referred for counseling. (Fiction)

Nonfiction Books for Adult Caregivers:

Doka, K. (2000). *Living with grief: Children, adolescents and loss.* Silver Springs, MD: Hospice Foundation of America.

Fitzgerald, H. (1992). *The grieving child: A parent's guide.* New York: Simon and Schuster.

Gaffney, D. (1988). *The seasons of grief: Helping your children grow through their loss.* New York: New American Library.

Grollman, E. (1967). *Explaining death to children.* Boston: Beacon Press.

Grollman, E. (1974). *Concerning death: A practical guide to the living.* Boston: Beacon Press.

Kubler-Ross, E. (1983). *On children and death.* New York: Macmillan.

Neuman, M. G., & Romanowski, P. (1998). *Helping your kids cope with divorce the Sandcastles way.* New York: Random House.

Rando, T. (1991). *How to go on living when someone you love has died.* New York: Bantam Books.

Stillman, P. (1990). *Answers to a child's questions about death.* Stamford, N.Y.: Guidelines Publications.

Wells, R. (1992). *Helping children cope with grief-facing death in the family.* London: Sheldon Press.

Books for Grieving Adults:

DiGiulio, R. (1988). *Beyond widowhood.* New York: The Free Press.

Didion, J. (2005). *The year of magical thinking.* New York: Knopf.

Dietz, B. (2000). *Life after loss: A personal guide dealing with death, divorce, job change and relocation.* (3rd ed.). Tuscon, AZ: Fisher Books.

Grollman, E. (1974). *Concerning death: A practical guide to the living.* Boston: Beacon Press.

Grollman, E. (1987). *Time remembered: A journal for survivors.* Boston: Beacon Press.

Kreis, B., & Alice P.(1982). *Up from grief: Patterns of recovery.* New York: The Seabury Press.

Kushner, H. (1981). *When bad things happen to good people.* New York: Schocken Books.

Mannino, J. D. (1997). *Grieving days, healing days.* Needham Heights, MA: Allyn & Bacon.

Lerner, G. (1978). *A death of one's own.* New York: Harper & Row.

Rando, T. (1993). *How to go on living when someone you love dies.* New York: Random House.

REFERENCES

Albom, M. (1997). *Tuesdays with Morrie*. New York: Random House.

American Association of Physicians Assistants. (2004). *Clinical practice guidelines*. Alexandria, VA: American Association of Physicians Assistants.

American Psychiatric Association. (2000). *DSM IV-TR*. Washington, DC: Author.

Arroyo, M. (2009). *Grief and loss journal*. Springfield, MA: Springfield College School of Social Work.

Banghwa, L. C., Hong, M., & Harrington, D. (2010). Measuring migratory grief and loss associated with the experience of immigration. *Research on Social Work Practice, 20*(6), 611–620.

Beem, E., Eurelings-Bontekoe, E., Cleiren M., & Garssen B. (1998). Workshops to support the bereavement process. *Patient Education & Counseling, 34*(1), 53–62.

Berendson, P. (2011). Staying passionate: Five keys to keeping the soul in our work. *The New Social Worker, 18*(1), 12–13.

Bernier, D. (1998). Coping strategies and burnout among veteran child protection workers. *Child Abuse and Neglect, 24*(6), 839–848.

Blum, D. (1993). Social work services for adult cancer patients and their families. In Stearns, N., Lauria, M., Hermann, J., & Fogelbergm, P. (Eds), *Oncology social work: A clinician's guide* (pp. 101–134). Atlanta, GA: American Cancer Society.

Bonnano, G. (2009). *The other side of sadness: What the new science of bereavement tells us about life after loss*. New York: Basic Books.

Bowlby, J. (1973). *Attachment and loss: Separation, anxiety and anger* (vol. II). New York: Basic Books.

Bowman, T. (1999). Literary resources for bereavement. *Hospice Journal, 14*(1), 39–54.

Bragdon, P. (2006). *Young male adults' experience of the death of a peer: Grief and bereavement*. Dissertations Abstracts Database.

Braza, K. (2002). Families and the grief process. *ARCH National Resource Center for Crisis Nurseries and Respite Care Services, Factsheet Number 21*. Retrieved January 10, 2002, from http://www.archrespite.org/archfs21.htm

Brenner, P. (1999). When caregivers grieve. In K. Doka (Ed.), *Living with grief: At work, at school, at worship* (pp. 81–92). Washington, DC: Hospice Foundation of America.

Bridges, W. (1980). *Transitions: Making sense of life's changes*. New York: Addison-Wesley.

Bronfenbrenner, U. (1996). Foreword. In R. B. Cairns, G. H. Elder, Jr., & J. Costello (Eds.), *Developmental science* (pp. ix–xvii). New York: Cambridge University Press.

Butler-Jones, C. (2003). *Loss and bereavement journal*. Springfield, MA: Springfield College.

Callahan, B. N. (1999). *Grief counseling: A manual for social workers*. Denver, CO: Love Publishing Co.

Callanan, M., & Kelley, P. (1997). *Final gifts: Understanding the special awareness, needs, and communications of the dying*. New York: Avon Books.

Campbell, S. (2002). Does therapy prolong the agony? *Psychology Today, 35*(4), 28.

Cassell, C., & Foley, K. (1999). *Principles for care of patients at the end of life: An emerging consensus among medical specialties*. New York: The Milbank Fund. Retrieved June 03, 2011, from http://www.milbank.org/endoflife/index.html#core

Christ, G. (2000). *Healing children's grief: Surviving a parent's death from cancer*. New York: Oxford University Press.

Christ, G. (2006). Providing a home-based therapeutic program for widows and children. In P. Greene, D. Kane, G. Christ, S. Lynch, & M. Corrigan (Eds.), *FDNY crisis counseling: Innovative responses to 9/11 fire fighters, families and communities* (pp. 180–211). New York: Wiley.

Christ, G., Kane, D., Horsley, H. (2011). Grief after terrorism: Toward a family focused intervention. In R. Neimeyer, D. Harris, H. Winokuer, & G. Thornton (Eds.), *Grief and bereavement in contemporary society: Bridging research & practice*. Routledge Press.

Chochinov, H. M., Hack, T., Hassard, T., et al. (2005). Dignity therapy: A novel psychotherapeutic intervention for patients near the end of life. *Journal of Clinical Oncology, 23,* 5520–5525.

Close, H. T. (2006). *Ceremonies for healing and growth.* Atlanta, GA: Self-Published.

Concerns of Police Survivors (COPS). Retrieved from http://www.nationalcops.org/

Corr, C. (2004). *Handbook of adolescent death and bereavement.* New York: Springer Publishing Co.

Corr, C. A., Nabe, C. M., & Corr, D. M. (1997). *Death and dying, life and living* (2nd ed.). Pacific Grove, CA: Brooks/Cole Publishing Company.

Crunkilton, D., & Rubins, V. (2009). Psychological distress in end-of-life care: A review of issues in assessment and treatment. *Journal of Social Work in End-of-Life & Palliative Care, 5,* 75–93.

Cskai, E., & Walsh-Burke, K. (2005). Professional social work education in end of life care: Contributions of the project on Death in America's Social Work Leadership Development program. *Journal of Social Work in End-of-Life & Palliative Care, 1*(2), 11–26.

Curtiss, G. (2007). *Helping older adults with grief.* Retrieved January 16, 2011, from http://connecticut.networkofcare.org/mh/library/hwdetail.cfm?hwid=aa122313#Why

Daaleman, T. P., & Frey, B. (1999). Spiritual and religious beliefs and practices of family physicians. *Journal of Family Practice, 48,* 98–104.

Dass-Brailsford, P. (2007). *A practical approach to trauma: Empowering interventions.* Thousand Oaks, CA: Sage Publications.

Davis, A. (2003). *Loss and bereavement journal.* Springfield, MA: Springfield College School of Social Work.

DeSpelder, L. A., College, C., & Strickland, A. L. (2009). *The last dance: Encounters with death and dying.* New York: McGraw Hill.

DeVeux, S. (2002). *Loss and bereavement journal.* Springfield, MA: Springfield College School of Social Work.

Didion, J. (2007). *A year of magical thinking.* New York: Vintage Books.

Dietz, B. (2000). *Life after loss: A personal guide dealing with death, divorce, job change and relocation* (3rd ed.). Tucson, AZ: Fisher Books.

Doka, K. J. (1995). *Children mourning, mourning children.* Washington, DC: Hospice Foundation of America.

Doka, K. J. (2002). *Disenfranchised grief: New directions, challenges and strategies for practice.* Champaign, IL: Research Press.

Doka, K., & Morgan, J. (Eds.). (1999). *Death and spirituality.* Amityville, NY: Baywood Publishing Co.

Drachman, D., & Ryan, A. S. (2001). Immigrants and refugees. In A. Gitterman (Ed.), *Handbook of social work practice with vulnerable and resilient populations* (pp. 651–686). New York: Columbia University Press.

Drench, M. E. (2010). *Loss, grief, and adjustment: A primer for physical therapy,* Parts I & II. APTA Continuing Education Series No. 27. Alexandria, VA: American Physical Therapy Association.

Durfee, M. (1997). *Facing the issues: Grief and mourning.* International Child Abuse Network. Retrieved January 25, 2004, from http://www.yesican.org/articles/article4-1.html

Elias, D. (2003). *Loss and bereavement journal.* Springfield, MA: Springfield College.

Erikson, E. H. (1950). *Childhood and society*. New York: Norton.

Erold, N. (2010). *Grief and loss journal*. Springfield, MA: Springfield College.

Fabry, M. (2011). *Addressing grief and loss in addiction counseling*. Retrieved January 29, 2011, from http://www.onlinewellnessassociation.com/pdf_articles/fabry_addressing_grief_and_loss.pdf

Fadiman, A. (1998). *The spirit catches you and you fall down: A Hmong child, her American doctors, and the collision of two cultures*. New York: Farrar, Straus & Giroux.

Field, M. J., & Cassel, C. K. (1997). *Approaching death: Improving care at the end of life*. Washington, DC: National Academies Press.

Figley, C. (1995). *Compassion fatigue: Coping with secondary traumatic stress disorder in those who treat the traumatized*. New York: Brunner-Routledge.

Finck-Samnick, E. (2010). *The professional resilience paradigm: Defining the next dimension of professional self-care*. Behavioral Health Central. Retrieved May 19, 2011, from http://www.behavioralhealthcentral.com/index.php/20101109241311/Special-Features/the-professional-resilience-paradigm.html

Fisher, J., & Brumley, D. (2008). Nurses' and carers' spiritual well-being in the workplace. *Australian Journal of Advanced Nursing, 25*(4), 49–57.

Flomenhaft, D. (2007). *The forgotten ones: The grief experience of adult siblings of WTC victims*. Retrieved July 11, 2011, from http://www.voiceamerica.com/episode/23957/the-forgotten-ones-the-grief-experience-of-adult-siblings-of-world-trade-center-victims

Gallup Poll (2007). *More than 8 out of 10 Americans identify with a Christian faith*. Retrieved from http://www.gallup.com/poll/103459/questions-answers-about-americans-religion.aspx#3

Gallup Poll (2002). *Americans' Spiritual Searches Turn Inward*. Retrieved from http://www.gallup.com/poll/7759/americans-spiritual-searches-turn-inward.aspx

Gelvick, W. (2011). *Secondary trauma and the legal process: A primer & literature review*. Retrieved February 1, 2011, from http://law.scu.edu/redress/secondary-trauma-a-primer.cfm#_ftn10

Georges, S. (2010). *Grief and loss journal*. Springfield, MA: Springfield College.

Gitterman, A. (Ed.). (2001). *Handbook of social work practice with vulnerable and resilient populations*. New York: Columbia University Press.

Grollman, E. (1996, April). Reflections on spiritual problems. *Journeys: Hospice Foundation of America Newsletter*, 1–4.

Gross, D. (2003). Good endings: Dealing with death in the nursing home. *Healthcare Review, 13*(2), 1–2.

Grossman, A. (2010). *Grief and loss journal*. Springfield, MA: Springfield College.

Haasl, B., & Marnocha, J. (2000). *Bereavement support group program for children: Leader manual*. Philadelphia, PA: Taylor Francis.

Harvard Health Publications. (2006). *Complicated grief*. Retrieved February 16, 2011, from http://www.health.harvard.edu/fhg/updates/Complicated-grief.shtml

Hauschulz, K. (2010). *Grief and loss journal*. Springfield, MA: Springfield College

Haven, T. J., & Pearlman, L. A. (2003). Minding the body: The intersection of dissociation and physical health in relational trauma psychotherapy. In K. A. Kendall-Tackett (Ed.), *Health consequences of abuse in the family: A clinical guide for evidence-based practice* (pp. 215–232). Washington, DC: American Psychological Association.

Hicks, S. (2010). *Grief and loss journal*. Springfield, MA: Springfield College

Highfield, M. E. F. (2000). Providing spiritual care to patients with cancer. *Clinical Journal of Oncology Nursing, 4*(3), 115–120.

Hildreth, K. (2002). *Loss and bereavement journal*. Springfield, MA: Springfield College School of Social Work.

Holloway, K. (2002). *Passed on: African American mourning stories*. Durham, NC: Duke University Press.

Holmes, T. H., & Rahe, R. H. (1967). The social readjustment rating scale. *Journal of Psychosomatic Research, 11*(2), 213–218.

Hooyman, N., & Kramer, B. (2006). *Living through loss: Interventions across the lifespan*. New York: Columbia University Press.

Horsley, H., & Patterson, T. (2006). The effects of a parent guidance intervention on communication among adolescents who have experienced the sudden death of a sibling. *American Journal of Family Therapy, 34*(2), 119–137.

Hudnall-Stamm, B. (2009). Professional quality of life: Compassion fatigue and Satisfaction Version-S. Retrieved July 27, 2011, from http://www.isu.edu

Hungerford, E. (2010). *Grief and loss journal*. Springfield, MA: Springfield College.

Hunt, B. (2007). Teaching a grief and loss counseling course. *Rehabilitation Education, 21*(2), 101–106.

Irish, D. P., Lundquist, K. F., & Nelsen, V. J. (Eds.). (1993). *Ethnic variations in dying, death, and grief*. New York: Taylor & Francis.

Jaycox, K. (2003). *Loss and bereavement journal*. Springfield, MA: Springfield College.

Kagan, R. (2004). *Rebuilding attachments with traumatized children: Healing from losses, violence, abuse, and neglect*. New York: The Haworth Maltreatment and Trauma Press.

Kaiser, L. (2002). *Loss and bereavement journal*. Springfield, MA: Springfield College School of Social Work.

Kelly, B., Edwards, P., Synott, R., Neil, C., Baillie, R., & Battishutta, D. (1999). Predictors of bereavement outcome for family carers of cancer patients. *Psycho-Oncology, 8*(3), 237–249.

Kennedy, A. (2004). Empty nest full heart. Workshop presented July 14, 2001, UCSC Extension. Retrieved January 10, 2004, from http://www.alexandrakennedy.com

Kessler, R. (2004). Grief as a gateway for teachers. In D. Liston & J. Garrison (Eds.), *Teaching, learning and loving: Reclaiming passion in educational practice* (pp. 137–152, Chapter 8). New York: RoutledgeFalmer.

Killner, S. K., & Crane, R. (1979). A parental dilemma: The child with a marginal handicap. *Social Casework, 60*(1), 30–35.

Kirby, M. (1999). Grief in the law enforcement workplace: The police experience. In K. Davidson & K. Doka (Eds.), *Living with grief: At work, at school, at worship*. Washington, DC: The Hospice Foundation.

Kissane, D. W, Bloch, S., McKenzie, M., McDowall, A. C., Nitzan, R. (1998). Family grief therapy: A preliminary account of a new model to promote healthy family functioning during palliative care and bereavement. *Psycho-Oncology, 7*(1), 14–25.

Kissane, D. W., Bloch, S., McKenzie, M., McDowall, A. C., & O'Neill, I. (2006). Family focused grief therapy: A randomized, controlled trial in palliative care and bereavement. *American Journal of Psychiatry, 163*, 1208–1218.

Klass, D., Silverman, S., & Nickman, S. (Eds). (1996). *Continuing bonds: New understandings of grief*. Washington, DC: Taylor & Francis.

Koenig, B., & Gates-Williams, J. (1995). Understanding cultural differences in caring for dying patients. *The Western Journal of Medicine, 163*, 244–249.

Koenig, H. (2002). *Spirituality in patient care: Why, how, when and what?* Radnor, PA: Templeton Foundation Press.

Konigsberg, R. D. (2011). *The truth about grief*. New York: Simon and Schuster.

Kramer, B. J., Pacourek, L., & Hovland-Scafe, C. (2003). Analysis of end-of-life content in social work textbooks. *Journal of Social Work Education, 39*, 299–320.

Kroeber, (2004). *Grief and loss journal.* Springfield, MA: Springfield College School of Social Work.

Kubler-Ross, E. (1969). *On death and dying.* New York: Simon and Schuster.

Kushner, H. J. (1981). *When bad things happen to good people.* New York: Schocken Books.

Larson, D. G. (1993). *The helper's journey: Working with people facing grief, loss and life-threatening illness.* Champaign, IL: Research Press.

Laudette, S. (2003). *Loss and bereavement journal.* Springfield, MA: Springfield College School of Social Work.

Lesser, J., O'Neill, M., Walsh-Burke, K., Scanlon, P., Hollis, K., & Miller, R. (2004). Women supporting women: A mutual aid group fosters new connections among women in midlife. *Social Work With Groups, 27*(1), 75–86.

Levin, A., & Greisberg, S. (2003). Vicarious trauma in attorneys, *Pace Law Review, 24,* 245–246.

Lichtenthal, W. G., Cruess, D. G., & Prigerson, H. G. (2004). A case for establishing complicated grief as a distinct mental disorder in DSM-V. *Clinical Psychology Review, 24,* 637–662.

Lindemann, E. (1944). The symptomatology and management of acute grief. *American Journal of Psychiatry, 101,* 141–148.

Livingston, R. (2010, June 1). In talks with dying patient, affirming life. *New York Times.* Retrieved from http://www.nytimes.com/2009/06/02/health/02case.html

Louden, J. (1997). *The woman's retreat book: A guide to restoring, rediscovering, and reawakening your true self-in a moment, an hour, a day or a weekend.* San Francisco, CA: Harper Collins.

Lynn, J., & Harrold, J. (2011). *Handbook for mortals: Guidance for people facing serious illness.* New York: Oxford Press.

Mannino, J. D. (1997). *Grieving days, healing days.* Needham Heights, MA: Allyn & Bacon.

Marine Corps Community Service. (2011). Leaders guide for managing marines in distress. Retrieved from http://www.usmc-mccs.org/leadersguide/Emotional/GriefLoss/symbolicloss.htm

McInnis-Dittrich, K. (2009). *Social work with older adults* (3rd ed.). Boston, MA: Pearson Education/Allyn & Bacon.

Miller, C. (2009). *Grief and loss journal.* Springfield, MA: Springfield College.

Moos, R., & Moos, B. (1994). *Family environment scale manual: Development, applications, research* (3rd ed.). Palo Alto, CA: Consulting Psychologist Press.

Morrison, M. J. (1999, May/June). Camp good grief. *Bereavement: A magazine of hope and healing,* 9–10.

Naierman, N. (1997). Reaching out to grieving students. *Educational Leadership, 55*(2), 62–65.

National Association of Social Workers. (2000). Cultural competence in the social work profession. In *Social work speaks: NASW policy statements* (pp. 59–62). Washington, DC: NASW Press.

National Cancer Institute. (2011). Grief, bereavement and coping with loss: Children's grief. Retrieved on January 21, 2011, from http://www.cancer.gov/cancertopics/pdq/supportivecare/bereavement/Patient/page9

National Center for the Advancement of Health. (2003). *Report on Grief and Bereavement. Washington, D.C.: National Center for the Advancement of Health.*

National Center for Health Statistics. (2006, June 28). *National Vital Statistics Reports,* 54, no. 19. Retrieved from http://www.cdc.gov/nchs

Ndikunkiko, C. (2009). *Loss and grief journal.* Springfield, MA: Springfield College School of Social Work

Neimeyer, R., & Currier, J. (2009). Grief therapy: Evidence of efficacy and emerging directions. *Current Directions in Psychological Science, 18*(6), 352–356.

Nichols, M. (2010). *Family therapy: Concepts and methods* (9th ed.). Boston, MA: Pearson Education.

Oliver, M. (1992). *The summer day. New and selected poems*. Boston, MA: Beacon Press.

Pausch, R. (2008). *The last lecture*. New York: Hyperion Press.

Pennebaker, J., Zech, E., & Rime, B. (2001). Disclosing and sharing emotion: Psychological, social and health consequences. In M. S. Stroebe, W. Stroebe, R. O. Hansson, & H. Schut (Eds.), *Handbook of bereavement research: Consequences, coping, and care* (pp. 517–539). Washington, DC: American Psychological Association.

Perschy, M. (1997). *Helping teens work through grief*. Philadelphia, PA: Taylor Francis.

Pfifferling, J., & Gilley, K. (2000, April). Overcoming compassion fatigue. *Family Practice Management*. Retrieved January 27, 2004, from http://www.aafp.org/fpm/2000/0400/p39.html

Pivar, I. (2010). Traumatic grief: Symptomatology and treatment for the Iraq War veteran. In National Center for Post Traumatic Stress (Ed.), *Iraq war clinician guide* (Chapter 11, 2nd ed.). Retrieved July 27, 2011, from http://www.ptsd.va.gov/professional/pages/tgs-treatment-iraq-war.asp

Pomeroy, E., & Garcia, R. (2009). *The grief assessment and intervention workbook: A strengths perspective*. Belmont, CA: Brooks/Cole, Cengage Learning.

Preston, K. (2010). *Grief and loss journal*. Springfield, MA: Springfield College.

Prigerson, H. G., Vanderwerker, L. C., & Maciejewski, P. K. (2007). Complicated grief as a mental disorder: Inclusion in DSM. In M. Stroebe, R. Hansson, H. Schut, & W. Stroebe (Ed.), *Handbook of bereavement research and practice: 21st century perspectives*. Washington, DC: American Psychological Association Press.

Public Broadcasting System (PBS). On our own terms: Bill Moyers Series on end of life. Retrieved from www.pbs.org/wnet/onourownterms/

Puchalski, C. (1999). A spiritual history. *Supportive Voice, 5*(3), 12–13.

Puchalski, C. M., & Romer, A. L. (2000). Taking a spiritual history allows clinicians to understand patients more fully. *Journal of Palliative Medicine, 3*, 129–137.

Ramos, J. (2003). Diversity in cancer care: Focus on Latino patients and families. *Association of Oncology Social Work News, 19*(2), 6–10.

Rando, T. (1984). *Grief, dying and death: Clinical interventions for caregivers*. Champaign, IL: Research Press Company.

Rando, T. (1991). *Grieving: How to go on living when someone you love dies*. New York: Bantam Books.

Rando, T. A. (1993). *Treatment of complicated mourning*. Champaign, IL: Research Press.

Reynolds, M., Miller, M. D., Pasternak, R. E., Frank, E., Perel, J. M., Cornes, C., et al. (1999). Treatment of bereavement-related major depressive episodes in later life: A controlled study of acute and continuation treatment with nortriptyline and interpersonal psychotherapy. *American Journal of Psychiatry, 156*(2), 202–208.

Rezenbrink, I. (2004). Relentless self-care. In J. Berzhoff & P. Silverman (Eds.), *Living with dying: A handbook for end-of-life healthcare practitioners*. New York: Columbia University Press.

Rickerson, E. M., Somers, C., Allen, C. M., Lewis, B., Strumpf, N., & Casarett, D. J. (2005). How well are we caring for caregivers? Prevalence of grief-related symptoms and need for bereavement support among long-term care staff. *Journal of Pain and Symptom Management, 30*(3), 227–233.

Romer, A. (1999). Taking a spiritual history allows clinicians to understand patients more fully: An interview with Dr. Christina Puchalski. *Innovations in End-of-Life Care, 1*(6).

Retrieved January 14, 2004, from http://www2.edc.org/lastacts/archives/archivesNov99/featureinn.asp#Puch

Rushton, G. C., Francomano, C. H., Kolodner, C., & Bernhardt, K. (2010). Genetics professionals' experiences with grief and loss: Implications for support and training. *Clinical Genetics, 77*(5), 421–429.

Schmuckler, C., & Laughlin, W. (1999). Professor and students empower families living with HIV/AIDS. *Syracuse University Magazine, Summer, 8.* Retrieved on December 17, 2003, from sumagazine.syr.edu/summer99/uplace/uplacepg8.html

Schoenfeld, D., & Quackenbush, M. (2010). *The grieving student: A teacher's guide.* Baltimore, MD: Paul Brooks Publishing Co.

Schut, H., Stroebe, M., Van Den Bout, J., & Terheggen, M. (2001). The efficacy of bereavement interventions: Who benefits? In M. S. Stroebe, R. O. Hansson, W. Stroebe, & H. Schut (Eds.), *Handbook of bereavement research* (pp. 705–738).Washington, DC, American Psychological Association.

Sharac, N. (2010). *Grief and loss journal.* Springfield, MA: Springfield College.

Shear, K., Frank, E., Houck, P. R., & Reynolds, C. F. (2005). Treatment of complicated grief: A randomized controlled trial. *The Journal of American Medical Association, 1*(21), 2601–2608.

Silva, M. (2003). *Loss and bereavement journal.* Springfield, MA: Springfield College.

Simons, R. (1987). *After the tears: Parents talk about raising a child with a disability.* New York: Harcourt Brace Jovanovich.

Stonberg, M. (1980). *Listen with your heart.* Boston, MA: Boston Social Work Oncology Group.

Stroebe, M. S., & Schut, H. (2001). Models of coping with bereavement: A review. In M. S. Stroebe, R. O. Hansson, W. Stroebe, & H. Schut (Eds.), *Handbook of bereavement research: Consequences, coping and care* (pp. 394–398). Washington, DC: American Psychological Association.

Sublette, K., & Flagg, M. (1992). *Final celebrations: A guide for personal and family funeral planning.* Ventura, CA: Pathfinder Publishing of California.

Suicide Action Prevention Network. (2002). *Supporting survivors of a suicide loss: A guide for funeral directors.* Washington, DC: Author.

Supportive Care of the Dying. (2004). Competency Standards/Assessment Tool. *Professional competencies.* Retrieved from http://www.careofdying.org

Suter, S. (2004). Personal Communication at Cincinnati, Ohio, November 15, 2003.

Tolle, E. (2005). *A new earth: Awakening to your life's purpose.* New York: Penguin Books.

Tomarken, A., Holland, J., Schachter, S., Vanderwerker, L., Zuckerman, E., Nelson, C., et al. (2008). Factors of complicated grief pre-death in caregivers of cancer patients. *Psychooncology, 17*(2), 105–111.

Townsend, M. (2002). *Loss and bereavement journal.* Springfield, MA: Springfield College School of Social Work.

Tyler, K. (2003). Helping employees cope with grief. *HRMagazine, 48*(9), 54–58.

U.S. Department of Health and Human Resources, Center for Disease Control. (2010). *Health, United States Chartbook.* Retrieved from http://www.cdc.gov/nchs/data/hus/hus06.pdf

U.S. Department of Health and Human Resources, Substance Abuse and Mental Health Services Administration. (2005). *Tips for survivors of a traumatic event: What to expect in your personal, family, work and financial life.* Washington, DC: Author.

Van Breda, A. D. (2011) Resilient workplaces: An initial conceptualization. *Families in Society, 92*(1), 33–40. DOI: 10.1606/1044-3894.4059.

Van Gerpen, R. (2011). Personal communication.

Viboch, M. (2005). *Childhood loss and behavioral issues: Loosening the link.* New York: Vera Institute of Justice. Retrieved on May 14, 2011, from http://www.vera.org/download?file=91/Childhood%2520loss.pdf

Viboch, M., & Parsons, J. (2004). *Loss screening interview*. New York: Vera Institute of Justice. Retrieved July 27, 2011, from http://www.vera.org/download?file=3026/Screening%25 20Tool%2520For%2520Loss-Public.pdf

Viorst, J. (1998). *Necessary losses: The loves, illusions, dependencies, and impossible expectations that all of us have to give up in order to grow*. New York: The Free Press.

Wain, H., Cozza, S., Grammer, G., Oleshansky, M., Cotter, D., Owens, M., et al. (2004) Treating the traumatized amputee. In I. Plovar (Ed.), *The Iraq war clinician's guide* (2nd ed.). Retrieved from http://www.ptsd.va.gov/professional/manuals/iraq-war-clinician-guide.asp

Waldsmith, L. (2000, February). For love of Ali. *Reader's Digest*, 78–85.

Walker, J. (1997). *Feeling light in the dark*. Northampton, MA: Pioneer Valley Breast Cancer Coalition.

Walsh, K., & Marcusen, C. (2010). *The cancer survival toolbox: Facilitator's manual*. Retrieved December 28, 2010, from www.cancersurvivaltoolbox.org

Walsh-Burke, K. (1992). Family communication and coping with cancer: The impact of the We Can Weekend. *Journal of Psychosocial Oncology, 10*(1), 63–82.

Walsh-Burke, K. (2000). Matching bereavement services to level of need. *The Hospice Journal, 15*(1), 77–86.

Walsh-Burke, K., & Cskai, E. (2005).Social work education in end of life care. *Journal of Social Work in End-of-Life & Palliative Care, 1*(2), 11–26.

Ward, J. (2003). *Loss and bereavement journal*. Springfield, MA: Springfield College School of Social Work.

Washington State Department of Social Services. (2009). *A behavioral health toolkit for providers working with children of the incarcerated and their families*. Retrieved from http://www.dshs.wa.gov/pdf/dbhr/youthtxtoolkit.pdf

Whaley, A. (2009). Survivors of Hurricane Katrina: Considerations and recommendations for mental health care. *Journal of Loss and Trauma, 14*, 459–476. DOI: 10.1080/15325020902925480.

Williams, A., & Merten, M. (2008). A review of online social networking profiles by adolescents: Implications for future research and intervention. *Adolescence, 43*(170), 253–274. DOI: 1518696481.

Wolfert, A. (2000). *Healing your grieving heart for teens: Simple tips for understanding and expressing your grief*. Fort Collins, CO: Companion Press.

Wolfert, A. (2004). *The understanding your bereavement support group guide: Starting and leading your bereavement support group*. Fort Collins, CO: Companion Press.

Worden, J. W. (1996). *Children and grief: When a parent dies*. New York: The Guilford Press.

Worden, J. W. (2009). *Grief counseling and grief therapy: A handbook for the mental health practitioner* (4th ed.). New York: Springer Publishing Company.

Zastrow, C., & Kirst-Ashman, K. (2001). *Understanding human behavior and the social environment*. Belmont, CA: Wadsworth/Thomson Learning.

Zoeller, M. (2006). Elderly face grief differently than do others. *Caring for the Ages, 7*(11), 1–23.

Zisook, S., & Shear, K. (2009). Grief and bereavement: what psychiatrists need to know. *World Psychiatry, 8*(2), 67–74.

INDEX